OCR Certi... Administration

Units 1, 2, 3 and 4

Level 3

Sharon Spencer

Endorsed by OCR

www.heinemann.co.uk
✓ Free online support
✓ Useful weblinks
✓ 24 hour online ordering

01865 888058

Heinemann
Inspiring generations

Heinemann Educational Publishers
Halley Court, Jordan Hill, Oxford OX2 8EJ
Part of Harcourt Education

Heinemann is the registered trademark of
Harcourt Education Limited

Text © Sharon Spencer, 2004

First published 2004

09 08 07 06 05 04
10 9 8 7 6 5 4 3 2 1

British Library Cataloguing in Publication Data is available
from the British Library on request.

ISBN 0 435 46230 X

Designed by Kamae Design Ltd
Typeset and illustrated by J&L Composition

Original illustrations © Harcourt Education Limited, 2004

Cover design by Tony Richardson at the Wooden Ark Ltd

Printed in the UK by Bath Press Ltd

Acknowledgements
Every effort has been made to contact copyright holders of material reproduced in this book. Any omissions will be rectified in subsequent printings if notice is given to the publishers.

Tel: 01865 888058 www.heinemann.co.uk

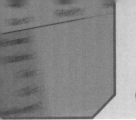

Contents

Please note:

The answers to the Over to You questions in this book can be found on the Heinemann website, at www.heinemann.co.uk/hotlinks. The express code for accessing the answers is 230XP.

Acknowledgements

I would like to thank the many people who have helped me to write this book and in particular Simon Richards, who showed great enthusiasm and confidence in my ability, Gay Watts and Peter Leggott, who both gave their time and knowledge freely.

At Heinemann, I would like to thank Anna Fabrizio for her patience and understanding when deadlines came and went, together with Jill Duffy, who showed me the way forward!

At home, I would like to thank Ian for taking the dog out when deadlines were near, Lucy for reading the manuscript and making many 'helpful' suggestions, Joe who said the manuscript was 'great' without reading any of it and Dave Preston who did read various chapters and made informed and helpful criticisms.

Sharon Spencer
June 2004

Introduction

You will find as you work through this book that administration is the core function of any business. It is essential that employers are able to find staff who have a thorough grounding in administration and a good understanding of how a business works.

The OCR Level 3 Certificate in Administration will give you the thorough grounding you require to start an interesting and rewarding career in administration. The skills you will learn in team working, planning, organising your time and writing documents will enable you to tackle almost any task that comes your way – with confidence.

This book will guide you through Units 1–4 of the work for the OCR certificate. Each unit in the book covers all the syllabus areas and assessment objectives required to obtain the qualification. Where appropriate, sample documents have been written so you can check that your work matches the standard required by the examination board.

I hope you enjoy using this book and wish you a very rewarding and successful career.

Sharon Spencer
June 2004

Producing complex business documents

Introduction

This unit covers all you need to know in order to write clear and concise business documents. At the end of the unit you will be able to do the following.

▶ Use accepted formats and conventions when composing business documents

▶ Analyse, extract, synthesise and adapt complex information to meet a given purpose

▶ Use appropriate tone, vocabulary and style of writing for a range of written communications

▶ Use English in all business communication that conveys meaning and is accurate

You will need to know the standard format and layout conventions of a number of business documents. You will already be familiar with some of these, such as letters, emails and memos.

The work in this unit is assessed in a three-hour examination. You will be given written information from which to compose a variety of business documents, which are shown in this book. The key to success is being able to extract information and convey it to others in a way that is clear, concise, accurate and appropriate to the situation within the given timescale.

▼ USE ACCEPTED FORMATS AND CONVENTIONS WHEN COMPOSING BUSINESS DOCUMENTS

There are many different types of business document that are used in the workplace. At Level 3 you will be expected to know how to present the majority of documents that are used in an office. You are not expected to learn about more technical documents such as invoices, quotations and tenders.

Most companies have their own house style. This means that the way in which documents are presented is standardised throughout the company. Therefore, if you receive a letter from the human resources department it will be set out in exactly the same way and contain the same elements as a letter from the finance department.

This book gives a standard approach for all the business documents; however, in the workplace you may find that there are subtle differences in the way documents are set out. You should always follow the house style of the company for which you are working, whether or not you feel it looks correct.

Business letters

Business letters are used to communicate with people outside of the organisation. They are formal documents and have a standard layout. Although the house style may vary in different organisations, there are various components which should appear in every letter. Look at Figure 1.1 on page 2 to see how a business letter is set out.

Table 1.1 on page 3 shows the items that must appear within a business letter.

Headed paper	**Angel Sounds** 12 Fore Street Cheltenham Glos GL1 2NO

Angel Sounds

Telephone: 01221 28391
Fax: 01221 28391
Email: info@angelsounds.co.uk

Reference	Our Ref ANG/SA/1
Date	2 May 2004
Special mark	**PRIVATE AND CONFIDENTIAL**
Name and address block	Ms K Lewis 8 Apsley Road CHELTENHAM Gloucs GL2 8NL
Salutation	Dear Ms Lewis
Heading	**Sales Staff**
	Thank you for your application form for the above position. We would like you to attend for interview at the store on 19 May at 2 pm. A short job description is enclosed for information.
Paragraphs of text	Please confirm that you are able to attend for interview by contacting Leila Grant on the above telephone number.
	Mrs Rebecca Cohen, the store manager, looks forward to meeting you.
Complimentary close	Yours sincerely
Signature space	
Designation	Leila Grant Personal Assistant
Enclosure	Enc
Copy indication	cc Rebecca Cohen

▲ Figure 1.1 A standard business letter

Table 1.1 Items that must appear in business letters

BUSINESS LETTERS

Type of paper	Use headed paper or template.
Reference	Use 'Our Ref' for company reference. Use 'Your Ref' for reference provided by customer. Both 'Our ref' and 'Your ref' may be printed on headed notepaper. Follow the company's house style, otherwise give initials of the person writing letter and person producing letter.
Date	Must be included. Use English format (day, month, year). Usually fully keyed, e.g. '21 February 2005'.
Special mark	This could be URGENT, CONFIDENTIAL, etc. Key in above the name and address block. Use upper case (blocked capitals).
Name and address block	Key each element on a separate line. Put the postal town in upper case. Postcode must be on a separate line. Separate the two halves of the postcode with one space.
Salutation (greeting)	Use the name of the person you are writing to (if known), e.g. Dear Mrs Vine. If you do not know the name, then use 'Dear Sir' or 'Dear Madam'. Do not use the first name in the salutation, e.g. 'Dear Mrs Joan Vine'.
Subject heading	If possible, use a subject heading to show the subject matter of the letter.
Main text	Have an introductory paragraph, followed by paragraphs explaining the purpose of the letter and finish with a summing up paragraph.
Complimentary close	This should match the salutation; 'Yours sincerely' if the salutation names the recipient, 'Yours faithfully' for 'Dear Sir' or 'Dear Madam'. The 'Y' for 'Yours' should have a capital letter, a lower case letter should be used for sincerely or faithfully.
Signature space	Leave a space large enough for the writer to sign his or her name.
Name and designation	This should appear under the signature space. Put the name and job title on separate lines. Use initial capitals for the job title e.g. 'Managing Director'.
Enclosures	If you are sending something with the letter then you need to indicate an enclosure. Use 'Enc' for one enclosure, 'Encs' for two or more.
Copies	Copies to others should be indicated as shown in Figure 1.1.
Punctuation	Use open punctuation (no punctuation) for items such as reference, date, name and address block, salutation and complimentary close. Use full punctuation for the body of the text.
Tone	Business letters must always be formal. Do not use slang or abbreviated words. Use simple and straightforward words that are easily understood.
Style	Use the KISS principle where possible; Keep It Short and Simple.

▶ Have all the information to hand before starting your letter. This might include account numbers, any previous correspondence or notes made during a telephone conversation. If you have to give information make sure it is correct.

▶ Make sure you spell the name and address details correctly, not only will it help in ensuring the letter is received by the correct person, but gives a good impression of your organisation and yourself.

▶ A good business letter will have an introductory paragraph, paragraphs of text giving the information required in the letter and then a short paragraph finishing off the letter. This gives a good structured approach that is easy to read.

▶ Once you have finished writing the letter, check to see if it is:
  – clear
  – correct
  – concise
  – logically structured.

OVER TO YOU!

Write a short business letter to the following company asking for a copy of its latest brochure and price list.

Phoenix Enterprises Ltd
1 Riverside Court
SHEFFIELD
S92 3NO

Memoranda

Memoranda, or memos as they are more commonly called, are used to communicate with other people within the organisation. They are never sent to people outside of the company. As a general rule, memos should only contain one topic.

As with business letters, your organisation may have a house style that sets out how the memo should look. You may well be given pre-printed memo paper to use. If this is not the case, then Figure 1.2 gives an acceptable layout.

Table 1.2 shows the items that must appear within a memo.

```
MEMO

TO:      Leila Grant        CC: John Westlake

FROM:    Rebecca Cohen

REF:     RC/TP

DATE:    23 June 2004

SUBJECT: Price list 2005

I attach a copy of the price list proposed for next year's
brochure. The figures have been based on a 5 per cent increase on
last year's figures.

Please check the prices and let me have any amendments you feel
are necessary. I would be grateful if you could let me have your
comments by Tuesday of next week.

Thank you for your help.
```

▲ Figure 1.2 The standard layout for a memo

Table 1.2 Items that must appear in memos

MEMOS

Type of paper	Use pre-printed paper or template.
To	Insert the name of the person to whom you are writing. Some companies also require the job title to be inserted.
From	Insert your name, and job title (if required).
Reference	Follow company house style, otherwise, give initials of person writing and person producing memo, e.g. 'MM/SLS'.
Date	Must be included. Use English format (day, month, year). Usually fully keyed, e.g. '21 February 2005'.
Special mark	This could be URGENT, CONFIDENTIAL, etc. Key in above the subject heading. Use upper case (blocked capitals).
Subject heading	Memos should have a subject heading.
Salutation and complimentary close	These are not used in memos. The writer of the memo may initial the memo at the bottom.
Enclosures	You should indicate these if attaching other documents. Use 'Enc' or 'Encs'.
Copies	If you are sending a copy to another person, then this should be indicated.
Punctuation	Use open punctuation for items such as reference and date. Use full punctuation for the body of the text.
Tone	Although you are writing to colleagues the tone should be relatively formal. Do not use slang or abbreviated words. Use simple and straightforward words that are easily understood.
Style	Use the KISS principle where possible; Keep It Short and Simple.

▶ As with any correspondence used in the business environment, the language should be formal. Do not use slang or contracted or abbreviated words.

▶ Memos should be structured appropriately. Use paragraphs and full punctuation for the body of the text and ensure that your text has a logical order.

▶ If you need to write to someone about more than one topic, it is usual to write a separate memo for each one. If this is not possible, you should use headings to show the different topics clearly.

OVER TO YOU!

Write a short memo to your tutor asking him or her to give you details of the house style of the college or training provider you attend.

Emails

Emails are now recognised as a very fast and efficient method of communicating with both customers and colleagues. However, it should be remembered that not all subject matter is suitable for email correspondence. Sensitive or highly confidential matters should not be dealt with by email unless you are absolutely confident that the email will not be seen by anyone other than the intended recipient.

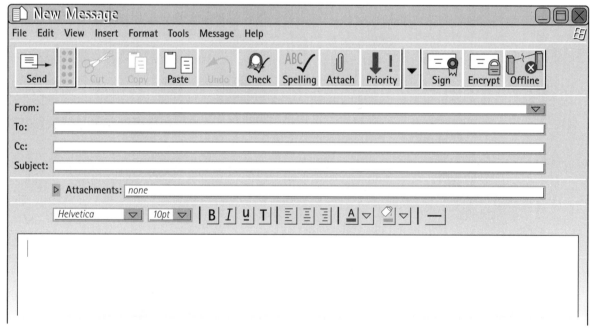

▲ Figure 1.3 Standard email format

Many people believe that an email is an informal method of communication and treat it accordingly. They use incorrect spelling and grammar, poor presentation and informal language. This is not acceptable. Any business communication, particularly with a customer, must be accurate and well written. This is because the standard of communication is a reflection on the company you are representing.

Emails are written on email 'forms' which are provided by the email software. There are a number of items that must be completed on the email form. Figure 1.3 shows a standard email format.

Table 1.3 Items to be included in an email

EMAILS	
From	The 'From' section should automatically be completed when you open a new email form. If you have a number of email addresses, check that you are sending your mail from the correct address. For the purposes of the examination, you may have to complete this box. If so, make sure that you copy the email address exactly as shown on the examination paper.
To	The 'To' section will display the email address of the person to whom you are sending the email. You may have to key this in from details given on a letter or other document. The email address should be copied very carefully otherwise it may be returned to you as an invalid address. If you email the same person regularly then you should add his or her name and email address to your address book, which is held on the computer. You can choose to send the email to a number of people at the same time. There are also ways of sending the same email to a number of people without having to enter all their addresses. If you are replying to an email received, then click on Reply. This is useful as it not only displays your own email address and that of the person you are replying to, but also keeps the previous correspondence on the message.
CC	This allows you to send copies of the email to other people. Enter in the email addresses of those you wish to receive copies.
Subject	It is very important that you enter a heading into the subject section, to give the recipient an idea of the contents.
Salutation and complimentary close	It is usual to start the email with some type of greeting. If you are writing to a customer, you should start your email with 'Dear'. Most companies feel it is acceptable to start an email to colleagues with 'Hi' or 'Hello'. To close an email, many people write a complimentary close such as 'Regards' or 'Best wishes', followed by their name and job title. Do not write affectionate closes such as 'All the best' or 'See you'.
Punctuation	The text of your email should be properly punctuated.
Tone	Emails should be written in an appropriate tone, particularly to customers. Do not use slang or abbreviated words.
Style	Use the KISS principle where possible: Keep It Short and Simple.

Hints for writing emails

▶ You should ensure that emails sent to colleagues and customers are written in an appropriate style. Do not use 'text' language, i.e. abbreviations, lower case letters at the start of sentences or all upper case letters.

▶ The main text of the email should be properly structured into sentences and paragraphs. If you need to write about two separate topics, send two separate emails.

▶ Keep your email short and to the point.

OVER TO YOU!

Draft an email that you would send to colleagues telling them about a meeting that has been arranged for Tuesday of next week. The meeting will take place in the staff canteen at 10 am. It is to discuss new working hours. All staff must attend. If there are any problems then Judy, head of Human Resources, must be contacted directly.

Faxes

Faxes are a very convenient way of communicating with customers. It is often customary for a company to have a printed cover page which must be sent with each fax. This sets out the name and address of the company together with other important details. If a cover sheet is used, the substance of the fax will not appear until page 2. Figure 1.4 shows the cover page of a fax document.

Hints for writing faxes

▶ Although faxes are more informal than letters, it is important that you use an appropriate tone and style. The language used should be formal with no abbreviations or slang.

▶ The main text of the fax should be properly structured into sentences and paragraphs.

OVER TO YOU!

Design a fax cover sheet that could be used at your place of training.

PHOENIX PLC
156 Newton Road
COVENTRY CV4 87G
+44 1225 628199
Fax message

To:	Laura Milward	From:	Martha Wilson
Fax:	+44 1803 212939	Pages:	1 of 7 pages
Phone:	+44 1803 299108	Date:	06/04/200-
Re:	Flooring Contract	CC:	

☐ Urgent   ☐ For Review   ☐ Please Comment
☐ Please Reply   ☐ Please Recycle

Message:

Laura

The flooring contract we discussed is attached (6 pages). Please ensure Alex signs this and returns it to us by the end of the week.

Many thanks

Martha

▲ Figure 1.4 Fax cover sheet

Table 1.4 Items to be included in a fax

FAXES

Company name and contact details	These details will be pre-printed on the cover sheet. If no cover sheet is available, they should be added to the fax so that the recipient knows who sent it.
To and from	Both of these should be shown on the fax cover sheet.
Pages	It is important to complete this in the way shown, i.e. page X of Y pages. This is so that the recipient will be sure they have received all of the pages transmitted.
Fax and phone numbers	These are the numbers relating to the company to which you are sending the fax. When using an international dialling code, remove the first number of the national dialling code.
Subject heading	It is very useful to give a subject heading so that the recipient knows what the fax is about.
Copies	If you send a copy of the fax to anyone else this should be stated.
Text	You can also use the fax cover sheet to write any messages to the recipient.
Tone and style	If it is being sent to a client, the tone of a fax should be just as formal as a business letter.

Agenda

These are used to set out the order in which items will be discussed at a meeting. An agenda will be issued a few days before a meeting is due to take place. Everyone who is due to attend the meeting should be given a copy.

It is customary for members of a committee to give 'agenda items' to the committee secretary if they wish to discuss a particular topic. The secretary will liaise with the chairperson regarding the order in which the items are to be discussed and then draw up an agenda accordingly.

There are certain standard items that should appear on every agenda. These give the meeting structure and help to ensure that nothing is forgotten. Figure 1.5 shows a standard agenda layout.

PARKER PRIMARY SCHOOL

Meeting of the Parker Primary School Governing Body to be held on 21 January in the School Hall at 7.30 pm.

AGENDA

1 Apologies
2 Minutes of previous meeting   } Standard agenda items
3 Matters arising

4 School calendar
5 Disciplinary policy   } Items to be discussed
6 Proposed computer suite

7 Any other business   } Standard agenda items
8 Date of next meeting

▲ Figure 1.5 A standard agenda layout

Hints for writing an agenda

▶ It is usual to number each item as shown in Figure 1.5.

▶ There is no need to expand on the items contained in the agenda, just topic headings are sufficient.

▶ The standard items should appear in the order shown in Figure 1.5.

▶ The items marked as standard in Figure 1.5 must appear on every agenda.

Table 1.5 Items to be included in an agenda

AGENDA

Name of committee	The name of the committee must be included at the top of the agenda.
Date, time and location of meeting	It is very important that all three are included on the agenda. They usually appear before the word Agenda.
Agenda	The word Agenda should appear near the top so that the document is easily identifiable.
Apologies	This is the first standard item to appear.
Minutes of previous meeting	It is customary for the minutes of the previous meeting to be agreed. This is done before the business of the current meeting. If any small amendments need to be made, the secretary will record them at this point in the meeting.
Matters arising	Any outstanding business, for example if a committee member has been asked to research a point and report back to the committee, will be dealt with at this point. The term refers to matters arising from the minutes of the previous meeting.
Current agenda items	These are the items to be discussed at the meeting. The chairperson usually decides the order in which these will be discussed.
Any other business	Members have the opportunity to discuss items not covered by other headings. For example, any late, but urgent topics may be raised at this point. It is also possible to raise issues that are going to be discussed fully in the next meeting.
Date of next meeting	It is customary to set the date, time and location of the next meeting at the end of the current meeting. This makes it easier to set a convenient date for all committee members.

OVER TO YOU!

Draw up an agenda for the Governing Body of Parker Primary School, using the information below. The meeting will be held in the school canteen at 7.30 pm on 8 September this year.

> Jane – Please add 'playground supervision' to the agenda for the next meeting. There have been some worrying incidents in the playground recently and I would like to have the Governors' views on putting together a policy for this.
> Thanks
> Yasmin

> Jane
> I would like to give a presentation to the Governing Body on the new computers that have been chosen for the computer suite. Could you make the arrangements for me please?
> Helena

Jane – Please could you add 'changes to funding from LEA' to the agenda for the next Governors' meeting. I think the changes are going to affect the school budget quite considerably and we need to discuss this in detail.

Thanks

Manjula

Chair's agenda

The chair's agenda gives more information than an ordinary agenda. It is customary to give a brief outline of each topic to be discussed in order to refresh the chairperson's memory. Figure 1.6 shows a chair's agenda.

PARKER PRIMARY SCHOOL

Meeting of the Parker Primary School Governing Body to be held on 21 January in the School Hall at 7.30 pm.

CHAIR'S AGENDA

1 Apologies for absence

Received from Julie Clark and Andrew Leonard.

2 Minutes of previous meeting

Small error under item 3; the estimate for the redecoration of the canteen is £2500, not £2850.

3 Matters arising

Yasmin Khan has now met with the local authority IT adviser and has agreed a training date; 4 May.

4 School calendar

Petra Hudson has now completed two designs for the new school calendar. The committee need to choose which to have printed. There is no difference in the cost.

5 Disciplinary policy

Kieran Jacobs will be presenting the new disciplinary policy. The Governing Body will need to formally adopt this if appropriate.

6 Proposed computer suite

Helena Craddock will provide information on the proposed computer suite. The cost for this project is in the region of £20,000 and can be funded over four years.

7 Any other business

Letters from the Local Authority regarding free school meals.

8 Date of next meeting

Suggest 4 March as the budgets for the coming year need to be finalised before the new tax year.

▲ Figure 1.6 A chair's agenda

▶ It is usual to give the name of the person who wishes to introduce a new topic.

▶ Only a brief outline needs to be given for each topic; just the most relevant points will be sufficient.

▶ The standard items of the agenda must also appear on the chair's agenda.

OVER TO YOU!

Using the information given in the exercise on page 11, draw up a chair's agenda for the next meeting of the Governing Body of Parker Primary School.

Minutes

During a meeting, the secretary or other designated person, should make notes of what has been discussed and agreed. The notes are used to produce formal minutes of the meeting.

How these minutes are presented will depend upon the committee's preferences. Some minutes are very formal with a prescribed layout, formal language and a complete transcript of the meeting. Others consist of little more than brief notes of the items that were discussed.

It is usual to number the minutes in the same way as the agenda. This provides an easy reference point. An action column is often provided so that any further action can easily be seen. Figure 1.7, on page 14, shows the minutes of the meeting for which the chair's agenda was produced in Figure 1.6. In this example, action points are included in the main text.

Table 1.6 Items to be included in the minutes

MINUTES	
Title	Minutes should have a title which includes the name of the committee, the date, time and location of the meeting.
Present	The names of all those present should be listed. If a person arrives late for a meeting, check how this is recorded at your workplace. Some companies require you to note the time of arrival.
Action	An action column is very useful as it allows members to see what they have to do for the next meeting. Generally, the initials of the person who is to take action are sufficient.
Closure	It is usual to note the time the meeting concluded.
Tone and style	Minutes should be formal and written in appropriate and business-like language. For example, Yasmin said that the fair had been very successful, instead of 'the fair was brilliant'. Use a variety of words instead of 'said', e.g. told, remarked, discussed. Do not repeat exactly what has been said.

Minutes of the Parker Primary School Governing Body Meeting, held on 21 January in the School Hall at 7.30 pm

Present: Gervase Pope (Chair), Yasmin Khan, Petra Hudson, Kieran Jacobs, Helena Craddock, Will Bletso (Secretary).

1 Apologies for absence

Apologies were received from Julie Clark and Andrew Leonard.

2 Minutes of previous meeting

Item 3 to be amended. The cost of the estimate for the redecoration should be £2500 and not £2850. The minutes were agreed as a true record of the meeting.

3 Matters arising

Yasmin Khan has now met with the School Liaison Officer. A date for training has now been agreed and will take place on 4 May at 9.30 am. Yasmin will inform all those involved in the training of the location and content.

4 School calendar

Petra Hudson showed the Governors the two designs for the cover of next year's school calendar. Both were attractive and some discussion took place as to the most suitable cover. A vote took place and the outcome was three votes for the photograph of the school and two votes for the child's drawing. It was agreed that the photograph would be used. The Governors thanked Petra for her hard work in designing the covers. Petra will now organise the printing of the calendar in due course.

5 Disciplinary policy

Kieran Jacobs explained the new policy to the Governing Body. Helena Craddock asked whether the policy had been devised in line with current government guidelines. Kieran advised the Body that it had been adapted from a model policy and was in accordance with current regulations. The Governing Body agreed to adopt the new policy with effect from the 1st of next month.

6 Proposed computer suite

Helena Craddock outlined the proposals for a new computer suite to be installed in classroom 5. This new resource would enable staff to teach children IT skills in a more coherent and structured way. Each class would be able to spend approximately 1 hour per week in the resource centre. Gervase Pope asked Helena about the cost of this project. Helena told the Governors that it would cost approximately £20,000 to furnish and equip the classroom. Government funding given specifically for such projects would amount to £10,000. This funding would be given in stages over the next four years. However, the leasing company that would provide the computer equipment offer a four-year contract which is of reasonable cost.

7 Any other business

Gervase Pope showed the Governors some letters received from the local authority regarding free school meals. The way in which the need for free meals is calculated is to change in the next academic year. This may result in a large number of families no longer being eligible for free meals. The Governing Body expressed its concern at this and it was agreed that Gervase will write to the local authority on behalf of the Governors.

8 Date of next meeting

It was agreed that the next meeting would take place on 4 March at 7.30 pm in the School Hall. The meeting was closed at 9.00 pm.

▲ Figure 1.7 Minutes of a meeting

Hints for writing minutes of a meeting

▶ Writing minutes is quite a skill. It is important that you record all the important points; however, as anyone who has ever attended a meeting will know, much of what is said is unimportant and irrelevant. The skill lies not in what you must include, but what you are able to leave out.

▶ There are many different acceptable layouts for writing minutes. If you are in the workplace, it would be sensible to check previous copies of minutes to see how the company prefers them to be set out. Discuss with your supervisor any changes you would like to make to the layout.

▶ Some minutes require the writer to quote direct speech. See page 47 for information on how to report direct speech.

OVER TO YOU!

Ask your tutor to show you the standard layout for minutes at your place of training.

Reports

The layout of a report will depend on whether the report is formal or informal. However, a well-written report will consist of the same elements:

▷ a paragraph outlining the purpose of the report

▷ the main substance of the report

▷ a conclusion or recommendations.

Informal reports may be written on a memorandum form. The use of headings, subheadings and numbering will make the report easy to read and understand. Figure 1.8, on page 16, shows an informal report layout.

Hints for writing reports

▶ Remember to use headings to divide your report into easy-to-read sections. Be consistent with the style of heading you use, keeping the same style for emphasis, font size and typeface throughout.

▶ Remain objective. If you have been asked to make a recommendation, do so in light of your findings. A report should not contain your personal opinion unless you can substantiate this by the findings of your investigations.

▶ Do not use phrases such as 'I think', or 'It seems to me'. Write in the third person and use phrases that do not relate to your personal opinion.

▶ Remember that a good report is just like a story, it should have a beginning, a middle and an end.

MEMORANDUM

To   Christina Borowski
From   Paul Matthews
Date   2 June 2004

REPORT ON OFFICE ENVIRONMENT

1 INTRODUCTION

This report was requested by Christina Borowski on 24 May. I was asked to investigate why the office environment was messy and cluttered.

2 THE OFFICE ENVIRONMENT

2.1 The office wastebins were noted to be full to the point of overflowing.

2.2 There are boxes of brochures in the corridor.

2.3 The stationery cupboard door is broken and therefore does not shut correctly.

2.4 Piles of paper have been left on top of desks.

2.5 Empty toner cartridges have been left under the photocopier.

2.6 Box files are stacked on top of filing cabinets.

3 STAFF INTERVIEWS

3.1 I spoke to the administrators, who told me that they found the office environment prevented them from working efficiently or effectively.

3.2 The staff do not feel they are responsible for emptying bins or dealing with empty toner cartridges.

3.3 The administrators stated that they are waiting for authorisation from their line manager to dispose of the boxes of brochures currently left in the corridor.

3.4 One or two staff admitted that they had fallen behind with their filing duties, which has meant that there are piles of paper waiting to be filed.

4 CONCLUSIONS

4.1 The boxes of brochures could easily be disposed of once the necessary permission has been obtained.

4.2 Staff should be encouraged to spend 10 to 15 minutes each day on filing to avoid large amounts of paper being piled up.

4.3 The wastebins should be emptied each day. This should be part of the cleaner's duties; however if this is not the case, then a member of staff should be made responsible for this.

4.4 Empty toner cartridges should be placed in the empty packaging and given to Jon Salter who will return them to the manufacturer for recycling.

4.5 Extra storage cabinets should be purchased.

4.6 The stationery cupboard should be repaired.

▲ Figure 1.8 A report layout

Table 1.7 Items that must be included in a report

REPORTS	
To	It is important that the report is addressed to a specific person. This can either be written as part of the memo heading or contained within the introduction.
From	The name of the person who has written the report must be also be present. Again, this can either be completed in the memo heading or put at the bottom of the report, usually with a signature.
Date	The date of the report must be present. If you are not using memo paper, ensure that you write the date at the bottom of the report, after the signature and name.
Heading	The report must contain a relevant and appropriate heading. If using memo paper put this after the To and From details. If preparing a formal report, its title should be the main heading of the document.
Introduction	The introduction should summarise the purpose of the report. If you have not used memo paper, it will need to contain details on who requested the report and when it was written.
Findings	Each finding should be displayed as a separate point.
Conclusion/ recommendation	A summary of your findings should be contained here. If you have been asked to make any recommendations, they should be included. Link your recommendations to your findings.
Tone and style	Reports should be factual and not full of your own opinions. Language should be relatively formal. As with all business documents, avoid slang and abbreviated words.

OVER TO YOU!

Write a short report on the canteen facilities either at your place of work or at college. Recommend two changes that could be made.

Articles

You may be asked to write an article for the following purposes:

▶ as a press release

▶ as part of a staff or company newsletter

▶ to give information to colleagues and/or customers

▶ as part of company promotional literature.

The layout of an article is very straightforward. Figure 1.9, on page 18, shows how an article may be displayed.

STUDENT RENTS GO THROUGH THE ROOF

The Student Union of Anytown University has today complained at the high cost of living in the town. According to research carried out by the union, student rents have risen by 25 per cent in the past year.

Students at the university now pay on average £60 per week for a room in a shared house. This is compared with £45 paid on average last year. Zara Gillick, president of the Student Union, said today that the findings of the research would discourage potential students from applying to study at Anytown. Zara said, 'This makes Anytown one of the most expensive universities in the country. The rise in rents appears to have come about because of a shortage of university accommodation, which has meant students have had to use the private sector.'

Letting agent, Nigel Woodward confirmed that rents had increased during the past year and said that private landlords now had a choice of people waiting for accommodation. 'It's all about supply and demand,' said Nigel. 'Unfortunately for students there is a shortage of all types of rented accommodation.'

A spokesman for the university agreed that there was a shortage of accommodation for students within the town centre. Malcolm Brown, Accommodation Officer, said, 'We are currently looking at alternative accommodation for students and hope that we will be able to meet their demands for good quality properties at reasonable rates for the next academic year.'

▲ Figure 1.9 Article layout

Hints for writing articles

▶ A well-written article will start with an overview or summary. This means the key facts should be present in the opening paragraph, i.e. what happened, to whom, when and where the event took place, and who was present. This will set the scene for the reader.

▶ The middle of the article will then give details of the event described in the overview. The paragraphs should be kept short and relate to one specific aspect of the main theme.

▶ The final section should also contain a summary in order to end the article appropriately. It should be different from the summary at the beginning.

▶ You may be restricted to the number of words that can be used to write your article. Most word processing software will count the words for you and this can be invaluable. As a general rule you should not have more or less than five per cent of the required number. For example, if you were asked to write a 200-word article, you should not have less than 190 or more than 210 words.

Table 1.8 Items to be included in an article

ARTICLES

Main heading	An article should usually have an appropriate main heading.
Subheadings	If the article is long or covers several different topics, use headings appropriately to make it easier to read.
Paragraphs	You must use paragraphs in order to break up the text and make it easy to read.
Tone and style	The tone should be suitable for the reader and the purpose of the article. Although the language does not need to be as formal as for other business documents, slang should be avoided. Pitch the language at the reader. Structure the text into paragraphs and use correct punctuation.

OVER TO YOU!

Write a short article about your course of study. Use no more than 300 words.

Job descriptions

Job descriptions are used to state the basic facts about a particular job and the role of the job holder. Some companies send these out with application forms so that prospective employees are aware of what will be expected within the job role. Other companies provide them once an employee has started their job.

The layout of a job description will vary from company to company; however, there are a number of common elements. It is usual to have the job title, the names or job titles of people the post holder will be responsible to and for, if appropriate, and duties of the job itself. Some job descriptions will contain details of salary, others just the grade. Figure 1.10, on page 20, shows the layout of a job description.

Hints for writing job descriptions

▶ It is important to ensure that you have all the necessary and most up-to-date information before you start to draft a job description.

▶ Each duty or responsibility should be summarised. It is not necessary to write paragraphs explaining each duty in full. However, it is important that the duties are described in sufficient detail to avoid confusion.

▶ It is usual to include a statement at the bottom that allows the post holder to be asked to undertake other duties that are not specified in the job description. This is important as it covers the organisation if it needs to ask the post holder to carry out other tasks. This also applies to the statement which allows the organisation to make changes to the job description itself.

PHOENIX PLC – JOB DESCRIPTION

Department: Administration

Job title: Administration supervisor

Responsible to: Administration manager

Responsible for: Administration officers (3 posts)

Job purpose: To supervise the administration officers, provide a high level of administration support to other departments and liaise with the administration manager as necessary

Salary scale: £15,000–£18,000 (Grade D)

Hours of work: 8.30 am–5 pm, Monday to Friday

Duties and responsibilities

1 To receive work from other departments and delegate as appropriate.

2 To liaise with other departments regarding specific requirements, deadlines, etc.

3 To supervise the work of the administration officers and delegate work as appropriate.

4 To liaise with the administration manager regarding workload, deadlines and other matters as appropriate.

5 To perform administrative tasks as necessary.

6 To ensure sufficient supplies of stationery and equipment are available in order for staff to carry out their duties efficiently.

7 To attend any training course considered appropriate by the administration manager.

8 To provide basic in-house training to administration officers as necessary.

9 To undertake any other relevant duties that may be identified.

This job description is not intended to be fully prescriptive and will be the subject of regular review and possible amendment. The post holder may be required to undertake related tasks that are not specifically mentioned above.

June 2004

▲ Figure 1.10 An example job description

OVER TO YOU!

As a group, gather together a number of different job descriptions and compare the styles, layouts and content.

Table 1.9 Items to be included in a job description

JOB DESCRIPTION

Department	The department in which the post holder will be working should be included.
Job title	The title of the post should be clearly displayed.
Responsible to and for	It is important that this is clear on the job description. The line manager will normally be the person to whom the post holder is responsible. If the post holder is responsible for other members of staff, this should be recorded.
Job purpose	A brief outline of the post should be included.
Salary scale	It is usual to include the salary scale or alternatively the grade of the post on the job description.
Hours of work	The hours of work are given, although many job descriptions will also carry a notice that the hours may be changed if necessary or extra hours worked if required.
Duties and responsibilities	A brief outline of the various duties and responsibilities will be given. It is usual to number these for clarity.
Date	It is important to date the job description to ensure the most up-to-date version is used.
Tone and style	Formal language and proper sentences must be used when drafting a job description.

Notices and leaflets

Notices and leaflets are used for the following purposes:

▶ to provide information on a subject

▶ to promote goods and services.

The layout of notices and leaflets should be eye-catching and interesting. It is helpful if graphics and pictures are included in order to break up the text.

A notice is a single piece of paper and a leaflet will consist of a folded piece of paper, usually A4 sized, in order to make several 'pages'. Figure 1.11, on page 22, shows the various ways in which a leaflet can be constructed.

An example of a notice layout is shown in Figure 1.12 on page 22.

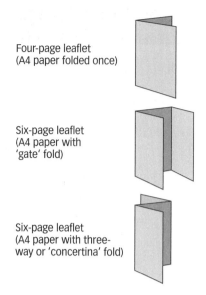

Four-page leaflet
(A4 paper folded once)

Six-page leaflet
(A4 paper with
'gate' fold)

Six-page leaflet
(A4 paper with three-
way or 'concertina' fold)

▲ Figure 1.11 Various types of leaflet

▲ Figure 1.12 A notice layout

Hints for writing notices and leaflets

▶ Follow the AIDA principle for writing promotional notices and leaflets:
  - **Attention:** the document must capture the reader's interest
  - **Interest:** aim to gain and hold the reader's interest
  - **Desire:** make your reader desire whatever it is you are offering
  - **Action:** tell the reader how to take action to obtain whatever it is you are offering.

▶ You must ensure that any information you give is correct, relevant and up to date.

▶ Use plenty of white space; do not have items too close together, which will make it difficult to follow. Don't have too many items on a page.

▶ Be sparing with the graphics: it is often better to use one large graphic than a number of smaller ones.

▶ Use bullet points to separate items where appropriate.

▶ Do not use more than three sizes of text or two styles of typeface in any one document – any more and it will look unprofessional.

▶ Although the language does not need to be formal, it is important that everything is correctly spelled and that there are no typographical or grammatical errors. Use words that your readers will understand.

▶ Do not go into too much detail, keep to the key selling points. Ensure you have included the relevant details of **what**, **where**, **when** and **how**.

OVER TO YOU!

1 As a group, collect as many different leaflets and notices as you can. Discuss the aspects of the leaflets that are attractive and work well.

2 Design a different notice for the Valentine's Disco shown in Figure 1.12.

Advertisements

As with notices and leaflets, advertisements need to be eye-catching and interesting to the reader. Advertisements are generally used for the following:

▶ to advertise goods and services

▶ to advertise job vacancies.

If you are preparing an advertisement for goods and/or services, you will need to give the document immediate appeal for the reader. Advertisements for job vacancies should be more formal.

Look at the advertisement for a job vacancy on page 24.

PHOENIX PRINTING LTD

Requires an

ACCOUNT MANAGER

A dynamic individual is required to join our accounts team. A minimum of five years' experience in commercial offset printing is essential. Digital workflow experience would be an advantage, although training can be given. The role involves liaising closely with customers and internal departments to ensure that our clients' requirements are met on time. Good communication and organisational skills are imperative. You will be joining an extremely successful and dynamic company, offering excellent future career and remuneration prospects. Salary is negotiable, but extremely attractive.

Please send your CV to

Murray.Lloyd@phoenixprintingltd.co.uk

or by post to:

Murray Lloyd, Manager,

Phoenix Printing Ltd, Riverside Court, Anytown AN1 3EP

Closing date 24 April 2004

▲ Figure 1.13 A job vacancy advertisement

Hints for writing general advertisements

▶ The tone of your advertisement should match the age and type of reader you have in mind. For example, if you were drafting an advertisement for a new games console, you would be able to make the tone much less formal than in an advertisement for financial services.

▶ The use of graphics should not be underestimated in an advertisement. You will not be expected to draw pictures in the examination, but if you wished you could indicate, by drawing a box, where you think a graphic image should be placed.

▶ The size of advertisement will dictate, to a large degree, the content of the text. The bigger the advertisement, the more expensive it will be. It is therefore important that you find out the size of the advertisement before you start to draft it.

▶ Smaller advertisements are booked by column size. For example, a small classified advertisement might be just 3 cm wide by 1 cm deep. If you have to design an advertisement for this size, you will need to be very economical in your wording. Abbreviated words (but only those that would be easy to understand) could be used.

OVER TO YOU!

As a group, collect a variety of advertisements that appear in local and national newspapers and magazines. Compare the style and design of these and decide which are the most eye-catching.

Instructions or guidance notes

As part of your job, you may well be asked to write instruction or guidance notes in order to help others complete tasks. There is quite a skill in writing these. They should not contain so much detail that they become difficult to read, but they must contain sufficient detail for someone to complete the task efficiently and accurately.

Look at the following instruction notes for operating a photocopier:

OPERATING INSTRUCTIONS FOR USING THE PHOTOCOPIER

1 Place the document to be photocopied face down on the flat glass screen. Line it up with the marked arrows.
2 Check the **number of copies** is set at 1.
3 Check that the **size** is set at 1:1.
4 Press **Enter**.

▲ Figure 1.14 Instructions for operating a photocopier

Hints for writing instructions or guidance notes

- Ensure that you have all the necessary information to hand before you start to write the instructions.
- If possible, work through the procedure or activity, writing down each action as a separate step of the procedure.
- Number the steps or use a flow chart (see page 220) so that the instructions are easy to follow.
- Avoid using overly technical language. Your aim is to make sure that anyone could follow the instructions.
- Do not assume any prior knowledge from the user. Just because something is obvious to you, it doesn't mean that it is obvious to everyone.
- Once you have written the notes, perform the task again, using your instructions to check for clarity and accuracy.

OVER TO YOU!

Write a set of instructions for logging on to the computers at your college. Ask a colleague to follow your instructions to see if they are clear and accurate.

Presentation materials

You may be asked to prepare presentation materials during your course of study or in the workplace. These require careful thought and planning to ensure that your message is passed across to your audience in an interesting and informative way.

The most common method of creating presentation materials is by using the software PowerPoint. This allows you to prepare 'slides' that will be shown on a computer screen or printed on to acetate and used on an overhead projector.

Presentation materials could include the following elements:

▶ graphs

▶ tables

▶ images

▶ pictograms

▶ diagrams

▶ bulleted text.

You will not be expected to prepare PowerPoint presentations in the examination; however, you could be asked to prepare notes that could be used by a speaker.

Hints for writing speaker's notes

▶ Ensure that the information you are using is complete, relevant and up to date.

▶ Keep to the point of the presentation; do not add unnecessary information.

▶ If you are explaining complex matters, provide examples for clarity.

▶ Language should be relatively informal, although slang should be avoided.

▼ ANALYSE, EXTRACT, SYNTHESISE AND ADAPT COMPLEX INFORMATION TO MEET A GIVEN PURPOSE

The assessment objective given for this section is complex. What it really means is that you must be able to understand the meaning of written information so that you can classify and sort it into relevant topics and headings. You should then be able to:

▶ critically analyse (evaluate) the information so that you can summarise the arguments or key points

▶ extract relevant information from one or more documents to meet a specified purpose

▶ select and adapt relevant information to reflect the specified purpose

▶ present this information clearly in documents that reflect the specified purpose, using your own format.

Critically analyse the content of documents

You will need to be able to analyse the content of various documents in order to adapt information for writing all types of business documents. You will need to be able to assess the relevance of the information and how you can use it. This is not always as easy as it sounds.

Look at the following message and decide what the key points might be.

MESSAGES

Kath

Have gone to pick up some brochures from the printers. It's annoying because they were supposed to be ready last week and I had made arrangements to collect them on Friday. The printers have done this before and if it happens again I shall have to think about finding a new company.

Anyway, it will probably take me around 1 hour to get the brochures and I might call in to see Graham King, you will remember he called us last week about some new stock he has received. It might be some use, and we can always do with new items for the shops. I don't know how long I'll be at Graham's.

I am expecting Martha Phillips to call this afternoon regarding her new contract. Tell her it's in the post (it's not, but I'll send it first thing tomorrow). Don't let her know that the contract is for only six months. I'll talk to her about it once she has seen it.

If Julie calls, tell her I can see her on Wednesday at 3 pm. If that's not convenient then she will have to wait until the 30th before I have another space. Its only about the training programme she's developed. Frankly, I don't think we'll have the money to fund it in any case.

Any other callers: tell them I'll ring them back either later on or tomorrow.

Denton

▲ Figure 1.15 A message

This lengthy message contains only a few relevant points. These are (in order of importance):

▷ Denton is out of the office and isn't sure when he will return

▷ if Martha rings, Kath is to tell her that the contract is in the post

▷ if Julie rings, Kath can offer her a meeting on Wednesday at 3 pm

▷ if anyone else calls, Denton will contact them later.

The rest of the message is irrelevant and indiscreet. Kath does not need to know much of the information provided and in fact the sentences relating to Martha and Julie put Kath in a difficult position as Denton is asking her to be less than truthful with them if they call.

If Kath was to select the necessary information and rewrite the message, she might produce something similar to Figure 1.16, on page 28.

MESSAGES

Denton has gone to the printers and will then go on to see Graham King. We do not know how long he will be.

If Martha Phillips calls, please tell her the contract is in the post.

If Julie rings, offer her an appointment at 3 pm on Wednesday. If this is inconvenient, Denton can meet with her after the 30th.

If there are any other calls, tell them that Denton will ring later or, if he's not back in time, tomorrow morning.

▲ Figure 1.16 The relevant information selected from the message in Figure 1.15

The point of this exercise was to find the key facts of the message. One of the skills you will need when writing business documents is to be able to understand and extract key or relevant facts from other sources.

Sometimes it can be be difficult to work out just what information the writer or speaker is trying to convey. This is often the case when you are looking at technical information.

You may need to extract relevant information from a source to incorporate into your own document. For example, if you were writing a report on the number of visitors to your sports centre during the past year, you would need to extract this information from various records. These might include records such as spreadsheets, till records and monthly reports.

On the other hand, you might need to condense a lengthy report or article into something more relevant and manageable to use, for example, in a presentation. You might also need to summarise records or reports into key points for your boss to save time.

You may need to use a variety of information sources in order to produce a report or article. Generally sources can be divided into two separate categories:

▷ **Primary sources:** These provide information that has been prepared specifically for the organisation. It may take the form of records such as sales figures, stock levels or responses from advertising. It may have been prepared in-house or by other organisations such as accountants or advertising agents on behalf of your company.

▷ **Secondary sources:** These cover a wide range of different sources and will not have been prepared specifically for the organisation. They might include the Internet, reference books, information from market research companies or government statistics and data. Generally the information gained from secondary sources will be much less confidential than that from a primary source.

If you need to undertake some research, you will be able to use the following sources to find information:

▷ libraries

▷ dictionaries

▷ reference books

▷ directories

▷ yearbooks

▷ encyclopaedias

- travel timetables
- trade handbooks
- travel guides
- hotel and restaurant guides
- telephone books
- the Internet
- trade associations
- local government.

OVER TO YOU!

The list above is not exhaustive. As a group, discuss other secondary sources of information that you could use.

Whatever the reason for extracting information, you will need to be able to pick up on the key points of a document and adapt them for your own purposes. This means that you may need to rewrite them in a style that suits your document, but which does not lose or change the original meaning of the text.

Whether or not you pick up the key facts quickly will depend on how you read the information in the first place. Think about the way in which you read the message in Figure 1.15 (page 27). Did you read it quickly, without taking in the meaning? Or did you read each word carefully, making sense of the message as you went along? There are several methods of reading text as shown in Table 1.10.

Table 1.10 Reading techniques

Scanning	This is looking over a piece of text quickly to find a specific piece of information. You might use this technique to find an item in an index.
Skimming	When you skim text you will look over it quickly to get a general idea of the content. When scanning you know what you are looking for, but with skimming you don't. You could use this technique for finding articles related to your study in a textbook.
Reading for study	This type of reading is used when you are making sense of the text in order to remember key points. It will take longer to use this technique and you will need to make notes, highlight key points and spend time reflecting on the content of the text.
Light reading	You use the light reading technique when you are reading a novel or magazine. You may not read or remember every word, but will read fairly quickly and understand the meaning of the text.
Sub-vocalisation reading	This is a slow and methodical method of reading whereby you voice the words to yourself. This technique is used when you are following instructions such as those for a recipe or a new piece of equipment.

One method of reading that will help you with your studies is the SQ3R method.

▶ **Survey:** Skim through the text to see what it is about and what you will be able to learn from the reading. It can be helpful at this stage to skim the comments on the back cover of the book, the foreword and the index to get a general idea of what the text contains.

▶ **Question:** Ask yourself what it is you expect to learn from your reading. Your objectives will be shaped by your reasons for study and your survey. It may be helpful to write down your objectives in advance to use as a reference point.

▶ **Read:** As you have made some preparations and you know what you are looking for, your reading should be easier. Skim the text to find any relevant sections and then read these carefully. Use notes or references for later use.

▶ **Recall:** Unfortunately, research has shown that we quickly forget most of what we read. Once you have completed the reading, try to fulfil the objectives you set from memory. This will let you know what you have learned and what you still need to know. If you are unsure, then refer back to the text.

▶ **Review:** Check that you have learned the relevant information against the piece of text. This is important, as it will show you whether you have remembered the information accurately.

OVER TO YOU!

Using the method shown above, survey the following article and decide what it is about. Classify the information into various sections, then analyse and evaluate the text, so that you finish with a list of headings under which the key facts have been placed in order of importance.

Health and safety in the workplace

There are many laws regarding health and safety at work and all employers must ensure that their premises are safe, not only for employees, but also for visitors. For employers with five or more employees extra regulations apply. These include preparing a written health and safety policy, appointing a health and safety representative from the staff and ensuring that findings from a risk assessment are recorded.

The risk assessment is essential for any employer and should be undertaken before work begins. This is not always possible and so employers should undertake risk assessments on a regular basis. This will highlight any unsafe working practices and any hazards that might be present.

As well as a risk assessment, employers and employees must be constantly aware of potential hazards, how to report them and how to deal with them. Procedures must be in place for reporting hazards as well as for emergency evacuation, fire drills and reporting accidents. A health and safety law poster must also be displayed in the workplace. Employees must attend any training that is provided by the employer.

The Health and Safety Executive sends inspectors to visit office premises as well as other types of workplace. They will carry out a number of checks and, if they find any problems, they will ask the employer to put them right within a specified time period. Failure to comply with this may result in a fine and the premises being closed. If the inspector finds a very serious hazard, he or she has the authority to shut the premises immediately and without notice.

The types of hazard in an office include filing drawers left open, fire exits blocked and items left in walkways. Employees also have responsibilities with regard to health and safety. They must behave responsibly at all times, report potential hazards, take care with equipment and use any protective equipment provided.

▲ Figure 1.17 A health and safety article

Now compare your list with the one given below.

Employers' responsibilities

▶ Employers must ensure their premises are safe for both employees and visitors.
▶ Employers must undertake risk assessments on a regular basis and preferably before work is begun.
▶ A health and safety law poster must be displayed.

Employers with five or more employees

Extra regulations apply and these include:

▶ the preparation of a written health and safety policy
▶ a health and safety representative must be appointed from within the staff
▶ findings from risk assessments must be recorded.

Employees' responsibilities

▶ To report potential hazards.
▶ To attend any training provided by the employer.
▶ To use protective equipment and clothing provided by the employer.
▶ To take care with equipment.
▶ To behave sensibly.

Procedures

Procedures must be in place for:

▶ fire drills
▶ emergency evacuation
▶ reporting hazards
▶ reporting accidents.

Health and Safety Executive

▶ Check premises to ensure that they are safe.
▶ Have the authority to ensure that employers make their premises safe.
▶ Employers can be fined or premises closed if found to be dangerous.

▲ Figure 1.18 Suggested list of key points

Your list may not be exactly the same as the one above; however, you should have been able to separate the text into broad categories and then place the various pieces of information under the headings.

Adapt information to reflect the specified purpose, document format and context

Once you have analysed the text and extracted the relevant information, you must be able to adapt it for use in your own documents. This may mean that you summarise a lengthy article into a much shorter piece to place in a report or you may have to rewrite something technical so that it is easy to understand.

When adapting text for your own purposes, there are a few things to remember.

▷ The text must still make sense; often people take out so much information that the remaining text makes little sense.

▷ The text must not have lost its original meaning. Be careful when you are summarising not to change any key points.

▷ Ensure that by changing technical words you do not alter the meaning of the text.

▷ Use your own words – it will be obvious if you have just 'lifted' the text from someone else's work and placed it in the middle of your own.

OVER TO YOU!

Have a look at the letter of complaint shown in Figure 1.20 on page 33. Separate the main points and place them in order of importance.

You have now spoken to Rose, the shop manager, about the letter of complaint. Below are the notes you made during your conversation with her. Rewrite these notes, putting the points in order of importance.

Mrs Sampson did return the shoes, but they were very worn and showed scuff marks, scratches and the heels were beginning to wear down.

The stitching was broken in some places, which was the probable cause of the water entering the shoes.

Mrs Sampson was shouting and caused quite a disturbance in the shop.

Rose offered the customer a credit note for £20, which she felt was fair in the circumstances.

Mrs Sampson threatened Rose and Sandra with legal action.

The Plymouth branch has sold many pairs of this particular shoe but has not received any other complaints.

▲ Figure 1.19 Notes made during conversation with Rose

Mrs J Sampson
123 Hallwell Road
PLYMOUTH
PL1 3NO

12 January 2004

Mr Peter Harmon
Managing Director
Harmon Shoes Ltd
4 Riverside Mews
MANCHESTER
M33 2PE

Dear Mr Harmon

I am writing to express my disgust at the way I was treated in one of your shoe shops the other day. Ever since you opened in Plymouth in 1981, I have purchased my shoes from you and have always found them to be very comfortable and reasonably priced. However, I certainly won't be giving you any more of my money, not with the way I've been treated.

I bought a pair of black leather shoes, lace-ups, about one month ago. They cost £45, which I thought was a bit steep, but as I liked them I paid the money. The first time I wore them, it started to rain and water came into the shoes. Obviously I took them back but the assistant, Sandra, told me that they were not designed for wet weather. How can that be possible in this country? It's always raining. In any case, shoes are supposed to be for walking in and obviously, as they are not slippers, it is likely they will be worn in the rain. I couldn't believe what I was hearing.

Sandra wouldn't give me my money back and so I insisted on speaking to the manager. Rose eventually agreed to talk to me but she wouldn't give me my money back either. I was absolutely furious and told them so. It is obvious that you do not train your staff. I could not believe they were so rude.

I want my money back and if I don't get it, I shall take this matter to the trading standards people. I have already told all my friends and family not to buy shoes at your shops and I'm sure you cannot stand all the bad publicity: the shop was empty when I was there and on the three occasions I have been back to get a refund.

Please send me a full refund immediately.

Yours sincerely

Janet Sampson

▲ Figure 1.20 Letter of complaint

Present documents for ease of use and to reflect the specified purpose

You should now be able to evaluate a piece of text and extract the key points and relevant facts. You now need to be able to present this information in a format that is clear and easy to use.

The best way to do this is to make a plan before you start to write. The list of points you make when evaluating a piece of text is a good place to start. You will have already placed items under various headings and then in order of importance. You can take this one step further by planning the order in which to use your headings and by ticking off the key points as you write them to ensure that you do not forget any important information.

Headings should be used where possible to separate the various topics within the text. These will make it easier for you to write and easier for people to read. Make sure that you paragraph the text so that it is broken up into short, clear blocks that are easy to read.

Use your list to work out the order in which you will present information. This should be the most logical order and should lead the reader from one idea to the next. As well as using headings, you can make your work logical and clear by using any of the following:

▶ flowcharts

▶ tables

▶ other visual aids

▶ appendices.

OVER TO YOU!

Using your lists from the exercise on page 32, write a short memo to Peter, outlining the complaint and the comments given by Rose.

▼ USE APPROPRIATE TONE, VOCABULARY AND STYLE OF WRITING FOR A RANGE OF WRITTEN COMMUNICATIONS

You have learned how to extract and adapt information for your business documents. Now you need to be able to write this information in an appropriate style for your reader.

Use of different styles of writing to suit different purposes

In the first section of this unit, you were given hints and tips for writing various business documents. For most, a formal tone should be adopted. However, there are exceptions to this and these might include articles, notices, advertisements and leaflets. Depending on the subject matter, a more informal tone may be appropriate because you are trying to attract and hold the reader's attention.

Regardless of the type of document you are preparing, you must ensure that your work is ordered logically and contains properly structured sentences and paragraphs, and that the spelling, punctuation and grammar are correct.

When you are preparing a document, think about the reader. For example, if you were writing a memo to your line manager, you would make the tone formal and respectful. A letter to an external customer would be formal and polite. You might adopt a more informal and chatty tone if you were writing an article. However, a very technical article for a trade magazine would require a formal tone with more complex language.

Use of appropriate vocabulary to suit specific purposes

It is important that the vocabulary you use is appropriate to the situation. Look at the following examples:

1 We have now been to see your property and think it's in a very nice state. We are sure it will sell for loads of money.

2 We have now visited your property and feel that, because it is in an excellent condition, it will fetch a high price.

Example 2 has a much more professional and business-like approach. You don't have to use very complex language to make your writing sound professional.

When choosing your vocabulary, keep in mind the following points.

▶ Try to avoid words such as like, good, nice, think.

▶ Do not use a word if you are not sure of its meaning. If you are in any doubt, look it up in a dictionary to check you are using it correctly.

▶ Try to avoid repeating the same word or phrase throughout a document.

▶ Where possible use the correct technical term. For example, you should write 'We will be sending you a quotation for the repairs', rather than 'We will be sending you a price for the repairs'.

▶ Do not use unnecessary words that add little to the meaning. For example, 'I never, ever eat meat'. The word 'ever' doesn't mean anything here: it is quite sufficient to say 'I never eat meat'.

▶ Do not use words and phrases such as 'like' and 'you know' in business documents. For example, 'It's like, you know, a real problem'.

▶ Try to avoid the use of clichés. These are phrases that have become ineffective through overuse. Examples of clichés include:

– at the end of the day

– at this moment in time

– in this day and age.

Given below are some words and phrases that should not be used when writing business documents:

▶ **Thankyou:** Thank you should always be written as two separate words.

▶ **Alright:** This should be avoided as much as possible. If you do need to use this phrase, write it as two separate words ('all right').

▶ **A lot or alot:** This should be avoided where possible. If you must use it, write two separate words.

OVER TO YOU!

Rewrite the following text to give it a more professional feel:

> Thanks for your letter. I have put some stuff in the post that tells you absolutely everything about our company. I hope you enjoy looking at it.
>
> Our goods have been selling really well for many years and our customers just love them. Our customer service is second to none and at the end of the day, this counts for a lot.
>
> I am sure you will really like us. Just give us a chance to show you just how good we really are. If you need to know anything else, give me a call.

Use of tone that reflects the needs of the recipient

If the tone of your document is incorrect, you could easily give the recipient the wrong impression or even upset them. Remember that when you are writing a business document you will not have the same opportunity to correct any misunderstandings caused by using the wrong tone as you would if you were communicating face to face. Look at the following examples.

1 It's not our fault that you didn't read the instructions properly. We will not be refunding your money.

2 Your failure to adhere to the manufacturer's instructions has nullified the guarantee. We are therefore unable to accede to your request for a full monetary refund.

3 Unfortunately, as the manufacturer's instructions were not followed correctly, the terms of the guarantee have been broken. This means that we will be unable to make a refund on this occasion.

All three examples say the same thing, but the tone that has been used makes them appear very different.

▶ **Example 1:** If you received this, you would probably feel very annoyed. The tone is defensive, stark and impolite. This is unacceptable in a business document.

▶ **Example 2:** This has a slightly better tone as it is more formal. However, the language is far too complex for the situation. This is also unacceptable.

▶ **Example 3:** This has a much better tone. The sentences have the same meaning as in examples 1 and 2, but the tone is much less defensive. It has been carefully worded so that the blame is not so direct. The use of the words 'on this occasion' makes the company sound much more reasonable than in either of the other examples.

The tone you use will depend on the person to whom you are writing. If you are writing to a new client, your tone should be welcoming, but formal. A memo to a director should be formal and respectful. A memo to a colleague can be relatively informal.

The message you are trying to get across should also be taken into consideration. For example, a letter of complaint should have a firm tone, although it should always be polite. A letter of apology should show some concern for the problem but should not be too humble, nor should it admit full liability. A letter to a potential new client should be welcoming and enthusiastic; however, it should not sound desperate or promise more than the company can deliver.

Getting the tone right will take a little practice. If you are unsure of the most appropriate tone, use one that is more formal rather than informal. By doing this you are unlikely to make a serious mistake.

Use of tact, diplomacy and persuasive language

Much of the information you will have access to in the workplace will be confidential. You must ensure that you respect this confidentiality in your communications to others, particularly those outside the organisation. If you are in any doubt as to what is confidential, check with your supervisor before sending the document. Generally, anything concerning personal or financial details should be checked carefully before being used.

When you are dealing with sensitive matters, remember to be diplomatic. Just because your boss has said that a particular customer is a pain in the neck, this does not mean you should repeat it. If you have to reply to letters of complaint, you must take a diplomatic tone. You should not agree with every word the customer writes, even if you feel they are justified.

Hints for writing letters of complaint

▶ If you have to complain to a company because of a problem you have experienced with either its products or services, you will need to take a firm, but polite tone. Before you start to write take into account the following:

- be clear about why you are complaining
- be specific about the problems you have experienced
- be clear about what you are expecting the organisation to do in response.

▶ Planning the letter before you start to write will enable you to focus on the problem rather than how you feel about the problem.

▶ A ranting letter of complaint that threatens the reader will not be taken seriously. It is much easier to ignore a customer who says 'your product (or service) is complete rubbish' than one who says 'I found that your product (or service) was of poor quality, because . . .'.

▶ It is essential that you are clear about your desired response to your complaint. If you are not, the company may well decide not to do anything. You must be realistic about the level of compensation you might receive.

▶ Use a firm and polite tone.

OVER TO YOU!

Write a letter of complaint for the following situation:
You recently bought an expensive outfit to wear to a wedding. On the day, the hem came undone and you found some of the stitching was loose. When you washed the garment it shrank, even though you followed the washing instructions. The garment is no longer wearable.

Hints for writing letters of apology

▶ All companies will receive letters of complaint from time to time. Many companies will have standard procedures for dealing with complaints and you must be aware of these.

▶ Plan your response to a complaint before you start to write your letter of apology. This will help you to focus on the problem. As a general guide use the following structure.

- The introduction should thank the customer for bringing the problem to your attention. You should express some regret that the customer has suffered inconvenience; however, you should not admit fault at this point.
- The main body of the letter should discuss the action that has been taken regarding the complaint. This might be that you have investigated the matter or that you are

passing on the complaint to the appropriate person. If you have already investigated the complaint, you should state the results of the investigation and any action you are taking to resolve the problem. If you are planning to give any compensation, state your proposal clearly.

– The final paragraph(s) should apologise again for the inconvenience caused and then express the hope that the customer will use your company again.

▶ Be factual and diplomatic. Do not admit full liability and do not name or blame others.

▶ Keep the letter concise, but make sure that this does not give the letter an abrupt tone.

OVER TO YOU!

Using the situation in the exercise on page 37, write a letter of apology in response.

You may also need to use persuasive devices, for example if you are writing promotional material or advertisements. Pay particular attention to the display and layout, information and wording, bearing in mind the mnemonic, AIDA (see page 23).

Make sure that the design of the material is eye-catching and the layout is clear. Do not forget to allow plenty of white space so that the document is easy to read. Make sure that important points are highlighted in some way; bold, large text or colour are all very effective.

The information you use in the document must be accurate and clear. Write in a way that is easy to understand. Use persuasive words that will appeal to the target reader, for example 'This product will enhance your lifestyle' will probably persuade more people to buy a product or service than 'Please buy this product'. Make sure that you have included all the answers to questions that the reader is likely to ask, such as 'What does it do? Where can I get it?'

All advertising is designed to promote something such as a product, company, service or point of view, and advertisements can be broadly categorised into two types – persuasive and factual. Persuasive advertisements use the devices described above, but factual ones tend to focus exclusively on facts and information, such as the details of a job or college course.

Hints on writing advertisements

▶ All advertisements are subject to scrutiny by the Advertising Standards Agency and they must be accurate, truthful and not misleading. Failure to comply with the regulations can result in prosecution in some cases.

▶ You must keep to the facts and not make statements that cannot be proved. This is why one leading alcohol manufacturer advertises their products as 'probably the best in the world' rather than 'the best in the world'. The first statement gives an opinion, the second a fact.

▶ You must include all the key points or information, adding extra details only if you have space.

▶ An interesting and eye-catching headline will immediately draw the reader's attention to the advertisement.

Write a small advertisement for your college course. You should use no more than 50 words. Make sure that you include all the key facts, such as the course manager's name, a contact telephone number and the hours of attendance.

▼ IN ALL BUSINESS COMMUNICATION USE ENGLISH THAT CONVEYS MEANING AND IS ACCURATE

It is essential for both examination purposes and the workplace that you are able to write documents that contain properly constructed sentences and are free of errors in spelling, punctuation and grammar.

Structuring sentences correctly

In order for your work to appear professional and well-written you will need to know how to structure your sentences correctly.

The following poem will remind you of the different words we use when writing. It was written by John Neale and published in 1886. The names given in capitals refer to the different types of words you use; the words in italics give examples.

The Nine Parts of Speech John Neale (1886)

Three little words we often see,

An ARTICLE, *a*, *an* and *the*.

NOUN'S the name of anything,

As *school* or *garden*, *hoop* or *string*

ADJECTIVES tell the kind of noun,

As *great*, *small*, *pretty*, *white* or *brown*.

Instead of nouns the PRONOUNS stand,

John's head, *his* face, *my* arm, *your* hand.

VERBS tell of something being done,

To *read*, *write*, *count*, *sing*, *jump* or *run*.

How things are done, the ADVERBS tell,

As *slowly*, *quickly*, *ill* or *well*.

A PREPOSITION stands before

A noun as *in* or *through* a door.

CONJUNCTIONS join the nouns together

As men *and* children, wind *and* weather.

The INTERJECTION shows surprise

As *Oh*, how pretty! *Ah*, how wise!

The whole are called 'nine parts of speech',

Which reading, writing, speaking teach.

Clauses

A sentence is made up of one or more clauses, such as:

I enjoy running.

This is a proper sentence made up of one clause. This sentence can be extended by adding another clause:

I enjoy running, my sister prefers cycling.

Subjects and verbs

A proper sentence must contain both a subject and a verb.

▶ **Subject:** The subject is the focus of the sentence. This could be a person, group of people, a place or an object.

▶ **Verb:** The verb describes the action that has taken place or is going to take place.

Some examples are shown below:

Susan answered the telephone. (subject: Susan, verb: answered)
A letter was sent to Mr Mantei yesterday. (subject: letter, verb: sent)

If you find this difficult, then ask yourself the following questions:

▶ Who, or what, did something? (to find the subject)

▶ What did the person or place or object actually do? (to find the verb)

If we do this with the original examples then we would find the following:

▶ Who answered the telephone? **Susan** (the subject)

▶ What did Susan do? **Answered** the telephone (the verb)

▶ What was sent to Mr Mantei yesterday? A **letter** (the subject)

▶ What happened to that letter? It **was sent** to Mr Mantei (the verb)

OVER TO YOU!

State the subject and the verb of the following sentences:

▶ Cassie won a prize for photography.

▶ The members voted against the motion.

▶ The documents are ready to send.

▶ Opportunities like this rarely occur.

▶ The journey to work takes one hour.

▶ Bristol has an international airport.

▶ The telephone has rung several times.

▶ Lorna was late for work.

▶ Waste paper should always be recycled.

▶ The skirts are priced at thirty-five pounds.

Conjunctions

The sentences in the exercise above are all simple sentences because they contain only one clause. Complex sentences will contain two or more clauses joined by a **conjunction**. Using conjunctions to join the sentences will make your writing more interesting and easier to read as the work will flow. Conjunctions are words such as but, so, yet, then, however, because, and. Look at the following example.

I enjoy running but my sister prefers cycling.
(clause 1)   (conjunction) (clause 2)

OVER TO YOU!

Use an appropriate conjunction to join together the following simple sentences.

▶ Lucy was late. Ismail arrived on time.

▶ I enjoy travelling. I do not like hot climates.

▶ The sun is shining. There is not a cloud in sight.

▶ The washing machine is not working properly. It needs to be repaired.

▶ The chairs are old. They are very comfortable.

Objects

As well as a subject and a verb, many sentences will also contain an object. The object is the person or thing that is affected by the action of the verb. For example:

Dalgit (subject) lost (verb) the letter (object).

This is a basic example, but it is possible to have more than one object in a sentence. For example:

Jasmine (subject) called (verb) Jack (object 1) on his mobile phone (object 2).

Nouns

Nouns are words that refer to people, places, ideas, animals and things. For example, Ivan, London, life, dog and book. Nouns can be divided into different categories:

▶ **Common nouns:** These refer to ordinary items such as bags, plates, computers.

▶ **Proper nouns:** These refer to specific people, places and items, for example, London, Margaret, Newtown College.

If you are using a proper noun in your writing, you must use a capital letter. Common nouns do not need a capital letter unless used to start a sentence.

Pronouns

Pronouns can be used as a substitute for a noun in order to make a sentence less repetitive. These are words such as he, it, they, we, us. The pronoun usually refers back to a particular noun that has already been mentioned.

Look at the sentences given below.

Mohammed attends Newtown College. Newtown College is a very friendly place and the lessons are fun. Mohammed is really enjoying his course.

This is very repetitive and difficult to read. The sentences below have been rewritten using a pronoun.

Mohammed attends Newtown College. It is a very friendly place, the lessons are fun and he is really enjoying his course.

The pronouns in this example have been used to replace the subjects of the sentences. You can also use pronouns to replace the object of the sentence as shown in the following example.

Andy sat on the broken chair and the chair fell apart under his weight.
Andy sat on the broken chair and it fell apart under his weight.

The pronoun you should choose will depend on the following:

▶ whether the pronoun is referring to the first, second or third person. The first person is the person who is speaking, for example I or we. The second person is the person spoken to, for example you. The third person is the person spoken about, for example he, she, it or they

▶ whether the pronoun is singular or plural

▶ whether the pronoun is replacing the subject of the sentence, the object of the sentence or indicating possession.

Table 1.11 shows the pronouns that can be used to replace the subject or the object of a sentence, together with the possessive pronouns that are used to show the possession of the noun. For example:

This book is yours. (where book is the noun)

Table 1.11 Pronoun table

Person	Subject	Object	Possessive
First singular	I	me	mine
First plural	we	us	ours
Second singular	you	you	yours
Second plural	you	you	yours
Third singular	he, she, it	him, her, it	his, hers, its
Third plural	they	them	theirs

Remember that these rules apply even if you have more than one subject or object in your sentence.

Common errors

The following section shows you some of the most common errors found in written documents.

Mixing singular and plural pronouns

One of the most common errors is to mix singular and plural pronouns. For example:

The company released their annual report last week.

This is incorrect, because 'company' is singular and 'their' is plural. The correct version of this sentence would be:

The company released its annual report last week.

Be careful not to make this mistake when you are writing business documents. Decide whether you will be writing on your own behalf or that of your company and then use either 'I' or 'we' accordingly. Once you have finished the document, check through to ensure you have been consistent throughout.

Avoiding the use of gender

Look at the following sentence.

The personal assistant will ensure her boss has everything he needs for the day ahead.

This is incorrect because we don't know that the personal assistant is a female or that the boss is a male. The correct way to write this sentence would be:

The personal assistant will ensure his or her boss has everything he or she needs for the day ahead.

This has lengthened the sentence and made it rather clumsy. Unfortunately there are no pronouns in the English language that relate to both men and women. If it is possible, you can avoid this situation by rewriting the sentence using the plural form.

Personal assistants will ensure their bosses have everything they need for the day ahead.

However there are occasions when you have no choice other than to use both 'his' and 'her'.

I or me?

It can be difficult to decide whether to use 'I' or 'me' in a sentence. The rule is to use 'I' for the subject and 'me' for the object. Look at the following example.

Lucy and me agree on this matter.

This is incorrect because both Lucy and me are subjects of the sentence. Therefore 'I' should have been used.

Lucy and I agree on this matter.

If you are still unsure try substituting 'I' with 'we' and 'me' with 'us'. If the sentence works, you will know you are correct. For example:

Can I visit Joseph tomorrow?

If you substitute the 'I' in this sentence with 'we', it still makes sense.

Can we visit Joseph tomorrow?

Avoiding pronoun confusion

As we have seen, pronouns replace nouns in a sentence. The distance between the pronoun and the original noun can cause confusion. Look at the following example:

Caroline told Ayesha that she had to cook dinner on Tuesday.

From this sentence we are not sure whether it is Caroline or Ayesha who has to cook dinner. One way of solving this problem would be to change the wording around. For example:

Ayesha was told by Caroline to cook dinner on Tuesday.

Caroline told Ayesha to cook dinner on Tuesday.

Who or whom?

People often get this wrong in their written work, probably because we do not tend to use the word 'whom' as often as we should in our speech. The rule for this is quite simple:

▶ Use 'who' if the person is the subject of the sentence.

▶ Use 'whom' if the person is the object of the sentence.

For example:

Mr Ashraf, who is our accountant, will be visiting us tomorrow. (Mr Ashraf is the subject.)

Yesterday John went to see Mr Ashraf, whom he had not met before. (John is the subject, Mr Ashraf the object.)

This rule can sometimes make the sentence seem too formal or awkward. If this is the case, try rewriting the sentence. For example:

John, who had not met Mr Ashraf before, went to see him yesterday.

That or which?

It can be difficult to know whether to use 'which' or 'that' in a sentence, particularly as computer grammar checkers often tell you to use 'that'.

▶ **Which:** This can refer to animals and things in both singular and plural form. You should not, however, use 'which' to refer to people. Use 'whose', 'who' or 'whom' instead. 'Which' is preceded by a comma and begins a non-restrictive clause, i.e. one that provides additional information. For example:

Gloria typed a letter, which she enjoyed composing, this morning.

▶ **That:** Again, this can refer to animals and things, but not people. 'That' begins a restrictive clause, i.e. one that defines the noun. For example:

The letter that Gloria typed was full of mistakes.

There are two common mistakes to avoid:

– Do not use 'that' when you should use 'who'. For example, 'It was Jack that paid the bill' is incorrect. The correct version is 'It was Jack who paid the bill'.

– Do not use 'what' instead of 'that'. For example, 'This is the house what Jack built' is incorrect. The correct version is 'This is the house that Jack built'.

Correct any errors you find in the following sentences.

▶ Lucy and me went for a long walk.

▶ Me and Pam are going to the cinema tonight.

▶ A solicitor must check their work very carefully.

▶ The business employed twelve members of staff in their despatch department.

▶ I apologise for our poor standard of customer service.

▶ Mark asked Milan if he could stay at his flat next weekend.

▶ It was Gill that forgot the lunch.

▶ Here is the book what I lost.

▶ Julian is the person which leaves the bathroom in a mess.

▶ Simon is someone who I would love to meet.

Tense

The tense of the sentence relates to when the action takes place. This could be the past, the present or the future.

Look at the following examples:

I **have been** working all day (past)
I **am** working all day (present)
I **will be** working all day (future)

One of the most common errors is to mix the various tenses incorrectly. Look at the following example.

I looked across the harbour and saw the boats bobbing up and down on the waves. The waves are crashing down and the lifeboat will be on standby.

This example starts in the past tense, moves into the present and ends in the future. In order to avoid this, check your work very carefully to ensure the tense remains consistent.

Agreement

You must ensure that the verb you use agrees with the subject of your sentence. For example:

We is going to the park later today.

This is incorrect. The rule is to use a singular verb for a singular subject and a plural verb for a plural subject.

We are going to the park later today. ('we' is plural)
I am going to the park later today. ('I' is singular)

This is very straightforward, but you need to bear in mind that one organisation is singular and so a singular verb must be used. For example:

The company is going from strength to strength.
Marks & Spencer is a very large company.

Words such as everybody, somebody, every, each, neither and nobody are all singular pronouns and will also require a singular verb. For example:

Nobody is going to leave the room until the bell rings.
Each girl has been given a gift.
Everyone has been asked to arrive at 8 am tomorrow.
Neither Harry nor Aisling has been asked to the party.

This can become confusing when you have two subjects in a sentence. For example:

The magician and his helper were given a round of applause.

This is correct because the two subjects have been linked by the word 'and'. Therefore the verb must be plural. However, if the sentence had used 'with' or 'as well as' then the verb would have been singular:

The magician, as well as his helper, was given a round of applause.

Redundant words

Redundant words are those that do not add any meaning to a sentence but are used to add extra expression. For example:

At the end of the day, I think it is absolutely the wrong thing to do, particularly in this kind of situation.

By removing the redundant words the sentence reads:

I think it is the wrong thing to do in this situation.

This sentence still means the same, but is much easier to read. Be careful not to use redundant words in your writing.

Rewrite the following sentences, removing any redundant words or phrases.

▶ At this moment in time, we cannot agree to your request.

▶ I categorically refuse to do this kind of work.

▶ It is a relatively simple task.

▶ It is particularly annoying to have to work late this evening.

▶ Basically, I dislike working with Pete, because if truth be told, I find him very irritating.

Double negatives

Two negatives in a sentence cancel each other out and therefore should not be used. Look at the following examples.

I have never had no cause to speak to him.
I didn't do nothing.

Both of these examples show that by using a double negative you change the meaning of your sentence. For example, if you never had no cause to speak to him, then you must have had some cause. Again, if you didn't do nothing, then you must have done something.

Occasionally, you will find people use double negatives in order to give the opposite meaning. For example:

I am not unhappy with this decision.

From this we can assume that as the writer is not unhappy with the decision, he must be happy with it. Try to avoid using double negatives in order to keep your writing clear and easy to understand.

Writing direct or reported speech

There are two ways in which you can write down what someone says in your business documents:

▶ direct speech

▶ indirect or reported speech.

Direct speech

Direct speech is most commonly used for stories, but can also be used for minute taking if it is important that you report exactly what has been said.

To write direct speech correctly you will need to use quotation marks to separate the spoken word from the speaker. Look at the following example:

The chairman asked Penny, 'Could you please tell us when the new computer suite will be ready? The work is now three weeks overdue.'

Penny replied, 'I know. The IT company has had problems with the cabling. The problems have now been resolved and the work will be finished by the end of the month.'

'Thank you for that,' said the chairman, 'we shall look forward to seeing the finished suite.'

When using direct speech the following rules apply.

▷ Each piece of speech is enclosed by inverted commas as shown in the example above.

▷ Each new piece of speech must start with a capital letter, even if it is not the start of a new sentence. The only exception to this rule is if the sentence is broken by the words 'he (or she) said'.

▷ Start a new line for each speaker.

OVER TO YOU!

Rewrite the following using direct speech.

> Kevin was late home from work. Where have you been, asked his wife Trudy. I've been worried sick about you. What's the big fuss, said Kevin. You know I had to finish that report for Harry, I told you that this morning. You never listen to me. Trudy hadn't listened to him that morning. She had been too busy getting the children ready for school, preparing packed lunches, feeding the dog, loading the washing into the machine and trying to get ready for her own day at work. Kevin, in the meantime had been enjoying a leisurely breakfast and reading the morning newspaper. Sorry, she said, I had forgotten that you were so busy.

Reported speech

This method is most commonly used for minutes and reports. The rules for reported speech are:

▷ the spoken words are often introduced by the word 'that'

▷ the verb changes to the past tense so that, for example, 'is' becomes 'was'.

▷ inverted commas are not used for reported speech.

Look at the following example:

The chairman asked Penny if she could tell the meeting when the computer suite was due to be completed as the work was already three weeks overdue. Penny told the meeting that there had been problems with the cabling, but these were now resolved. It was expected that the work would be completed by the end of the month. The chairman thanked Penny for the information and said that they looked forward to seeing the computer suite.

This is a full version of events. However, if you were writing minutes of this conversation, you could write a much shorter version.

The chairman asked about the completion of the new computer suite which was now overdue. Penny explained that there had been problems with the cabling, but it was expected that the work would be completed by the end of the month.

If you were writing minutes of a meeting, it would be best to use the shorter version shown above. Any general comments or distractions that are not relevant to the discussion should be left out of the minutes, particularly those that are inappropriate.

Rewrite the following using reported speech.

> 'Have you any questions on this topic before we move on?' asked the chairman.
>
> 'Yes, I've got one,' said Marcus. 'How will we be able to implement these changes in such a short space of time? It seems to me that there is an awful lot of work to be done.'
>
> The chairman asked Richard to answer this question.
>
> 'Well,' said Richard, 'it will mean that staff will have to work extra hours, including weekends, but as they are under the threat of losing their jobs, they won't complain too much.'
>
> 'How long do you think it will take?' asked Marcus.
>
> 'About six weeks in total,' replied Richard.

Punctuation

As well as making sure that your sentences are grammatically correct, you will need to ensure that your work has been properly punctuated. Given below are some rules of punctuation that you need to learn and apply to your own writing.

Capital letters

This is an area where people make many mistakes. The rules, however, are quite simple. You should use capital letters for the following:

- the first letter of every sentence

- for the personal pronoun 'I'

- for the first letter of proper nouns such as names, places, titles of books and films, days of the week, months of the year, public holidays.

- for the first letters of the titles of specific people, organisations and events. For example, Mr Roberts, Prime Minister Blair, Automobile Association. Be careful here though, as you do not need to use a capital letter for titles such as managing director or chief executive unless you are referring to a specific person

- for the first letter of the words in the name of a specific event. For example, The Royal Hospital Summer Fête

- for initials in people's names, such as Mrs S Spencer, and initials in abbreviations, such as AA

- at the start of direct speech.

Do not use capital letters for the following:

- seasons of the year, such as spring and summer

- job titles that do not refer to a specific person. For example: 'the role of the personnel officer, or human resources manager as it is widely known, is very important'

- events that are not specific. For example: 'charity sales or bazaars are often held to raise money for local charities'.

Rewrite the following sentences, inserting capital letters as appropriate.

▶ mark and patti are going to visit nepal next summer.

▶ the managing director, alex grey, made an announcement to his staff.

▶ my birthday party is going to be held at the white horse inn.

▶ the university of wales offers a wide range of courses.

▶ the hotel is famous for its wonderful french cuisine.

▶ where will you be spending christmas day this year?

▶ i could meet you on thursday 2 may.

▶ the prime minister visited the royal united hospital last week.

Full stops

Don't forget to use a full stop at the end of each sentence.

Commas

Commas are important as they provide natural pauses in our reading. If they are not present then it can be difficult to make sense of the text. It is also important, however, to ensure that the comma does not alter the meaning of the text. Look at the following example:

The teacher said the student was a fool.

Without any commas you would assume that the teacher felt that the student was foolish. If you now look at the sentence with commas inserted, you can see it means something quite different:

The teacher, said the student, was a fool.

You should use commas for the following:

▶ separating lists of words, for example, 'Bring a pen, pencil, rubber and ruler to class.'

▶ to separate different parts of an address (except between the county and the postcode) if it is written on one line. For example, '12 Ashley Avenue, STROUD, Gloucs GV3 8WN'

▶ to separate clauses or phrases. For example, 'As the weather was fine, we went for a picnic.'

▶ in speech, to show the name of the person being spoken to. For example, 'What time will you come home, Sarah?'

▶ before or after phrases that refer to a person. For example, 'Mrs Green, the dentist, lives in the large house opposite the village green.'

▶ before and after a clause that adds a thought to an original statement. For example, 'My brother, who is the eldest child, has a birthday next week.'

- before and after words or phrases that add emphasis to the sentence. For example, 'We will, of course, honour our agreement.'
- before or after words such as 'however', 'moreover', etc. For example, 'I like Jack. However, I don't like his wife, Judy.'
- before the word 'but'. For example, 'Joe is hopeless at French, but is very good at football.'

OVER TO YOU!

Rewrite the following sentences, inserting commas where necessary.

- ▶ Max is a tall blond and handsome boy.
- ▶ My mother who is quite elderly will be visiting us soon.
- ▶ The address is 10 Lavender Grove St Ives Cornwall TR3 8NO.
- ▶ It seems to me however that you do not agree with the chairman.
- ▶ To make a cake you will need flour sugar milk butter and eggs.
- ▶ Josephine our hairdresser works from her home.
- ▶ The books should be sent to Paris France.
- ▶ As far as I know the trains are running on time.

Exclamation marks

The exclamation mark is used to show a strong feeling or emotion. It should not be used in business documents, although it can be used in advertisements or notices. It is used instead of a full stop and the following word will start with a capital letter. For example:

Fantastic! That's the best news I have heard today.

Question marks

The question mark is used at the end of a sentence that poses a direct question, and it replaces the full stop. Indirect questions do not need a question mark, for example:

He asked if I could lend him some money.

Colons

A colon is used before a list, quotation or summary. It may also be used after expressions such as 'for example', 'the following', or 'namely'.

You may also wish to use a colon instead of a full stop between what would otherwise have been two sentences when the second part gives an explanation or further details to the first. For example:

Please arrange a meeting for later today: the matter is extremely urgent.

Semicolons

The semicolon marks a longer pause than the comma. It is useful when writing what would otherwise have been two sentences that could have been written independently but are close in sense. Semicolons are used to:

▶ link two or more sentences instead of using and, or, but, etc. Each sentence makes sense on its own, but they work better linked together. For example:

Cassie went to school today; her sister stayed at home.

The company is performing well; profits have risen steadily.

▶ mark a list of phrases or items introduced by a colon (see above). You would use this when the items are too long or complicated to use a comma:

Please bring to the meeting: a copy of the agenda; the full set of accounts; and the confidential report regarding personnel issues.

You may also use a semicolon before 'however'. For example:

I like milk chocolate; however, I don't like white chocolate.

Parentheses

Parentheses (or brackets, as they are more commonly known) are used to separate words or phrases that are not necessary in the sentence. For example:

Yesterday (which was Tuesday) was my mother's birthday.

The words in brackets add detail to the sentence, but do not add to the meaning. The sentence would still make sense without the words in brackets.

En dashes

En dashes are often confused with hyphens, but they are longer than hyphens (the width of a capital letter N) and their use is very specific.

You may use an en dash to introduce an explanation of what has been written before. For example:

Nadine was entered for Producing Complex Business Documents and Creating IT Solutions for Other Users – two of the components that make up the Certificate in Administration.

A double en dash may be used like parentheses to explain or add information that is not essential to the sentence. For example:

I am convinced – as you know – that the conference will be a success.

The en dash can also be used to show the omission of words in certain circumstances. For example:

Monday – Friday (missing word 'to').

It is also used to indicate a range of numbers such as 2–120.

Rewrite the following sentences, inserting punctuation as necessary.

▶ Goodness me he said I can't believe my eyes.

▶ He asked me if I would like a cup of tea

▶ Please excuse me I have a dreadful cough

▶ He went to the cinema his sister went to the park

▶ Their itinerary included Paris Bonn Munich Rome Greece Amsterdam and Venice.

Apostrophes

Apostrophes cause no end of trouble, but there are just two simple rules for using them:

▶ to show possession

▶ to show omission.

To show possession

The apostrophe should be used when an item 'belongs' to someone or something. For example:

The dog's lead was on the chair. (The lead belongs to the dog)
The manager's diary was black. (The diary belongs to the manager)

You could turn round the second sentence above and say:

The diary belonging to the manager was black.

If you are not sure whether to include an apostrophe, then try saying the sentence using the word 'of', for example, the diary of the manager. If, by adding the word 'of' the sentence works, you will need an apostrophe.

Singular words which end in 's' will need an apostrophe + 's'. For example:

James's bike; Thomas's book; the boss's diary.

Plural words that end in 's' will only need the apostrophe. For example:

The accountants' calculators; the lecturers' notes; the students' bags.

Plural words which do not end in 's' will need an apostrophe + 's'. For example:

Men's shoes; women's handbags; children's toys.

Plural words which end in 'es' will only need the apostrophe. For example:

The boxes' lids; the coaches' drivers; the businesses' accounts.

To show omission

If you join two words together, for example, can not into 'can't', will not into 'won't', did not into 'didn't', an apostrophe is required to show where the letters have been omitted.

A common mistake is to confuse 'its' and 'it's'. If you are unsure as to which version to use, then try substituting 'its' with 'it is'. Look at the following example:

The dog wagged its tail.

You cannot say the dog wagged **it is** tail and so the word does not need an apostrophe. Now look at the following example:

The sun is shining: it's a lovely day.

'The sun is shining, it is a lovely day', does make sense – therefore an apostrophe is required.

Another common error is to confuse 'your' and 'you're'. Again, try replacing the 'your' with 'you are' and see if the sentence still works. For example:

Your visitor has arrived.

Replace the 'your' with you are and the sentence doesn't make sense. Now look at the following example:

I hear you're having a party.

Replace the 'your' with 'you are' here and the sentence works. You are having a party.

OVER TO YOU!

Rewrite the following sentences, using apostrophes where necessary.

▶ Your coat is lovely, its new isnt it?

▶ Dont do as I do, do as I say.

▶ Davids left his coat here.

▶ The dog hurt its front paw whilst out walking.

▶ Please take this to St Thomas Hospital.

▶ Lets have a picnic tomorrow.

▶ The ladies bags were left on the desk.

▶ The companies aims were very similar.

▶ Darius car is bright red.

▶ The womens career prospects are particularly good.

▶ The childrens toys were left all over the floor.

▶ The directors home was very luxurious.

Spelling

Many people say that learning to spell is not as important as it used to be because computer text can easily be checked by using a spelling checker. This is definitely not the case. Although spell checkers are useful tools, they are not always accurate, for the following reasons.

▷ They do not understand the context of the word. For example, if you were to key in the sentence 'Let's watch the whether forecast to see weather it's going to rain', the spell check would not find any errors. This is because both words, whether and weather, are correct but have just been used incorrectly.

▶ You are usually given a number of options to choose from. Some of these options are given because the spelling is similar; however the word may be quite incorrect. For example, if you key in the word 'liase', which is a common misspelling of the word 'liaise', the first option you are given is 'lease'. This is clearly incorrect. The correct spelling 'liaise' is the third option. If you are not sure which is the correct word, this can lead to errors. If, however, you looked up these examples in the dictionary, the meanings of the words would make it absolutely clear which was the correct option to use.

Below are some rules that will help you improve your spelling.

Singular to plural

This often causes some confusion; however, the rules are quite straightforward.

Table 1.12 Some common plural endings

Word ends in:	Add	Examples
S, X, Z, CH SH or SS	ES	Glass – glasses, box – boxes, buzz – buzzes, church – churches, bush – bushes
F or FE	Change to V and add ES with some exceptions	Calf – calves, scarf – scarves, shelf – shelves, roof – roofs
Y after a vowel	S	Day – days, toy – toys
Y after consonant	Remove the Y and add IES	Baby – babies, spy – spies, dolly – dollies
O	Usually just add S, with some exceptions	Piano – pianos, hero – heroes, potato – potatoes, tomato – tomatoes

Adding prefixes

Prefixes are added to the beginning of words, for example, dis + appear = disappear. If you are adding a prefix to a word, you do not need to add or subtract any letters, either to the original word or the prefix.

I before E

Try to remember the rhyme:

I before E except after C or when pronounced other than EE

For example:

Believe, pier, shield
Receive, deceive, conceit
Weigh, eight, height.

Anti or ante

These can cause problems, but remember the following:

- ante means before
- anti means against.

Therefore use 'e' for prefixes and 'i' for words that mean 'against'. For example:

antedate, antenatal, antecedent
antibiotics, antidote, antiseptic.

Double consonants

When a word containing ll is joined to another word, the double L becomes single. For example:

Skill + full = skilful, full + fill = fulfil, un + till = until, well + come = welcome.

Double the last consonant in the words shown below when using the present and past tense:

refer	referring	referred
prefer	preferring	preferred
transfer	transferring	transferred
permit	permitting	permitted
admit	admitting	admitted
regret	regretting	regretted
commit	committing	committed
equip	equipping	equipped
occur	occurring	occurred
label	labelling	labelled

Single consonants

The words shown below keep a single consonant when used in the present and past tense:

offer	offering	offered
suffer	suffering	suffered
differ	differing	differed
develop	developing	developed
interpret	interpreting	interpreted
focus	focusing	focused

Dropping the E before ING

With the words shown below, drop the 'e' before adding 'ing':

use	using
advertise	advertising
arrive	arriving
acknowledge	acknowledging
continue	continuing
advise	advising
insure	insuring
ensure	ensuring
separate	separating
have	having
interfere	interfering

Homonyms

Homonyms are words that sound alike but have different meanings. It is very important that you learn the meanings of the examples below so that you can use them correctly.

aid	aide	dependant	dependent
aloud	allowed	discreet	discrete
assent	ascent	draft	draught
bare	bear	draw	drawer
birth	berth	flair	flare
board	bored	formally	formerly
border	boarder	grate	great
borne	born	hear	here
cannon	canon	hire	higher
ceiling	sealing	horde	hoard
censor	censure	key	quay
cereal	serial	knew	new
check	cheque	licence	license
coarse	course	lightening	lightning
council	counsel	miner	minor
compliment	complement	missed	mist
currant	current	naval	navel

Homonyms continued:

no	know	see	sea
or	ore	sight	site
pain	pane	stationery	stationary
passed	past	steal	steel
patients	patience	story	storey
peace	piece	straight	strait
peek	peak	summery	summary
pendant	pendent	sweet	suite
pour	pore	tail	tale
practice	practise	there	their
presents	presence	threw	through
principal	principle	vain	vein
right	write	wave	waive
review	revue	wear	where
roll	role	weather	whether

Similar words

These words are pronounced differently but are similar enough to cause confusion. Find out what each word means and learn to spell it correctly.

accede	exceed	attendants	attendance
accept	except	desperate	disparate
access	excess	devise	devise
adapt	adept	formally	formerly
addition	edition	loath	loathe
adverse	averse	lose	loose
advise	advice	personal	personnel
affect	effect	potion	portion
alley	ally	prescribe	proscribe
allude	elude	president	precedent
allusion	illusion	proceed	precede
ascetic	acetic	slither	sliver
assistance	assistants	suit	suite

Rewrite the following sentences correcting any errors you may find.

▶ Elisha excepted the gift from Ben.

▶ Wellcome to our new home, said Daniel.

▶ Ellie searched in vane for her lost purse.

▶ I am refering to you, said the teacher.

▶ We will be advertiseing the job in the local paper.

▶ Maybe you should have a coarse of antebiotics if you are feeling unwell.

▶ I am offerring you the oportunity of a liftime.

▶ We need to order some more stationary.

▶ You will need to state your wieght and hieght.

▶ How many silk scarfs do we have in stock?

▶ The advertiseing company were dissappointed with the response to their campaign.

▶ The bored of directors were dissmayed to see profits had fallen.

▶ Jacinder decided to higher a boat for the weekend.

▶ As it was only a miner error, the driving examiner aloud Maggie to pass the test.

▶ Lorna wanted to insure that everyone chequed there bags before they left the key.

▶ Harry was offerred a peace of Nat's birthday cake.

▶ Ursula advissed Beth to take her complaint to the principle.

▶ I cannot except your answer and would advice you to revise more thoroughly.

▶ Kate preceded to drive from her home to college.

▶ The affect this will have on the new addition of the book is huge.

Promoting effective working relationships

Introduction

This unit will teach you how to work effectively with others, both colleagues and customers. By the end of the unit you should be able to do the following.

Element 1

▶ Work with others to set realistic objectives

▶ Contribute to planning as a member of a team

▶ Agree working arrangements with others

▶ Carry out your own responsibilities

▶ Communicate effectively with others

▶ Contribute to the working of the team

▶ Maintain effective working relationships

▶ Work with others to monitor progress

▶ Review the effectiveness of the team

Element 2

▶ Follow organisational procedures for working with customers

▶ Present a positive image to customers

▶ Use appropriate tone and manner when working with customers

▶ Interact effectively with customers

▶ Identify customer needs

▶ Convey information to customers clearly and accurately

▶ Convey information to colleagues clearly and accurately

▶ Build effective working relationships

▶ Identify problems and suggest solutions

▶ Check customers' requirements have been met and identify any follow-up action

The unit is divided into two separate elements. Element 1 requires you to work effectively with others in team activities. You need to show your tutor or assessor that you can make a real contribution to teamwork because he or she will complete two witness statements reviewing your performance during the activities. The assessment requires you to write two separate reports, each reviewing a team activity.

Element 2 requires you to deal effectively with customers, handle enquiries from them and deal with problems efficiently. In the assessment you will be observed dealing with a customer on the telephone or in person on two separate occasions and again two witness statements will review your performance.

The assessments for both units take place in college or at your workplace and your reports and the witness statements will then be submitted to OCR.

Element 1 Working with colleagues

Importance of effective teamwork

People often say that they prefer to work on their own rather than as part of a team. They perceive that teamwork is all about having to do what someone else says, that the work will take longer, that they will be watched all the time and that the work will not be of such a high standard as if they were doing it by themselves.

However, team working can be a very positive experience. A good team will share the load equally, members will remain motivated and enthusiastic, people's skills can be used to their best advantage and all team members can learn something about themselves and the people with whom they are working. The work can be completed efficiently and effectively with the minimum of fuss. A good team will ensure that all members know what they have to do, who to report to and when the work must be completed. Help and support should be easily obtained and the end result will be of a high standard.

▲ Figure 2.1 An effective team working together

Teamwork is beneficial to an organisation because:

▶ clear and realistic objectives can be set

▶ everyone will be working to the same goal

▶ work may be completed more quickly

▶ there is less duplication of work

- communications are improved

- staff are more motivated because teamwork brings benefits

- the quality of work is better as people's strengths can be utilised

- there is greater flexibility; team workers will learn more skills as they work together

- there is better co-operation between workers

- teams take ownership of the task.

You can see from the list above that these benefits act as a good incentive to organisations to promote working in teams.

Working as part of a team can be much more effective than working individually. We have already looked at the benefits that teamwork brings the organisation; there are also benefits to the individual. These include:

- help and support from other team members; this could be practical or emotional

- social benefits

- the opportunity to learn new skills

- the opportunity to share and exchange ideas

- the opportunity to take responsibility

- enhanced job satisfaction

- assistance with problem solving.

So, from the lists of benefits we can see that if a team works well together there will be benefits to both the team members and the organisation, which will lead to greater job satisfaction, increased productivity and a higher standard of work.

CASE STUDY 2.1 – Elegant Designs Ltd

Kulvinder works as a personal assistant for a company called Elegant Designs Ltd. The company manufactures classic clothing for women aged 30 plus. Elegant Designs is committed to community involvement and regularly raises money for its adopted charity, St David's Hospice, a local hospice that provides care for the terminally ill.

Kulvinder has been asked to work as part of a team to organise the latest charity event. The brief is that the event should take the form of a fashion show at a nearby country house hotel. Immediately after the show, there will be a reception at which wine and canapés will be served. The event should be of approximately two hours' duration and the date is in three months' time, on Friday 20 April.

It is anticipated that approximately 300 people will attend this event and the company wishes to make no less than £1000 for the charity's funds. The company has given the team a budget of £500 as its contribution towards the cost of the event.

The team consists of:

▶ Kulvinder – personal assistant from the human resources department

▶ Georgina – a fashion designer and stylist

▶ Luke – production assistant

▶ Jane – financial controller

▶ Hannah – administration assistant from the administration department

▶ Jack – warehouse manager.

The team has been told that no one is expected to spend more than three hours each week on planning this event.

CASE STUDY 2.2 – Newtown College

Lena is currently attending Newtown College and is studying for the Certificate in Administration award at Level 3. She has been placed in a group with four other students to form a team for their Unit 2 activity. The students have been taken from each of the three levels. The team has been asked to prepare a course booklet and PowerPoint presentation for the college open evening. The booklet will be handed out to prospective students and the presentation will be run on screen without a presenter. Apart from these facts, the team is not given any other restrictions.

The team has four weeks to prepare this information. Their tutor has told them that they will be working on the task during their lessons, which will give them eight hours in total. They have also been told that they will need to do extra work outside of class time in order to get this completed by the deadline.

The team members are:

▶ Lena (Level 3)

▶ Elizabetti (Level 2)

▶ Mark (Level 2)

▶ Bethan (Level 1)

▶ Isaac (Level 1).

Forming your team

It is likely that you will be given the opportunity to choose your team members for the team activities required for this unit. However, in the workplace, teams are usually carefully chosen either for their workplace skills, such as finance, personnel or administration, or for each team member's characteristics.

There has been a great deal of research into team dynamics (i.e. the way in which teams work together). Dr Meredith Belbin, a researcher from Cambridge, has conducted many studies into the way people interact when working as part of a team. He believes that, although individuals can never be perfect, it is possible to put together the perfect team. From his studies he concludes that people tend to conform to one of nine team roles, each of which has typical features, strengths and weaknesses. Psychometric tests have been developed so that individuals can establish their 'team role' and managers can ensure that each team comprises of a mix of team roles to ensure effective working.

The nine team roles are divided into three main categories:

▶ **action-oriented roles:** shaper, implementer and completer finisher

▶ **people-oriented roles:** co-ordinator, teamworker and resource investigator

▶ **cerebral roles:** plant, monitor evaluator and specialist.

These roles are explained further in Table 2.1.

Table 2.1 Belbin's team roles

Belbin team-role type	Contributions	Allowable weaknesses
PLANT	Creative, imaginative, unorthodox. Solves difficult problems.	Ignores incidentals. Too preoccupied to communicate effectively.
CO-ORDINATOR	Mature, confident, a good chairperson. Clarifies goals, promotes decision-making, delegates well.	Can often be seen as manipulative. Off-loads personal work.
MONITOR EVALUATOR	Sober, strategic and discerning. Sees all options. Judges accurately.	Lacks drive and ability to inspire others.
IMPLEMENTER	Disciplined, reliable, conservative and efficient. Turns ideas into practical actions.	Somewhat inflexible. Slow to respond to new possibilities.
COMPLETER FINISHER	Painstaking, conscientious, anxious. Searches out errors and omissions. Delivers on time.	Inclined to worry unduly. Reluctant to delegate.
RESOURCE INVESTIGATOR	Extrovert, enthusiastic, communicative. Explores opportunities. Develops contacts.	Over-optimistic. Loses interest once initial enthusiasm has passed.
SHAPER	Challenging, dynamic, thrives on pressure. The drive and courage to overcome obstacles.	Prone to provocation. Offends people's feelings.
TEAMWORKER	Co-operative.	Indecisive in crunch situations.
SPECIALIST	Single-minded, self-starting, dedicated. Provides knowledge and skills in rare supply.	Contributes only on a narrow front. Dwells on technicalities.

It is not essential to have nine people in a team in order to get the correct mix. Belbin believes that people can take on more than one role within the team. What is important is that there is a balance of roles within the team.

You may have a copy of the Belbin tests in your college or workplace. Find out if it is possible for you to take the test. The results will be very interesting and you may learn more about how you interact with others.

Team roles

It is a good idea to give team members specific roles and it is particularly important to appoint a team leader. The team leader will have the following responsibilities:

▶ to co-ordinate the team activities

▶ to delegate work appropriately and when necessary

▶ to be the first point of contact for problems, delays, etc.

▶ to keep a check on progress and monitor events

▶ to keep the team on target

▶ to help promote teamwork and the group identity

▶ to oversee meetings and take the role of chair if necessary

▶ to motivate team members.

Although the team leader will have overall responsibility for these tasks, some of these can and should be delegated to other team members. For example, another team member who chases up work and makes regular reports to the team leader can undertake monitoring progress.

If you are dealing with finance of any type, for example if you are collecting money for a trip or organising a charity event, then it is sensible to appoint one person to look after the money and keep detailed records. This will help minimise any problems later on.

Someone who is willing to take notes on behalf of the team is essential. All decisions and actions can be recorded and given to the team after the meeting. This will help ensure that decisions and agreements that have been made are remembered and acted upon where necessary. There is no need to write up notes in the style of formal minutes; however, this is a useful structure and will ensure that items are not forgotten.

Giving a specific role to each team member will help the team bond, ensure that everyone is fully involved and make co-ordination of the activity much easier. The group will have an identity and be fully aware of the aim of the activity. If you are working with people you know well, you will be able to utilise their known strengths and avoid their known weaknesses.

▼ CONTRIBUTE TO PLANNING AS A MEMBER OF A TEAM

The initial team meeting

The first team meeting is crucial to the success of the team. It is at this meeting that you will appoint your team leader, exchange ideas and information and, most importantly, plan the work of the activity.

The first thing you should do is to appoint the team leader. Once this has been achieved, you already have a point of contact and someone who will be able to co-ordinate the rest of the work.

▲ Figure 2.2 A team meeting

Setting overall objectives

The activity will seem much more achievable and realistic if clear objectives are set at the initial team meeting. The benefits of setting objectives are:

▶ everyone is fully aware of the purpose of the activity

▶ the standard of the activity can be set

▶ the final deadline for the activity can be set.

Depending on the brief you have been given, some of your objectives will already be set. For example, deadlines for completion of the activity and the quality of the finished product. However, it is useful if the team leader goes over these with the rest of the team so that he or she can be assured that the team are fully aware of what they are doing and why.

Exchanging ideas and information

Once the objectives have been set, the real planning can take place. If you have been given a very specific brief, as in case study 2.1, the planning should be fairly straightforward as it will relate to getting things done correctly and on time.

However, if you have been given a brief that is much wider, as in case study 2.2, then time should be spent deciding how the team will tackle the activity. This has to be undertaken fairly quickly, and preferably at the initial team meeting, so that the team can then get on with planning the workload.

One of the problems of meetings during which people are invited to share ideas is that they can quickly get out of hand. A good chairperson will be able to stop the meeting from disintegrating. Some of the problems that can occur in this situation are:

▶ people refusing to listen to others

▶ several people speaking at once

▶ ideas being dismissed without thought or consideration

▶ those who are dominant monopolising the meeting and demanding that their ideas are accepted

▶ quieter members of the team not having a chance to put ideas forward.

The key to running a successful meeting is to have a good chairperson. He or she will need to have the following characteristics and skills:

▶ patience, tact and diplomacy

▶ ability to listen

▶ ability to think quickly

▶ ability to summarise the information exchanged

▶ ability to keep order

▶ ability to include everyone in the meeting.

A team leader who can also chair meetings effectively will make the process much more positive. However, it is not necessary for the team leader to chair every meeting, this could be taken in turns.

The following methods can be used to ensure team meetings are productive and everyone is given the opportunity to contribute.

Setting a time limit for discussion

If a time limit is set for a discussion on a particular topic, this has the effect of focusing the minds of the team members. This will help keep discussions to the point and will help resolve disagreements. It can also be helpful to gather together the various ideas during the allocated time and then ask team members to vote at the end of the time allowance. This is a democratic way of deciding issues and ensures that decisions are made.

Asking for individual input

Another way of working is to give each team member an outline of the problem several days before the meeting in order to allow for preparation. This approach is useful as it is then possible to assume that all team members have had an equal opportunity to research their ideas and present them at the meeting. This also gives quieter or more intimidated members of the group the opportunity to have their say.

At the meeting the chair would ask individuals or small groups to present their ideas. Other team members would be able to ask questions or clarify the information. Again, at the end of the session it would be possible to vote for the preferred solution.

Brainstorming

Brainstorming can be used to gather ideas from the group and to encourage the flow of creativity. However, this has to be managed well in order to be effective. A good brainstorming session will motivate team members, create new ideas and help solve problems.

In order for brainstorming to work well it needs to be structured and requires the team leader or chairperson to manage the process. The structure of the session will use the following elements.

▶ **Define and agree objectives:** This is quite straightforward as you will have already agreed the objectives of the activity at the beginning of the meeting.

▶ **Brainstorm ideas and suggestions within an agreed time limit:** The team leader or chairperson will need to keep this part of the session in order. He or she should encourage each member of the team to participate and remind the group that all suggestions are valid. Every idea should be written on a flip chart or whiteboard so that everyone can see what has been said and the direction the discussion is taking. It is useful if a time limit is set for this part of the activity.

▶ **Categorise the results:** Once the suggestions have been made and recorded, the various ideas should be categorised. This should help the team to see the various links between suggestions. Refining the ideas under new headings will also assist this process. In this way the weaker suggestions can be grouped along with other themes, thus avoiding the need to reject any contributions. It is important to remember that all suggestions, unless inappropriate in some way, are valid and should be treated as such, even if you think they are unrealistic or won't work.

▶ **Assess, evaluate and analyse the results:** The group should then look at each of the categories and discuss the validity of the ideas, etc. The various categories can then be condensed into a realistic set of options and ideas that can be used.

▶ **Draw up an action plan:** Once the final set of options and ideas has been drawn up, it is possible to write an action plan of how to tackle the work.

Brainstorming can be used for ideas on how to undertake activities as well as deciding what form the activity should take. For example, Kulvinder's team in case study 2.1 could use brainstorming as a method of deciding on the tasks that need to be completed, the timescales for each task and the method for completing each one.

Hold an initial team meeting to decide on the team's objectives and the topic for presentation. You should also allocate roles and hold a brainstorming session to obtain ideas.

Organising work into manageable tasks

Once you have decided what you are going to do, you will need to work out how to organise the various tasks. This is a good idea as it will make the work seem much more manageable and it will be easier to distribute tasks to the team. The first thing to do is to group similar tasks together. Look at the case studies shown below.

CASE STUDY 2.1 – Elegant Designs Ltd

Kulvinder's team have called an initial meeting to sort out the event. Kulvinder was appointed team leader, Jane will look after the finances and Hannah has agreed to act as meeting secretary.

The team had a brainstorming session to agree on the tasks that needed to be completed. This is their list:

Charity evening			
Book	**Documentation**	**Financial**	**Miscellaneous**
Hotel	Tickets	Obtain quotes	Log ticket sales
Models	Publicity	Calculate ticket price	Organise catwalk
Hair and make-up artists	Checklist	Collect/bank money	Transport to venue
Flowers	Schedule of tasks	Keep financial records	
Band			
Caterers			
PA System			

The team realises that there will be other tasks to add to this list, but this gives them something to work with and they will be able to start distributing tasks.

CASE STUDY 2.2 – Newton College

Lena's team has also had an initial meeting and Lena has been appointed team leader. The team agreed to take it in turns to write meeting notes and Elizabetti volunteered to take the notes of this session.

The team had a brainstorming session to get ideas for the event. Elizabetti's final list is on page 71.

Course open evening

Booklet: A5 size, 24 pages

Booklet content

2 pages for each unit, giving unit outline and assessment criteria	(10 pages)
2 pages for diploma units, outline and criteria	(2 pages)
2 pages for comments from existing students	(2 pages)
2 pages for information about and comments from lecturers	(2 pages)
3 pages giving information about college and facilities	(3 pages)
1 page regarding course fees and financial assistance	(1 page)
1 page regarding progression and career prospects	(1 page)
1 page from college Student Union	(1 page)
1 page with introductory text from Principal	(1 page)
1 page for entry criteria	(1 page)

Pictures of college, students, lecturers and anything else that is interesting

PowerPoint presentation

1 slide for introduction

1 slide for course content

1 slide for each unit

2 slides for diploma units

1 slide for students' comments

1 slide for entry criteria

1 slide for career prospects/progression

The team is pleased with the work so far. However, before they can finalise the structure for the booklet and presentation, they need to know the following.

▶ Is there a budget for the booklet?

▶ Where will the event take place?

▶ When will the event take place?

▶ How many people are expected?

▶ Who will be issuing invitations/publicity, etc?

▶ How many booklets should they print?

▶ Should the booklets be printed or photocopied?

Lena has agreed to request a meeting with the tutor to discuss these issues and the team has agreed to have a meeting after classes as soon as Lena has obtained the information.

You can see that the two teams have listed the various tasks in groups. It is now much easier to see the type and amount of work that needs to be undertaken. By grouping similar tasks you will benefit because:

▶ you will be able to see the resources that will be necessary, for example, paper, toner, photographs

▶ you will be able to prioritise more easily. For example, in case study 2.1 there are a number of things that need to be booked. This can now be organised into a fairly straightforward task

▶ it will be possible to see if anything has been forgotten, as similar items will act as a reminder. For example, when the team members are considering the items that need to be booked they may well be reminded of others

▶ your workload will already have a structure that will be useful when drawing up schedules and checklists.

Agreeing individual responsibilities

After the team has determined what has to be done, tasks can be allocated to individuals. This can cause problems when people think they have been given the difficult, boring or lengthy tasks. In order to avoid arguments and disputes there are a few methods that will help allocate tasks. It is not suggested that you should choose one of these methods as the only way of allocating tasks. A combination of the methods below can be used after taking into consideration the amount of time each person has available, their skills, preferences and the urgency of the work.

Using strengths and weaknesses

One method is to allocate tasks according to the team members' strengths and weaknesses. This will help ensure that the work is carried out to a high standard. The disadvantage of using this method is that people often enjoy working on something new and are therefore reluctant to take on work that is the same or similar to their usual tasks. If this is the case, try to compromise as a team, either by allowing individuals to try something new under the supervision of a more experienced person or by asking people to work together. It is worth remembering that a few well-chosen words of flattery will probably encourage even the most reluctant person.

Another problem that can arise using this method is that some roles are larger than others. For example, the role of the secretary or finance officer is often quite involved. In order to overcome this problem, two or more people could take on the larger roles, with perhaps the skilled person in charge and the other acting as an assistant.

Asking for volunteers

Asking for people to volunteer can work reasonably well, but you may find that all the best jobs are taken immediately, which leaves the team with a number of unpopular tasks to be shared among the rest. It is possible, however, to use this method to good effect if you ask each team member to volunteer, in turn, for at least one task. This means that everyone will have a chance to pick something they would like to do. This can either be continued until all tasks have been allocated or you can then share out the unpopular tasks using a different method.

Autocratic task allocation

It may be the case, particularly in the workplace, that the team leader allocates the tasks as he or she feels appropriate. Although this might seem unfair, the team leader may have decided that by taking this action, the tasks will be allocated promptly with little or no discussion or argument. The disadvantages of using this method include resentful and dissatisfied team members who may not show much commitment to the team.

One way of using this method is to allocate the tasks on this basis at the start and then once the team has settled down and are working well together, to allow more choice.

Most importantly, after you have agreed the task allocation you need to ensure that all team members are clear about their responsibilities. The meeting secretary should either include this information on the minutes or write a memo outlining the various responsibilities, which can be handed out shortly after the meeting has taken place.

Identifying resources

Once the team has allocated the tasks, it is important to think about the resources that will be necessary to achieve them. This must be done as early as possible so that items can be ordered or booked as necessary. The ordering process will differ according to your workplace or college's procedures.

Given below is a list of resources you should consider.

▶ **Stationery items:** to include headed paper, compliments slips, pens, pencils and so on. If you are going to use a large amount of headed paper or envelopes, it is sensible to put in a request immediately as there might not be sufficient amounts in stock.

▶ **Equipment:** photocopiers, guillotines, shredders, whiteboard, flip chart, PA systems, computer presentation equipment, etc. You will need to find out whether your workplace or college has the required equipment. If so, book it with the person responsible for this. If not, you will have to negotiate a budget and find a company that hires the equipment you require.

▶ **Rooms:** for events or meetings. If you are booking rooms outside of your organisation, this should be done as soon as possible. Some colleges and workplaces have meeting rooms that need to be booked in advance. If possible, draw up a schedule which includes meeting times so that you can book the necessary rooms at one time.

▶ **Labour:** If part of your activity requires extra labour (for example, staff to host an event or prepare a mail shot), try to organise this well in advance. If you are asking people to work outside their normal hours, you may need to get permission from their managers.

Determining priorities

This is an important part of the planning process. You will need to prioritise work for the following reasons:

▶ to ensure that the work flows in a logical order

▶ to ensure that tasks that require booking or ordering are completed in time

▶ so that urgent work is carried out first.

To help you prioritise, look at the various tasks you have to do and grade them into the categories shown in Table 2.2 on page 74.

Table 2.2 Prioritising work

Order	Category	Type of work
First	Urgent and important	Tasks that are crucial to the overall job.
Second	Urgent and important	Tasks that others need you to complete before they can start their own work.
Third	Urgent	Tasks that are very close to their deadline (or are overdue).
Fourth	Urgent	Tasks that may need time to sort out. This might be because others are involved or research needs to be undertaken.
Fifth	Important	Tasks that must be carried out, but are not necessarily or currently urgent. Filing should be included in this category.
Sixth	Routine	These might include routine tidying, sorting of files, clearing out old paperwork, etc.

Don't forget that if you ignore categories four, five and six for too long then these tasks will move up to categories one and two. If you have several tasks in category one, decide how long each will take to complete. If possible, try to do the shorter tasks first because this will clear some of your workload immediately, you will feel motivated as you have managed to get some work out of the way and you will be relieved of some pressure.

If you cannot decide the category of a task, ask yourself the following questions.

▶ If I don't do this today, what are the consequences?

▶ Will I be holding others up by not completing this task?

▶ Who gave me the task; was it a manager or supervisor?

▶ How long will it take?

▶ Could the deadline be moved if necessary?

The answers to these questions should help you determine the urgency and importance of the task.

Identifying timescales and deadlines

A large part of the planning process should be to organise the timescale of the activity as a whole and the individual deadlines for tasks. The timescale may well be given to you as part of the brief. It is important that you decide on individual deadlines for the tasks so that:

▶ tasks are completed on time to aid the workflow

▶ team members have a firm date by which they must complete the work

▶ problems can be seen in advance

▶ sufficient time can be allocated to acquire resources

▶ contingency planning can be built into schedules

- a realistic timescale can be set for completion of tasks and the activity as a whole

- extra time can be allowed if the deadlines cannot be met.

This should be carried out as early as possible and preferably at the initial team meeting. When allocating time for tasks, always be as generous as possible and also allow extra time for problems. For example, if you know that a task will take two or three days, allow a three-day period, but allow a five-day period on the schedule, just in case the team member cannot complete the task on time.

It is particularly important to allow extra time when dealing with external suppliers such as printers or stationery suppliers. These often take longer than expected and if you have a problem, for example an error on the printed invitation or goods arrive broken, you need sufficient time for replacements to be issued and delivered.

Identifying possible problems and solutions

There is always the possibility that the work will not be completed exactly as planned. A good team will have anticipated problem areas and agreed upon a contingency plan to cover the unexpected from the outset. It is, however, very difficult to anticipate everything that might go wrong and it would be unproductive to spend too much time planning for problems. The key to dealing with the unexpected is to be able to use your initiative and be well prepared. If you can do this and remain calm in a crisis, you will be able to overcome most disasters.

A good plan of work will include the following.

- Extra time for completion of work, receiving of goods and checking details. This will help ensure that if things do go wrong you have the time available to sort out a solution.

- Details of people, companies and resources that could be used in an emergency. For example, if your printer cannot deliver the goods on time, you should have the details of a alternative company that could help. If you organise external services on a regular basis, you will soon learn which companies are reliable and which are not.

- Who to report to if things go wrong. It is essential that you know who to report to if you have a problem that is outside the authority or experience of your team.

OVER TO YOU!

Within your team, allocate tasks and agree individual responsibilities. Work out the resources that you will require and identify the deadlines you will need to keep.

CASE STUDY 2.1 – Elegant Designs Ltd

Kulvinder's team decided to allocate groups of tasks to the various individuals according to their strengths. The group were happy with the allocation as the activity will form part of their day-to-day workload.

Shown below are the various responsibilities of each of the team members:

▶ Kulvinder: team-leading; monitoring progress; co-ordinating work; liaising with St David's Hospice; preparing publicity material; liaising with directors

▶ Georgina: booking hair and make-up artists; organising models; designing layout

▶ Luke: designing tickets; researching music options; organising catwalk

▶ Jane: all financial work

▶ Hannah: booking hotel, flowers and caterers; dealing with distribution of tickets and publicity material

▶ Jack: dealing with transportation of goods to and from venue; assisting Luke with catwalk, sound and lighting.

It has been agreed that when new tasks are added to the list, they will be shared according to current workload and availability.

The timescale for this activity is quite short and there are many arrangements to be made. Hannah has agreed to produce a checklist and schedule for each member of the team so that the work is completed efficiently.

The team has discussed possible problem areas and they are concerned about the following.

▶ The equipment required – for example, sound and lighting – has not been used for some time and may not be complete or working.

▶ It may be difficult to book the required number of models at such short notice.

▶ The date of the fashion show is just before the release of their company's new collection. They are concerned that showing last season's clothes will give the wrong impression, but are not sure that the new collection will be ready in time.

▶ Jane already has a very heavy workload and she is concerned that she will not have sufficient time to carry out her tasks.

As a team, they decided upon the following contingency plans.

▶ Booking the venue and the models as the first priority.

▶ Luke should check the equipment immediately and report to the team if there are any problems.

▶ Georgina should discuss the problem with the collection with her line manager and the production department. If the new collection is not ready, they will have to use their Classic range. This is a collection of clothes aimed at the professional, older woman. This range is fairly stable as the designs are usually updated each season in terms of colours and detail, but not redesigned to keep in line with high fashion.

▶ Hannah and Kulvinder have agreed to assist Jane with the financial elements of the event.

Hannah said she would be able to spend some time devising the schedule and individual checklists that afternoon. The team agreed to meet first thing the next day to be given their lists and to go over the work that needs to be completed immediately. Table 2.3 shows the team checklist that Hannah has prepared.

This is a basic schedule that can be used for monitoring purposes as there is a column for 'signing off' tasks that have been completed. Items can easily be added to the schedule if required.

Table 2.3 Checklist for the charity fashion show

Date	Task	Team member	Completion date for task	Comments	Date Completed
20/01	Contact suitable hotels for availability and costs	Hannah	22/01	Obtain details of 3 hotels	
20/01	Check sound and lighting equipment	Luke	02/02	Report any problems to Kulvinder	
23/01	Visit hotels for suitability	Georgina, Luke, Jack	24/01		
24/01	**Team meeting**	**All**		**Select venue**	
25/01	Book hotel	Hannah	25/01	Hannah to confirm booking to team	
25/01	Research printers for tickets and publicity material	Hannah	29/01		
26/01	Book models	Georgina	29/01	5 models required	
26/01	Design tickets	Luke	29/01		
26/01	Book hair and make-up artists	Georgina	29/01		
26/01	Research music options	Luke	29/01	Preferably jazz band	
26/01	Book flowers	Georgina	29/01	Georgina will order flowers to match theme of event	
27/01	Liaise with St David's Hospice	Kulvinder	27/01	Contact: Maggie Wyndham	
30/01	**Team meeting**	**All**		**Discuss costs. Approve ticket design. Discuss publicity. Approve band**	
30/01	Calculate ticket price	Jane	30/01		
30/01	Prepare publicity material	Kulvinder	02/02		
30/01	Book band	Luke	31/01		
30/01	Organise catwalk	Luke	02/03		
02/02	Report progress to Directors	Kulvinder	02/02		
03/02	Send publicity material/ tickets to printers	Hannah	04/02		
04/02	**Team meeting**	**All**		**Approve publicity material Progress report**	
07/02	Receive publicity material/tickets from printers	Hannah	07/02		
08/02	Organise transportation of equipment to hotel	Jack	28/02		
10/02	Distribute publicity material	Hannah	12/02		
15/02	Log ticket sales	Jane	19/04		
10/02	**Team meeting**	**All**		**Discuss progress and ticket sales**	
10/03	**Team meeting**	**All**		**Discuss progress. Check confirmation for all bookings**	
15/03	Select garments for show	Georgina, Luke, Hannah	16/03		

Table 2.3 Continued

Date	Task	Team member	Completion date for task	Comments	Date Completed
28/03	**Team meeting**	All		**Discuss progress and ticket sales**	
10/04	Calculate ticket sales	Jane	12/04		
12/04	**Team meeting**	All		**Discuss final arrangements**	
13/04	Liaise with St David's	Kulvinder	13/04		
17/04	Give hotel numbers for catering	Hannah	17/04		
18/04	Gather resources required for event	Hannah, Jack, Georgina	19/04		
20/04	Transport materials to venue	Jack			

CASE STUDY 2.2 – Newtown College

Lena has also prepared a checklist for her team. This is shown in Table 2.4.

Table 2.4 Lena's checklist

Lena	Elizabetti	Mark	Bethan	Isaac
Write copy for unit outline and assessment criteria	Write copy for diploma units	Interview existing students for comments pages	Interview lecturers	Ask Student Union for information
Research information regarding course fees and financial assistance	Research information on college and facilities	Research entry criteria for course	Take suitable photographs of the college and students using digital camera	Assist Bethan with photographs
Speak to Principal regarding introduction	Research progression and career prospects	Design layout of booklet	Key in text in a suitable format	Assist Mark and Bethan
Monitor progress	Show group how to use PowerPoint			Speak to lecturer regarding queries

Comments

▶ Open evening is 30 March.

▶ All copy must be ready by 12 March.

▶ All photographs must be ready by 15 March.

▶ Final design of booklet must be completed by 22 March.

▶ Final design of PowerPoint presentation must be completed by 25 March.

▶ Team meetings will be held on the following dates: 9 March, 16 March, 23 March. These will be held during lesson time (1.30–3.30 pm) in Room 203. Any problems, please report to Lena.

▼ AGREE WORKING ARRANGEMENTS WITH OTHERS

Agreeing the decision-making process

Once the team has determined the tasks to be completed and allocated who will be tackling each task, it needs to decide and agree on the methods of working. It may seem unnecessary to do this; however, there will be many benefits to agreeing the processes and procedures that the team will use. The benefits can include:

▶ everyone knows what to do

▶ there will be standard procedures so work will be completed in the same way

▶ the processes and procedures will have been agreed so there is less room for argument or disagreement

▶ people will know who to go to for help and support

▶ it will be easier to monitor progress.

How you agree the decision-making process will depend on the level of authority of your team members. If your team has a hierarchy with a manager or supervisor at the top, they will probably make most of the decisions, allowing the team members to make their contribution.

However, if you have a team that has equal authority, you will need to work out a method of decision making that is acceptable to the majority. Your team may decide that all decisions have to be voted up with the majority vote winning. This is probably one of the most democratic methods of decision making.

You will also, as a team, need to decide on the level of authority for each team member as they work through their individual tasks. For example, will team members be allowed to make decisions that may affect the rest of the team or the activity as a whole? If so, will they need to discuss this with the team, just tell the team leader or will it be a matter that must be voted on? These decisions will be affected by the type and overall importance of the team activity.

Procedures for monitoring progress and reporting back

In order to ensure that the work is completed on time, it is essential to monitor its progress. It is sensible if one team member takes the responsibility for doing this, so that work is not duplicated and progress can be updated regularly. It can be useful if the team leader is the person who monitors progress as he or she will be able to see if anyone is struggling or not able to meet the deadline.

There are a number of ways of monitoring progress, some rather basic, others much more sophisticated. The most suitable method for your team will depend on the number of team members, the length of the activity and the complexity and type of activity. The methods include the following.

▶ **People reporting their progress on a daily or weekly basis:** This works reasonably well as long as each team member co-operates. If people forget to let the team leader know then they will have to be chased, which can be very time consuming.

▶ **Team member checking on progress:** Another method is for the person monitoring progress to make contact with each team member on a regular basis in order to establish progress. They will then update their records and be able to assess whether the work is on target. This is probably the most effective method, but also the most time consuming.

▶ **Using task checklists:** Each member is given a checklist to complete when they have either finished the task or completed specified parts of the task. The checklist would then be handed back to the person monitoring progress on a regular basis. Again, the problem with this method is making sure that each team member co-operates with the reporting process.

▶ **Schedule:** Some schedules include a column that can be used to 'sign off' tasks once they have been completed. The person monitoring progress can complete the schedule using information given by the team members or each member can complete it themselves once the task has been completed. Schedules provide a good method of ensuring that work is on target; however, as with all other methods, it does rely on team members giving the information regularly.

▶ **Planning software:** Some companies use planning software that can be accessed by all members of the team. Information can be entered into the program and crucial dates and notices can be displayed easily and quickly.

Once you have established how progress will be monitored, it is essential to ensure that all team members fully understand the process and are happy to co-operate by giving accurate information at the appropriate time.

OVER TO YOU!

In your teams, agree a reporting and monitoring process that can be used for your activity.

Identifying health and safety issues

The team should consider health and safety issues when devising their tasks and activities. If the activity is of a general nature carried out within the workplace, the team will not need to spend much time on this activity. Your organisation should already have procedures in place for risk assessment and of course you should have received training on the use of equipment, working safely and reporting hazards. If the activity requires you to use equipment you are not familiar with, you will need to ensure that you receive the appropriate training.

However, if the activity involves work or people outside of the organisation, a health and safety risk assessment needs to be carried out. For example, if you were to hold a coffee morning at your college in order to raise money for charity and were inviting local people to attend, you should undertake a risk assessment to check that there are no health and safety hazards or issues that could have an impact on your event.

It is especially important that a risk assessment is undertaken if you are inviting external people to an event or holding an event outside your workplace. If you were to hold a large event, for example a firework display, it is sensible to speak to the local Health and Safety Executive to see if there are any regulations to which you must adhere.

Public liability insurance is another area that should be considered in conjunction with health and safety. If you are hosting an event that involves anyone from outside the company, you will need to check that your public liability insurance will cover this type of event. If in any doubt, speak to your supervisor or line manager.

Liaising with people outside the team

Part of your activity may involve working with people from outside your team or organisation. If this is the case, it is a good idea to nominate one of your team members to act as liaison officer. There are several benefits to this:

▶ the person or people from external organisations have a point of contact

▶ a good working relationship can be established and maintained

▶ the team member liaising with external contacts is fully aware of any agreements that have been made

▶ the work will be easier to manage.

OVER TO YOU!

In your team, carry out a risk assessment for your activity. Decide how the team will liaise with external contacts.

CASE STUDY 2.1 – Elegant Designs Ltd

Kulvinder's team were worried about reporting progress and keeping each other informed as they are all very busy people.

Hannah suggested that a copy of the schedule should be held on the computer network and that when a task was completed the team member would complete the appropriate column. This would mean that progress could be checked at a glance. It would also cut down on paperwork and time. The team accepted this suggestion. Kulvinder could then look at the schedule on a weekly basis and chase anyone who had missed a deadline. Full progress would be discussed at team meetings. It was also agreed that if anyone had a problem they should contact Kulvinder in the first instance.

Kulvinder volunteered to liaise with the directors of Elegant Designs and St David's Hospice as she had worked with them on previous occasions. This would ensure that she could maintain a good working relationship with them.

As Elegant Designs will be hosting a public event they will need to ensure that they have sufficient public liability insurance to cover the event. The hotel will also have a current public liability cover and so the event should be well protected.

CASE STUDY 2.2 – Newtown College

Lena and her team will hold a team meeting each week during their lesson time. The team agreed that progress could be reported at that time. Lena has told the group that she is usually available in the college library each day between 3.30 and 5 pm so if anyone has a problem they could go and speak to her then.

Isaac agreed to act as liaison between Pam, their lecturer, and the group. This is because Pam spends more time with the Level 1 group and so Isaac is able to speak to her on a regular basis.

The group did not consider that there were any health and safety issues involved in the work that they were going to undertake.

▼ CARRY OUT OWN RESPONSIBILITIES

So far we have looked at the responsibilities of the team as a whole. As a team member, you will have specific responsibilities towards your team.

Planning and prioritising work

Once you have been allocated your tasks you will need to plan and prioritise the workload. This is essential for the following reasons:

▶ to ensure that you do not forget to do anything

▶ to ensure that you have sufficient time to complete the tasks

▶ so you do not hold up the work of others

▶ to ensure a smooth and efficient workflow.

The first thing you should do is work out the order in which the tasks should be undertaken. You can use the same method for prioritising as discussed on pages 73–74.

Once you have prioritised the work, you can draw up a plan or schedule. This will help you keep on track. Write any deadline dates in your diary or electronic organiser as well as on the planner or schedule.

When you are devising a schedule remember to give yourself sufficient time to complete each activity. It is better to overestimate the time required to do a task so that you do not miss your deadlines. Remember, things nearly always take longer than you think and you must include time for interruptions, distractions and contingencies.

The quality of your work is also very important, particularly if it is going to be part of a presentation or report. Give yourself plenty of time to gather together the necessary resources; these should be to hand before you start the task. If you need to undertake any research or find information, this will need to be part of the plan. Don't leave these until the last minute. If you have everything you need before you start and plenty of time to do the task, your work should be of a high quality.

Reporting problems

Unfortunately, no matter how thorough the planning process, sometimes things go wrong. If this occurs, the best thing you can do to resolve the matter is to report the difficulties you are having to your team. Tell your team leader or the person appointed for this situation immediately you are aware that you have a problem. This will then give the team time to sort things out. You will find that the team will be far more sympathetic if you are likely to miss a deadline if they know in plenty of time. They may also be able to lend practical support and help by assisting you with the task.

Failure to report problems will have an impact on the team and the activity. Possible consequences of failing to report problems include:

▶ you will miss deadlines

▶ your work will not be of a sufficient quantity or quality

▶ you may hold up the work of others

▶ the activity will not be as successful

▶ if the activity is part of your employment, then more serious consequences such as disciplinary action could be taken.

Respecting confidentiality

Much of the information we handle in the workplace could be seen as confidential. It is important that you respect this confidentiality and keep your knowledge to yourself. In the workplace you may have to deal with staff records, financial information or marketing statistics. All of this information would be considered confidential, even between different departments.

If you are working in a cross-departmental team, it can be difficult to differentiate between confidential and non-confidential information. Think before you speak or give information to others. If you feel that it could be confidential, have a quiet word with your team leader or manager. If you are working on a sensitive project, your team leader should brief the team as to the level of confidentiality.

If you are working with external contacts, you must be particularly careful not to give out confidential information. If in doubt, speak to your line manager or supervisor.

Remember not to leave confidential papers and reports lying on your desk. Keep a folder handy on the desktop so that you can quickly and easily remove the papers from the sight of others. If you have confidential information on the computer screen, change the screen when others approach. Use passwords and other security measures on the computer and remember to log yourself out of the system if you have to leave your desk. Try to get into the habit of doing this whenever you leave the room.

Reviewing your own work

Reviewing your own work on a regular basis is essential if you are to stay on track and produce work of a high standard. If you have drawn up a sensible and well thought out plan, the review should be simple. You will be able to check that you are on target by referring to your plan and you will see how much work you still have to complete.

Checking the quality of your work will take longer. You should check your work for basic mistakes on a regular basis. Make use of the grammar and spell-checking facilities if you are preparing documents on the computer. Read through your documents before you hand them to others and be especially careful if your work contains figures. Double-check facts and figures with the original source to be sure that you have copied them correctly.

You can also enlist fellow team members to help you by reading through your documents to see if they can find any mistakes. If you do this, don't forget they are also busy and may not be able to check your work immediately.

Using initiative to solve problems

If you encounter a problem with your task, you may, with a little thought, be able to solve the problem without involving the rest of your team. As mentioned earlier, a little forward planning for problems can go a long way. Have a list of suppliers and contacts you can use if your original choice lets you down. Be prepared to work a little later in the evening or take a shorter lunch break in order to get work completed.

You must be careful though not to exceed your authority, for example, by incurring extra expense for your organisation without obtaining permission from your supervisor or manager. Do not make promises to colleagues and customers that you cannot keep.

Keep an open mind and try some lateral thinking when a problem occurs. You may find that taking a different approach will solve what might seem to be a difficult problem. Listen to others or ask them how they would approach the problem; you may find they have had previous experience and know just what to do.

OVER TO YOU!

As an individual, draw up a plan of work, prioritising your own tasks, and show how you will be able to meet your deadlines.

▼ COMMUNICATE EFFECTIVELY WITH OTHERS

In order for your teamwork to be successful, you will need to be able to communicate effectively with others. To do this you will need to be able to do the following:

- listen to others
- speak clearly and coherently
- put your thoughts into a logical order
- provide others with accurate information
- give constructive criticism
- co-operate with others
- use an appropriate tone
- use appropriate body language
- be aware of barriers to communication.

Provide and obtain accurate information

Unless you use accurate and up-to-date information your work will be worthless. You should always endeavour to find the most recent information and resources available.

It is particularly important that you do not give out inaccurate information to others if they are using it for their own reports. You could end up costing your organisation a great deal of money if decisions are made on the basis of inaccurate information.

If you are collating facts and figures from documents within your organisation, you can check they are accurate by proof reading your work very carefully. If you are not sure if the facts or figures are correct, you can easily ask the author of the work. If, however, you are using external sources for your research, such as the Internet, it is much more difficult to check for accuracy. In this case, you should tell your team members or supervisor that you cannot be absolutely sure of the accuracy.

Consult and liaise with others

Remember, when you are working in a team, you are working with others. This means you should consult with them whenever appropriate. For example, if you run into difficulties or need to change your plans, you should have the courtesy to tell your team members. This becomes essential if any of the changes are going to impact on their work. An email will suffice if your changes are minimal and have little or no effect on the work of others. If, however, your changes mean that the plan has to be altered or a deadline is going to be missed, you should have a word with your team leader.

If you are asked to liaise with others as part of your task, make sure you contact them on a regular basis. If you have agreed to speak or meet with a colleague or customer, do so at the appointed time, even if it is just to make contact with them.

Make constructive suggestions

When asked to give an opinion or make a suggestion, make sure you keep your comments constructive. It can be very easy to make negative comments about someone's ideas or work, but this does not help the team and can make the person feel embarrassed or humiliated.

If you cannot find anything constructive to say, then say nothing. This is a much more tactful and diplomatic approach than upsetting people. If you are pressed for an opinion, be as tactful as you can without being hurtful.

Being constructive in your criticism or suggestions means looking at the work or ideas from a number of points of view. Try to avoid giving your first opinion, think about it first. When you give your opinion or make suggestions, avoid saying 'I think' all the time, use phrases such as 'do you think . . .' or 'have you considered . . .'. This is much more acceptable to the person to whom you are giving the criticism.

Given below are some rules for making constructive criticism.

▶ **Know why you are making the criticism:** Before you speak, be clear about your objective. What is it you want to achieve? If your objective is to show your anger or annoyance, think again. You will not achieve your objective and will make things difficult between you and your colleague.

▶ **Be specific:** Don't be vague with your criticism. If you have to tell someone that their work is full of errors, be specific about the problems. Don't say 'You have made lots of mistakes lately', say 'The report you handed me yesterday contained three factual errors'. If you are vague, you are inviting the other person to become defensive on the grounds that you are being unfair. A specific example will stop this.

▶ **Don't be personal:** It can be very demotivating if criticism is directed to someone as an individual. 'The report you handed me yesterday contained three factual errors' is much less personal and therefore easier to accept than 'You made three errors in your report'.

▶ **Ask for feedback:** If you have made suggestions for improvement or change, ask the person to contribute to this. If you impose your suggestions on the other person without inviting feedback, you will only make the situation worse as the person will feel that you are attacking them.

▶ **Summarise the meeting:** It is a good idea to summarise the problem and the possible solution with the person before the meeting closes. This will ensure that both parties are clear about what has been agreed.

Discuss and co-operate with others

Teamwork is all about learning to co-operate with others. You will need to be able to compromise. This can be very difficult for some people, who feel that they must be right all the time or that all their ideas or suggestions should be adopted by the team.

If you are in a situation where people are fighting for their own way, do try and think of a middle way that will allow both parties to keep some of their ideas and their dignity intact. This will help to diffuse any potentially explosive situations.

When working with a team, and particularly at team meetings, learn to discuss your thoughts and ideas. This means asking others for their opinion and then accepting it with good grace, even if you don't agree with what they have said. When others give you their thoughts and ideas, don't dismiss them without thinking first. Remember to make only constructive criticisms.

If you are asked to do something, accept the task without argument and with good humour. Team members who moan continually, argue over every little detail and refuse to accept criticism are very difficult to work with.

Style and manner of address

The style and manner of address you should use when communicating with your team members will depend upon the culture of your organisation and the level of authority of your team members.

Some companies address everyone by their first name, including the managers and directors, but others are more formal and expect people to be addressed by their title and family name. As a general rule, you should address managers and senior staff in a more formal way, unless you have been specifically told to use their first names. This rule also applies to external contacts and customers.

The style and manner of address used at team meetings will depend on the formality of the meeting or organisation. Even if the meeting is very informal, it is courtesy to address your remarks through the chairperson. This ensures that only one person is speaking at any time and that the meeting remains orderly.

Using language and tone appropriately

The language and tone you use when verbally communicating with others is extremely important. Inappropriate language or the wrong tone can cause endless problems and misunderstanding. What is the difference between language and tone?

▶ **Language:** the words or vocabulary that are used.

▶ **Tone:** the way in which something is said.

We discussed the use of language and tone in written communications on pages 34–39. The same rules apply to verbal communication.

Where possible use words that are easy to understand and that will clarify the meaning of what you are saying. If you do have to use technical language, make sure that the person you are speaking to is familiar with the terms. Check their understanding, tactfully of course, before proceeding.

Do not use slang or current expressions to your work colleagues or customers. You should not swear. Try to keep to the point and refrain from giving your own opinion unless you have been asked to give it.

▲ Figure 2.3 Make sure that the language you use is appropriate for your audience

Using diplomacy and tact

An essential skill for team working is the ability to be diplomatic and tactful. This will involve thinking about what you say before you say it. Remember, once you have said something it can be very difficult to take it back. A few words spoken out of turn can leave the recipient feeling very hurt and upset. A few moments of thought could have avoided this situation.

It is particularly difficult to be diplomatic and tactful if you have to tell people things they would rather not hear. For example, if you have to make a complaint about the standard of a colleague's work. In this case, you should prepare for the interview in advance and try to think of ways of addressing the problem without saying outright that their work is not of the standard required. You shouldn't lie to others, but leave out details that might be hurtful. Remember that criticism should be constructive and positive. Sarcasm and rudeness should never be used in any situation.

When dealing with external contacts and customers it is essential that you remain tactful and diplomatic. If, for example, your colleague has given out some incorrect information, do not say 'Oh yes, Mike always gets this wrong, he's useless'. It is embarrassing for Mike, gives the wrong impression of the company and reflects badly on you.

Importance of listening

Do not underestimate the importance of being a good listener. It is something that needs to be worked at because most of us are not naturally good at listening to others. A good listener will not just keep quiet while the other person is talking, they will actually hear what the other person is saying. This is called 'active listening' and requires you to be involved in the following:

▶ commenting on what you are hearing

▶ adding to the conversation

▶ changing the direction of the conversation when appropriate in order to move it forward.

An active listener will be absorbed in what is being said and will understand it at an emotional level. He or she will be able to pick up on nuances and underlying meanings. Paraphrasing, i.e. feeding back and checking facts, will also be part of the active listener's skills. This ensures that the listener has heard and understood correctly.

Think about your own listening skills. When a friend is telling you something, do you switch off in order to think about your more important and interesting story that you are going to tell next? If so, you will need to practise your listening skills in order to become an active listener, not a passive one.

In order to take an active listening role, you need to allow others to speak. This may sound strange, but your behaviour may prevent others from having their say. When speaking to others, remember the following.

▶ **Don't interrupt:** When people are trying to speak, do not talk over them. This means allowing them to start and finish their conversation before you speak. Sometimes this can be difficult, particularly if you disagree with what they have to say. It is, however, extremely rude to talk at the same time as someone else and this can soon lead to arguments and disagreements.

- **Allow others to speak:** Failing to do this is different from interrupting a conversation as this type of behaviour prevents others from speaking at all. Even if you think you have all the answers or that your information is more important than anyone else's, do give others the chance to have their say. Encourage others to respond and contribute to the meeting – you will be surprised at how much you can learn from others.

- **Don't be dismissive:** Even if you don't agree with what someone is saying, try not to be dismissive. Listen carefully to what the person is saying, you might be missing the point. If you really do disagree with the person, be tactful and diplomatic.

- **Welcome the contribution of others:** In order for the team to be successful it is essential that each team member feels that any contribution they make will be valid and equal. If the team is dominated by one or two members, or if the contribution made is readily dismissed, eventually people will stop contributing. This situation will lead to just one or two people running the team, which is not what teamwork is about.

Identifying essential information and passing it on

If you are an active listener, it will be much easier to identify essential information. An active listener will make notes during a conversation that can be used as a reference point later. Try to get into the habit of making notes during conversations, without losing your listening skills.

Once you have been given essential information, you will need to pass it on to the appropriate people, quickly and accurately. It is a good idea to pass on information immediately you receive it. This way it will be fresh in your mind and, if you have made notes, accurate. A quick email to team members may well be sufficient; you can always give further information if necessary at a later date.

Failure to pass on information promptly can hold up the work of others or may mean that they work with inaccurate information. This can cause many problems and can easily be avoided.

CASE STUDY 2.2 – Newtown College

Lena's team have now had their second team meeting and everyone has managed to write the copy on time. The photographs have been taken and the team is on target to finish its activity by the deadline date.

The team was just discussing the final layout of the booklet when Isaac remembered that he had forgotten to tell the team that Pam, the lecturer, had said that there were too many pages in the booklet and that it should be limited to 20 pages.

Although the team members were quite cross with Isaac, Lena managed to turn the discussion to cutting four pages from the booklet. This caused an argument as no one would agree to cut any of their work. Mark suggested that Isaac's information should be cut the most as he made the mistake. He also said that some of the photos Isaac had taken with Bethan were not very good and so these could be left out. Isaac started to feel that he was being bullied and the rest of the team then turned on Mark.

OVER TO YOU!

As a group, discuss how Lena could deal with the difficult situation in the case study on page 89. Then decide how the cutting of the information from the booklet could be agreed in a way that was acceptable to all the team.

▼ CONTRIBUTE TO THE WORKING OF THE TEAM

A team will only be successful if all members work together for the good of the team. Remember, the team activity is not meant to show off your skills as an individual. In order to work well with others you will need to do all of the following.

Support and respect others

Supporting your team members is an essential skill of team working. This means giving moral support as well as practical help. The importance of active listening and allowing others to have their say has already been mentioned. You should also be able to respect the strengths and abilities of your team members and offer support in the form of allowing them to use their respective talents and abilities. Don't be quick to dismiss others, you may be surprised at what they are able to achieve.

A good team will not only allow each member to make a contribution by having their say, it will also allow each member to actively take part by using their skills and talents. If you know that one of your team members has a particular skill, for example in art or design, encourage them to use their talents when appropriate.

Don't be scared to allow others to use their talents. Some people feel threatened when colleagues are given the opportunity to display their skills as they feel that the colleague will look better than them. Remember this is a team activity and the success of the team will be reflected on all team members. Therefore, always choose the best person to do the job, as their success will make you look successful as well.

Offer help

It can be difficult to help others, particularly when you have a full workload. However, the team will be much more successful if members can assist others when necessary. A few minutes giving a colleague a hand when they are overloaded can save hours later.

Offering help does not mean that you should take over someone else's work. Offer practical support in small ways, such as talking over a problem or doing some photocopying or basic research. You should not allow your team member to offload their work onto you: they must be able to do their own task. However, if they have run into problems, giving a few minutes of your time will be much appreciated. Remember, you might be the person who requires help in the future.

Don't wait to be asked if you see someone is struggling. Everyone has their pride and your team member may not want others to know they have encountered a problem. Volunteer to help out before the problem becomes a real issue. Remember though, that the way in which you offer your help is also important. You should tactfully ask your team member if you can lend a hand. Don't point out that they are struggling or unable to cope. A few words along the lines of 'I've got a few minutes to spare – is there anything I can do?' is much more diplomatic than 'I suppose I'd better help you or we'll never get this finished'.

If you really cannot spare the time to help a team member, encourage them to speak to the team leader. It may be the case that there is someone else in the team who can lend support at that particular time.

By helping your colleagues you will also be doing yourself a favour; you will have a reputation as someone who is helpful and pleasant to work with. This will be noted by your supervisor or line manager. It will also mean that your colleagues are far more likely to help you when you have a problem.

Co-operate

The team will be much more successful if it recognises that it is a team and not just a few individuals being forced to work together on an activity. The team will only be successful if members co-operate with each other. This means they will do the following:

▶ listen to each other and allow everyone to make a contribution

▶ keep to the reporting procedures that were agreed at the initial meeting

▶ help and support each other when necessary

▶ behave appropriately towards each other

▶ be prepared to be flexible

▶ be prepared to share the workload

▶ share resources as required

▶ ensure that their work integrates with the work of others

▶ keep everyone informed of progress, problems, deadlines, etc.

In order to do all of the above, you will need to make a conscious effort to consider your team members. Always keep in mind how you would feel if your team members did not co-operate with you.

Fulfil your commitments

If you have agreed to do something, make sure that you do it. The team will only work if everyone takes their commitments seriously and works hard to complete their tasks at the agreed time and to the agreed standard. This is one of the most important aspects of team working. If you fail to deliver your work on time, you will hold others up. If you fail to deliver the work at all, you will be letting down your fellow team members. Think about how it would affect you, both in terms of your workload and how you would feel, if your team members did not complete their tasks.

Reporting on work

Team meetings should be held on a regular basis so that the progress of the team can be monitored and problems or difficulties can be resolved. As a team, you may use team members to report on progress or you may have one person who chases progress reports on a regular basis.

Whatever method your team uses to report on progress, it is essential that you give an accurate report on your personal progress. If you haven't completed a task, say so. Do not be tempted to lie about your progress; you will probably be found out and you will put extra pressure on yourself.

If you are unable to complete your tasks as agreed, inform the team. It is far better to tell people in advance so that a solution to the problem can be found. Don't be tempted to say you have got further with a task that you really have. This may come back to haunt you if you find that later on you have a difficulty with the task and require help.

When problems occur, it is essential that you follow the procedures for reporting problems and difficulties. Tell those that are involved in monitoring progress and, if you have a team leader, have a quiet word with him or her.

OVER TO YOU!

As an individual, make a note of when you think you co-operated particularly well with your team and/or helped some of your colleagues. Then make a list of the occasions when other members of your team have helped or co-operated particularly well. Are the lists well balanced? Could you be making more of a contribution to your team?

▼ MAINTAIN EFFECTIVE WORKING RELATIONSHIPS

Part of the skill of being a good team worker is your ability to be able to work with others. This can sometimes be very difficult, particularly if you do not like them or have little respect for their ability. You will need to be able to put aside your personal likes, dislikes and prejudices and be able to work with others with an open mind. You never know, you may well have been wrong in your assumptions about them.

Dealing with different personalities within a team

Teams can often fail when the mix of personalities clash. As mentioned earlier on page 64, Dr Belbin felt that in order for a team to be successful a balance of personalities was required. Unfortunately, it is not always possible to achieve a balance within a team. In this case the team members have to work to the best of their ability to ensure that the team works effectively.

In order to do this, the team will need to make allowances for others and to take into account their basic personality types. Professor Cary Cooper, a management expert, identified three types of personality that he felt were essential to a successful team.

▶ **Good communicators:** An effective communicator is an essential member of any team. Use the communicator within your team to keep people informed and updated. If possible, ask this person to take on the role of monitoring progress.

▶ **Social emotional leaders:** A social leader will look after the welfare of the team. They are interested in the welfare of others and have a caring personality. They may be able to prevent arguments and disagreements between others.

▶ **Task people:** These people will want to get on with the task, be co-operative and assist others. They may shy away from leadership roles, but will be happy to contribute to the team both in the decision-making process and in carrying out the tasks. As a team, you must be careful that you do not overload these helpful members with tasks that no one else wants to do or take advantage of their good nature.

One of the most important aspects of teamwork is to recognise the roles that the team members are able to take and to make use of their strengths. It is, however, equally important to recognise that there will be roles that are unsuitable for certain personality types and that they should avoid these roles. Each team member should feel comfortable with his or her role, otherwise the team will not work effectively.

We have already discussed the importance of co-operation within a team. Another important team skill is that of effective negotiation. This means that the team should be able to resolve difficulties and work together without arguments or conflict.

It is unrealistic to expect team members to always agree with each other and show the necessary amount of respect and co-operation. However, a successful team, will learn to accept that there will be differences among team members, come to expect them and have strategies to overcome them.

Remember that the team should be working together to complete an activity and this means that each member has an equal part to play. As part of effective negotiation, you will need to be prepared to do the following:

▶ listen to the opinions and views of others

▶ treat each person's contribution equally

▶ keep your criticisms constructive

▶ make suggestions rather than tell others what to do

▶ contribute to discussions

▶ use tact and diplomacy where appropriate.

If you follow these rules, you will become an expert and valued team member. If agreement is made by majority vote, abide by this and do so with good grace.

OVER TO YOU!

In your team, discuss the consequences of reporting Georgina to senior management instead of having a quiet word with her as in the case study on page 94. How do you think this would have affected the team's working relationship?

CASE STUDY 2.1 – Elegant Designs Ltd

Kulvinder's team are making good progress with their activity. The venue, flowers and music have all been booked. However, when Kulvinder looked at the schedule she found that Georgina had not signed off her tasks relating to the booking of hair and make-up artists. She sent Georgina an email asking if this had been completed. Georgina did not reply for several days and then sent an email saying that it was all in hand, but not actually completed.

At the next team meeting Kulvinder asked Georgina for an update on this task. Georgina became very defensive and said she had been far to busy to do this task by the deadline. When she did try to book the make-up and hair artists she found that her regular people were already fully booked.

This caused a great deal of annoyance to the rest of the team. Georgina refused to accept that this problem was her fault and then left the meeting saying she was too busy to argue with them.

Kulvinder felt she had been placed in a difficult position. The hair and make-up artists were essential for the fashion show and as Georgina had left the meeting it was not known whether she had any other arrangements in hand. The team wanted to report Georgina to a member of the senior management as they felt she had behaved very unprofessionally.

Kulvinder decided to have a private word with Georgina the next day and told the team that she would then decide what was the best way forward. The following day she asked Georgina to spare her a few minutes. Kulvinder explained that the team had felt let down and that perhaps Georgina could have handled the criticism a little better.

Georgina told Kulvinder that she had recently had some personal problems and was also under great pressure at work. She said that after the meeting she had contacted another company that Elegant Designs have used in the past and that it was able to supply the staff for the event. She had made a provisional booking and would confirm it later that day.

Creating a positive image

We all know people who moan continuously – those who always have a negative answer to any question. These people are very difficult to work with as it can be impossible to get them to show any enthusiasm or optimism. If allowed to continue, these people can easily demotivate or demoralise the team.

In order not to fall into the trap of moaning and complaining, think before you speak. As mentioned earlier, if you cannot say something positive or constructive, don't say anything at all.

A positive image will also be a professional image. Most professional people do not waste their time complaining – they take action to change a poor situation. A positive approach will allow change to happen and will help the team to remain motivated.

In order to create a positive image, try the following.

▶ **Remain calm in a crisis:** Flapping about in a panic will do nothing to resolve the situation and will stop you from thinking logically. By remaining calm you will appear to be reassuring and positive, which will help the team resolve the situation rather than make a poor situation worse.

- **Don't let the behaviour of others affect you negatively:** If your instinct is to react negatively to the comments of others, try to keep this under control. Accept constructive criticism gracefully. If you feel the criticism is not constructive, then say so, calmly and politely.

- **Don't gossip about others:** Although it can be highly entertaining to gossip about others it will not do your image much good. Don't forget that people will gossip about you as well. If there is an argument or conflict within your team, try not to join in or take sides. Work towards resolving the conflict where possible.

- **Don't moan or complain:** We all have something to moan about from time to time, but do avoid listing your complaints at great length. If you have a problem, then say so with the minimum of fuss. Your team members will respect you for not whinging and be far more likely to lend a hand.

Personal qualities of effective team members

In order to be an effective team member you will need to have certain qualities. Some of the following have been discussed earlier in this section:

- be kind and considerate towards others

- be honest and reliable

- be an active listener

- have a positive attitude towards your work and team members

- be tolerant of others

- be loyal and fair

- be courteous and polite

- be calm and reassuring

- be helpful and supportive

- show commitment to the work and the team

- respect the views and opinions of your team members

- be willing to give praise where appropriate.

You may find it difficult to behave in this way all of the time; however, if you keep in mind that these are the required qualities of a good team member, you will be well on the way to effective team working.

Identifying problems with working relationships

No matter how hard you try, there will still be occasions when problems arise within a working relationship. These generally fall into one of two categories.

Personality conflicts

Occasionally you will come across a person you find very difficult to work with. This may be caused by one or more of the following reasons:

- they do not value your opinions, views or suggestions
- they may try to make you look foolish in front of others
- they work in a different way from you, which you find difficult to understand
- they are self-opinionated and won't listen to others
- they are sarcastic or rude or make hurtful comments
- they have a volatile temperament, which makes it difficult to approach them
- they may dislike you and make this clear to you and others
- they may talk about you behind your back
- they may be particularly critical of your work, especially in front of others
- they may deliberately prevent you from working effectively, perhaps by withholding information from you or refusing to help you when required.

If you come across someone who behaves in one or more of these ways, you will need to consider carefully how you can deal with this person. Retaliating by using the same behaviour towards them is not the solution. A better way of dealing with the problem is to find out why their behaviour is poor.

Remember that it is easy to think you have been slighted in some way or to misinterpret someone's behaviour. Take time to think about the way in which this person behaves towards others. If it is the same, you still have a problem but you will know it is not personal, which makes it much easier to deal with.

Try one or more of the following strategies to improve your working relationship.

- Approach the person who is upsetting you and ask if you can have a quiet word. If possible, go somewhere private and tell them how you feel about their behaviour. They may not be aware that their attitude is upsetting you. Try to remain calm and don't use an accusatory tone.

- Be patient; it may be that the person has problems outside work or perhaps is under great pressure at work.

- Speak to someone else about your problem; choose someone you trust and explain to them what the problem is. If they know the person in question, they may be able to give you some advice on how to deal with them.

- Discuss the matter with your team leader or supervisor. You should take this action if you feel the situation is in danger of becoming out of hand. Be careful not to moan about the other person, just state the facts clearly and concisely. Ask for advice on how to cope with the situation.

- If all else fails, make a formal complaint. Your college or workplace will have grievance procedures in place for dealing with these situations. If you are sure you cannot resolve the situation in any other way, or if you feel threatened or bullied, then you may have to take this action.

Work conflicts

Occasionally you may find that you or your team members will disagree on an issue that leads to conflict within the team. If the team have enjoyed an effective working relationship until this point, it will probably be reasonably easy to resolve the problem.

If a conflict over work arises bear in mind the following.

▶ Working relationships will not be helped if you lose your temper. When you are putting forward your views, speak calmly and logically. Keep to the point of your argument and state your case concisely using well thought out reasons to support your case.

▶ Do not personalise your argument. Keep to the facts and avoid making it personal. Don't make accusatory statements to your colleagues.

▶ Be prepared to compromise. If you refuse to change your opinion or compromise with others you could end up looking foolish, particularly if the rest of the group have reached an agreement. Never make silly threats that you are obviously not going to keep.

▶ Avoid childish behaviour such as shouting, storming off, crying or sulking. It won't win you an argument and your reputation within the team will be irreparably damaged.

▶ Don't fall into the trap of arguing for the sake of it. Look at the issue and judge whether it really is so important to you. If the matter is relatively minor, ask yourself whether the argument is really worth it.

▶ Remember that eventually an agreement must be reached, so do not delay making a decision just for the sake of it, particularly if it looks as though you will have to compromise in the end.

By taking on board some of the above points, you will demonstrate that you are a reasonable and well-balanced member of the team. This means that the others will respect your judgement and will be more prepared to listen to you in the future. This may mean that when an issue that is important to you arises you are better placed to win your argument.

▼ WORK WITH OTHERS TO MONITOR PROGRESS

The importance of this has already been discussed on page 80. In order for the monitoring process to work properly it requires the co-operation of all team members. As well as monitoring progress against the plan, as a team you should monitor your progress against your original objectives. This will help ensure that the outcome of the activity is successful.

Progress meetings

As a team, it is a good idea to have regular progress meetings where each member of the team reports on his or her progress so far and gives a brief outline of the tasks he or she have not yet completed. This will ensure that the team is kept up to date and if it looks as though there might be problems, there is an opportunity to find ways of resolving them.

As a team member, you should prepare a short report to take to the progress meeting. Your task checklist, which should be up to date, will give you a basis from which to work.

Look at the tasks you have been allocated and write a brief outline of the progress on each. It is important to make written notes as it is easy to forget things at the meeting. Note the deadline dates for each task and check that you are still on target to meet them. If you are not, then calculate the amount of time you think you will need and make a note of this.

If you have any other problems with your tasks, for example you need more resources or are having problems using special equipment, make a note of this as well so this can then be discussed at the meeting.

Once each team member has given a progress report, the team will be able to look at its progress overall. It will be able to assess the following:

- the likely success of the team against the objectives
- whether the team will be able to meet the overall deadline
- whether any team members require help or assistance
- if any further resources need to be acquired
- if there are any other requirements for equipment
- whether any additional tasks need to be added to the list
- whether the objectives of the team need to be amended
- whether the plan of work needs to be adjusted.

The progress meeting can also provide an opportunity to motivate the team. A good team leader will praise those who have completed their work on target or have made a substantial contribution to the activity. He or she will also be able to encourage those who are encountering a difficulty. A show of support from the team will help motivate any member who is finding the work difficult or time consuming.

OVER TO YOU!

As a team, hold a meeting to discuss the progress of the activity. Are you likely to meet your targets? Are you working in line with your objectives? If necessary amend your plan.

▼ REVIEW THE EFFECTIVENESS OF THE TEAM

Once the team has completed its activity, a review or feedback meeting should be held so that the team can reflect upon its performance.

No matter whether the final outcome of the activity was a success or not, there are always things that can be learned. The meeting should give each member an opportunity to reflect on his or her own contribution and the team as a whole should be able to reflect on its strengths and weaknesses.

The review or feedback meeting should be treated as seriously as any of the previous team meetings. It should be remembered that at this meeting you are still part of the team and it is not an opportunity to blame others or point out individual weaknesses.

The final outcome of the activity should be reviewed against the original objectives. Take each objective that you set yourselves at the initial team meeting. Did the team achieve each of the objectives? It is hoped that the answer to this will be yes. But if not, you will need to analyse as a group why the team was unable to meet the objectives. Perhaps the objectives were unrealistic or it may be that the team was not sufficiently committed to the activity.

If the team has been successful, each of the team members should be able to congratulate themselves on their contribution to the success. If it has been unsuccessful, each person should be prepared to take on board some of the failure.

Learning from experience

At the team review it is a good idea to spend some time asking each team member what they have learned from the experience. It is likely that the range of answers will be quite wide. Some people will have learned how to co-operate or communicate effectively, others may have found that they have learned new skills that they will continue to use outside the team.

Be wary of those who say they have learned nothing; these will usually be the people who contributed the least to the team and let the team down on occasion. There will always be those who find teamwork very difficult. You may find it takes a while before it dawns on them just how useful the experience has been.

As a group, it might be useful to note down how the team could have been more successful. With the benefit of hindsight it is much easier to see how things could have worked or how you could improve the team's performance. It is worth taking the time to go through this at the review meeting as this will prove to be part of the learning experience.

Evaluating strengths and weaknesses of the team

Don't be afraid to discuss, as a group, any problems or difficulties that were encountered during the activity. You must remember, however, that this is not an exercise in blaming others or embarrassing them. The point of this part of the review is to see how the group worked together, what could have been improved and the aspects that worked well. A typical strength could be that the team communicated well. A weakness could be that not all team members attended all the meetings. This forms an important part of the review as a great deal can be learned from this evaluation in terms of team dynamics.

Identifying and evaluating the factors contributing to success or failure of the team

Use this part of the review to discuss why the team was successful, or not. As a group, you should look at the factors which led to the success or failure of the team. These might include the following:

▶ the activity brief

▶ the feasibility of the objectives set

▶ the amount of time you had to complete the activity

▶ the commitment of each individual

▶ the availability of resources and equipment

▶ the amount of time each individual had to spend on the activity

▶ the team dynamics

▶ communication within the group

▶ contact with external customers or suppliers.

If, for example, you had a straightforward brief, plenty of time to complete the activity and sufficient resources, these factors would certainly have helped the team be successful. However, if you were given only a short space of time, little in the way of resources and an unrealistic brief, obviously these factors would have presented difficulties for the team.

Analysing different working relationships

It is very useful to analyse the different working relationships that took place in your team. You don't need to assess individuals at this point, rather the way in which the team conducted itself. For example, were there occasions when members of the group needed to compromise? If so, how did this affect the success or failure of the group? If a group member lost his or her temper, what happened? Did the rest of the group give way, or did they negotiate to find an acceptable alternative? These are the aspects of working relationships that should be considered.

When you are reviewing this part of the activity as a group, remember this is not intended to allow team members to vent their frustration or personal feelings on the others. If a working relationship was difficult, it should be discussed, but try to focus on the behaviour of the team members and not their personalities.

Identifying individual contributions

As part of the team review you should spend some time analysing your own performance. It is sensible to do this before the review meeting so that you are properly prepared. Ask yourself the following questions.

▶ What was your input into the activity?

▶ What did you do well?

▶ How could you have improved your own performance?

▶ Do you think you communicated well with other team members?

▶ If you had difficulties with team members what did you do to overcome these?

▶ Did you complete all your tasks? And to the best of your ability?

▶ Did you contribute to the planning process?

▶ Did you always complete your tasks on time?

▶ Did you contribute ideas and suggestions to the team?

▶ How did you relate to the other team members?

▶ Did you use the correct procedures for reporting progress?

▶ How committed did you feel towards your team?

▶ Did you assist any of your team members over and above your allocated tasks?

▶ What were your strengths?

▶ What were your weaknesses?

▶ What have you learned from the experience?

▶ How could you improve your performance in the future?

At the team meeting the individual members should be prepared to discuss their own performance in the light of the above. It must be remembered though, that this is not an opportunity for team members to be rude or hurtful. If there are any comments to be made on an individual's contribution, they should be given in the form of constructive criticism.

Improvements for the future

This is a very important part of the review. You should have gained enough from the experience to be able to see where you can improve your performance in the future, both as a team member and as an individual.

If, as a team, you have completed a thorough review of the items mentioned above, it should be fairly obvious where there are areas for improvement. Look at the areas in which the team had difficulties and see how these could be avoided in the future. If the difficulties could not have been avoided, perhaps the way these were handled could have been better.

Even if you think the team was a great success and all objectives were met, there is usually room for improvement. The team might feel that it would have been helpful if there had been more team meetings or if one team member had been elected to check the quality of work. As a group, make a list of the small improvements that could be made for future teamwork.

From an individual point of view, there is almost always room for improvement. Think carefully about how you could improve your performance in the future. You may find that there are only areas that you consider quite insignificant such as checking your work more carefully or reporting progress more promptly. Remember that making small changes over a period of time add up to quite significant change. Improving your performance in this way will make you a much more professional and reliable worker and team member.

CASE STUDY 2.1 – Elegant Designs Ltd

Elegant Designs have held their charity event and it was a great success, raising over £1000 for the St David's Hospice. The team worked well together and, with one or two exceptions, met their deadlines and completed their tasks without assistance.

The team held a review meeting for the event and it was agreed that overall the team met the objectives of the activity. They felt that the main strength of the team was that they were able to sort out difficulties that arose. The weaknesses of the team included not paying sufficient attention to detail and that the reporting back procedures should have been enforced more strictly.

The team felt that the factors that contributed to the success of the team included the fact that they had sufficient resources to carry out the tasks and that there was a good working relationship within the team. It was agreed that Kulvinder was an excellent team leader who worked well with everyone. The team felt that, generally, the working relationships were good as everyone made an effort to help each other and co-operate.

It was felt that future improvements could include paying more attention to detail and having stricter controls on reporting progress. It was also felt that team meetings could have allowed more time for people to discuss their problems.

OVER TO YOU!

Hold a feedback meeting once you have completed the activity. Reflect on the areas identified on page 99.

Lena's team have also completed their activity. The booklet and presentation looked very professional. Their lecturer and the Principal congratulated them on their performance.

They held a feedback meeting and agreed that overall the activity had been a great success. They had met all of the objectives and deadlines.

Factors that contributed to the success of the team were having plenty of time to carry out the activity and the fact that the team worked really well together. Lena had been a good team leader and Elizabetti had worked well with everyone, encouraging and motivating when necessary. Elizabetti had also spent quite a lot of her free time helping Bethan and Isaac.

The team identified improvements for the future including remembering to pass on information quickly and accurately. It would also have been a good idea to ask their lecturer to put the answers to their questions in writing so that they wouldn't have wasted time and effort completing extra work. It was agreed that they should have been able to discuss possible solutions to problems without arguing or blaming each other.

Assessment requirement 1

The assessment of this element is in two parts.

▶ **Part 1:** You must take part in two different team activities. Each activity should be complex and require you to carry out a variety of tasks. You must meet assessment objectives 1–8 for each of these activities. The evidence required for this part of the assessment will take the form of a witness statement that has been signed and evidenced by your tutor or supervisor.

▶ **Part 2:** You must produce a review of the effectiveness of the team for both team activities. This review will be your evidence for meeting assessment objective 9.

OCR provides a Candidate Information Sheet which tells you the type of information to include in your review. Use the bulleted points as headings in your review, this will ensure that you do not forget any of the assessment objective criteria.

You do not need to write a huge amount, 2–3 sides of A4 paper will be sufficient. You may handwrite or type but a typed review looks more professional.

Remember, the examiner or moderator will be looking at your review to check that you have covered all of the assessment objectives on each occasion of team working. It is therefore much better if you produce two separate reports, one for each activity.

When you are writing your review, remember to include the necessary information for the examiner or moderator to be able to understand the nature of the team activity, who was in your team, the roles you took and the task(s) you undertook. You should bear in mind that the examiner or moderator does not know who you are or what you were asked to do. Therefore you must ensure that you have explained the activity in sufficient detail for him or her to be able to understand what is was you were trying to achieve.

Once you have finished your review, read it through and check very carefully to see whether you have covered all the assessment objectives in sufficient detail.

Shown below are the reviews Kulvinder and Lena prepared for their team activities.

CASE STUDY 2.1 – Elegant Designs Ltd

Review of team activity: Organising a charity event

The nature of the activity in which I participated

My job is personal assistant in the human resources department for a company that designs and manufactures women's clothing. I was asked to be part of a team to organise a charity event for our local hospice, St David's Hospice.

The event was a fashion show at a local country house hotel. The money made from ticket sales to the event would be donated to the charity. Approximately 300 people were expected to attend and refreshments in the form of wine and canapés were to be served.

The team consisted of myself, Luke, Georgina, Jack, Jane and Hannah. We all work in different departments and have different types of job. We were given a brief to work from and had approximately three months to complete the activity.

How the team organised itself and planned to meet its objectives

The team held an initial team meeting during which we set the aims and objectives of the activity. We also made a list of the tasks that would need to be completed. We decided to allocate tasks according to our specialist areas and this made the allocation quite straightforward.

The team devised a plan of action and Hannah draw up a schedule so that team members were fully aware of the work to be completed and the deadline dates. We also agreed monitoring and reporting procedures.

My role and the tasks I had to complete

At the initial team meeting I was elected team leader. My main responsibilities were to liaise with the directors of Elegant Designs and the staff at St David's Hospice. I was also in charge of monitoring progress and co-ordinating the work. I also prepared the publicity materials.

How we dealt with problems or setbacks

We did not have many problems or setbacks apart from meeting deadlines. As most of the tasks involved the booking of items such as the venue, models, make-up and hair artists this meant that they had to be completed almost immediately. Some of the team found this difficult as the activity had to be fitted around their normal work.

A problem did arise with the printing of the tickets. The printers sent us a copy to proof check, but unfortunately we did not find an error until after they had been returned. Luckily we did spot the mistake before the tickets were printed, but this could have caused a real problem.

One of the team did not complete her task on time and although this did not hold anyone up, it could have had a serious impact on the success of the task. Because the team member failed to complete the task, the supplier was unable to help us at short notice. After I had a quiet word with her, she was able to find another supplier.

Maintaining good communication and effective working relationships

As a team, we met on a regular basis, which helped us to maintain a good working relationship. We used the schedule, which was held on a shared area of the network, to record progress and I called the team together on a regular basis to ensure that they were able to meet their deadlines.

We did have one problem with a team member who would not report progress. However, after a quiet word, she improved her performance.

How certain working relationships helped the team

Hannah worked very well with everyone and gave help and support to several team members when they were overloaded with work. Jack and Luke co-operated and liaised well and worked hard to ensure that all the necessary equipment arrived at the venue on time.

As we all work for the same company, we are familiar with each other's personalities and behaviour and I think this helped as we were already used to each other. The team really wanted the event to be a great success and so we all worked well together and co-operated in order to make this happen.

Overall strengths/weaknesses of the team

We felt that the level of communication and co-operation within the team was our greatest strength. We were able to sort out any difficulties within the team. The allocation of tasks according to our specialist areas was also a strength as we all knew how to do our work.

We did not have too many weaknesses, but overall we could have paid more attention to detail. A few mistakes were made which meant we had to do work again or alter our arrangements. The error on the ticket is an example of this. Another weakness was that some of the team members did not report progress as promptly as agreed and this meant I had to spend time chasing them.

Overall success of the team

Overall, the event was a great success and our company raised over £1000 for the charity. The directors congratulated us on our work and the local hospice wrote to us thanking us for organising the event so well.

As a team, we were also successful because we were able to get on with our work and complete the activity on time and without too many problems.

My contribution

I felt my contribution to the team was very useful as I monitored the progress and kept the team on target. I feel that I handled some difficulties within the team well and helped maintain good working relationships.

Improvements for future activities

Our experience with the tickets made us aware that we should check things much more thoroughly in the future. A stricter control on progress reporting would also be an improvement as it would have cut down the amount of time spent on chasing things.

One improvement would be to ensure that there was sufficient time at team meetings to discuss things in greater detail.

Importance of teamwork

This activity proved that working in a team can be a very efficient way of completing tasks. Organising this event involved a great deal of work and, as there was not much time in which to complete it, I do not think it could have been achieved in any other way.

As a team, we all had different skills and strengths, and we were able to utilise these in order to complete the work as quickly and as efficiently as possible.

Review of team activity: Preparing a booklet and PowerPoint presentation

The nature of the activity in which I participated

Pam, our lecturer, asked the team to prepare a booklet that could be used at our college open evening. The booklet should explain the Certificate in Administration course and give some general information about the college. We were also asked to prepare a PowerPoint presentation that would be shown on a monitor. This would not be used as part of a talk, but just to give information.

I was placed in a team with the following students: Elizabetti (Level 2), Mark (Level 2), Bethan (Level 1) and Isaac (Level 1).

We were told that we could spend four lessons (eight hours) in total on the activity and that if we needed extra time we would have to meet outside class time.

How the team organised itself and planned to meet the objective

We held a meeting to discuss what we were going to do. We had a brainstorming session and came up with quite a lot of ideas. I was appointed team leader as I am the Level 3 student. The team decided on the number of pages that the booklet should contain and the content.

We had a discussion and gave out the tasks to each team member. Each person had to research some information for the booklet and write up the copy. Bethan and Isaac agreed to take photographs using Bethan's digital camera. I agreed to draw up a checklist so that we all knew what we had to do. We would have team meetings in our lessons so that we could talk about any problems we had.

My role and the tasks I had to complete

As team leader part of my role was to ensure that the work was completed on time and to help solve any problems. I also had to write the pages containing information on each unit of the Certificate in Administration and also the assessment criteria. I was also in charge of monitoring progress and chairing team meetings.

How we dealt with problems or setbacks

The main problem we had was that Isaac forgot to tell us that Pam had said the booklet could only have 20 pages instead of the 24 we had planned. As we had already written all of the content, this was very annoying.

We dealt with the problem as a team by looking at the material we had prepared and trying to work out how we could redesign the layout to keep the information. This was not possible and so we had to cut some of the information and photographs. This proved to be difficult as no one wanted to have their work removed from the booklet. In the end we compromised and each of us had to go away and reduce our own work. Although this took extra time, it avoided arguments.

Maintain good communication and working relationships

We had a team meeting each week in our lessons and we used these to check on progress and discuss any problems. I told the team that I was available in the library most afternoons and so they could find me there if they had a problem.

We all helped each other complete our tasks and agreed on all of the decisions. The team were really committed to doing a good job and so we made an effort to work well together.

How certain working relationships helped the team

Bethan and Isaac worked really well together, taking the photographs and saving them on the computer. Elizabetti helped us all by showing us how to use PowerPoint. If she had not been so helpful, I don't think we would have finished the task on time as no one else knew how to use it. Elizabetti also helped Bethan and Isaac with writing their copy for the booklet.

Overall strengths/weaknesses of the team

The strengths of the team were that we all worked together to do a really good job on the booklet and presentation. We helped each other and we all tried to complete our tasks on time.

Our weaknesses were arguing when something went wrong. This didn't really help the situation and sometimes a team member would get upset. I think we should have handled the problems in a better way.

Overall success of the team

We were very successful as we completed our activity on time and we were very pleased with the booklet and presentation. Pam said our booklet was excellent and the Principal congratulated us as well. We met all our objectives.

My contribution

I think I helped the team by listening to their problems and helping them find solutions. I kept the team motivated at team meetings and made sure we kept to our deadlines. I was also pleased with the information I wrote for the booklet. The others said I was a good team leader and that I was approachable.

I felt our team worked really well together, but we could improve the way we handled problems. We should have checked our facts before preparing the booklet and this is something I would do in future as we all wasted quite a lot of time writing unnecessary material.

Importance of teamwork

It is important to be able to work as part of a team. Our booklet turned out well because we had lots of ideas and input from all of the team members. We all helped and supported each other and this made the work much more enjoyable.

We were able to complete this task on time because we all worked hard to get it finished. The reason for this was because we didn't want to let our colleagues down.

OVER TO YOU!

Write a review of your team activity using the format shown above.

Element 2 Providing effective service to customers

This part of the unit discusses the importance of dealing with customers efficiently, effectively and in a way that provides a high level of customer service. In order to meet the assessment requirements you will be observed dealing with customers by your tutor or supervisor.

▼ FOLLOW ORGANISATIONAL PROCEDURES FOR WORKING WITH CUSTOMERS

Importance of customer service

Customer service is probably the most important aspect of any business as without customers there would not be a need for the business. The market place is now extremely competitive and the one way in which your organisation can stand out from the rest is by offering a high level of customer service.

Finding new customers for your organisation can be a very costly business. It is much more cost effective if an organisation has customers that return again and again. Customer loyalty is very important for organisations and they will often offer a great deal to keep their customers.

Even organisations that don't have competitors in the usual sense, such as hospitals, schools and government agencies, must provide a high level of customer service in order to avoid bad publicity and complaints.

What exactly is meant by the term 'customer service'? It can be summed up as 'what the organisation does to meet customer expectations and produce customer satisfaction'. It is also the way in which procedures are put in place to enable an organisation to deal with a customer in an efficient and effective manner. The procedures should ensure that customers feel that they are valued, listened to, appreciated and have received a high level of service. There are two parts to the customer experience:

▶ how the customer has been treated

▶ how the customer feels that he or she has been treated.

These are two separate issues and it is when the customer feels that he or she has not been treated appropriately that problems arise.

An organisation that provides a high level of customer service will have customers who have had a good experience of dealing with it. The customer will have had his or her questions answered promptly, the goods or services will have arrived on time and in good condition and any difficulties will have been resolved in a way that is acceptable to both the customer and the organisation. All of these will have been achieved at minimum cost to the organisation.

It is important to remember that everyone who works for an organisation is involved in customer service, even if they do not meet customers face-to-face. The way in which the telephone is answered or the prompt despatch of goods or information all add to the customer's experience. You should therefore aim to present a positive image to your customers at all times.

▲ Figure 2.4 Always present a positive image to your customers

Maintaining and improving customer service

In order for organisations to thrive they must constantly maintain and improve their level of customer service. As already mentioned, the market place is very competitive and if a customer can expect to receive the goods or services at a similar cost, they will choose their supplier according to the level of service they receive.

Organisations will know that this is the case and will strive to improve their level of service. They will research their customers' needs and wants and try to provide them at a minimal cost. They will value the opinion of their customers and will try to make the customers' experience of dealing with them as pleasant and efficient as possible.

Identifying potential customers

Before you start to work on customer service you should be aware of who your customers are. Remember: customers are not limited to people who use your company for buying goods and services. Almost everyone you come into contact with in business is a potential customer. Customers can also be internal or external.

External customers

These are people who do not work for your organisation. They may be either people who buy goods and/or services from your organisation or people who supply your organisation with goods and/or services.

Internal customers

Your colleagues will from time to time be internal customers. They become customers when you provide them with information, type their documents, do their photocopying, and so on. Internal customers need to be treated with the same courtesy you would extend to external customers.

Procedures for working with customers

Most organisations now have proper procedures for dealing with customers both face-to-face or by telephone. Their purpose is to ensure that any customer who deals with the organisation will receive the same treatment. This standardised approach benefits the organisation in the following ways:

- the staff will know what to do
- customers will be treated equally
- customers will receive a consistent service
- procedures can be designed to allow staff to obtain and record customer feedback
- training staff will be straightforward.

There may be a number of customer service procedures in place, as shown in Table 2.5.

Table 2.5 Customer service procedures

Procedure	Purpose
Style of address	The standard greeting given by anyone who answers the telephone or greets visitors. For example, 'Hello, Elegant Designs, Sandra speaking.' or 'Hello, how may I help you?'
Prompt service	Many organisations state the acceptable time delay before the telephone is answered or a visitor is greeted. The usual standard is that the phone should be answered within 3 rings. Visitors should not be left unattended for more than 1 or 2 minutes.
Dealing with complaints	This procedure will set out how a customer complaint should be dealt with and may include the limit of authority (see below). It will also include the timescale for dealing with the complaint.
Scope/limit of services that can be provided	This will set out what the member of staff can offer the customer in terms of service and show the limits of either the service offer or the compensation that can be given to a customer in the event of a complaint.
Recording customer information	The organisation may have procedures for obtaining information and feedback from its customers. The procedures must ensure that the gathering of this information is done so lawfully and within the restrictions of the Data Protection Act.

Recording of customer information

These days it is possible for organisations to find out a great deal about you as a customer without even asking you a question. Supermarkets and other stores make good use of their computerised tills to record what you buy and how often you buy it. They can then improve their customer service by sending you special offers that relate to products you buy on a regular basis.

Companies can buy mailing lists of names and addresses of people who match their customer profile. So, for example, a company selling pet accessories might purchase a mailing list from a company that sells pet insurance.

In order to give some protection to individuals, the Data Protection Act 1998 was devised. It contains eight principles to help ensure that information is handled properly. The data must be:

▶ fairly and lawfully processed

▶ processed for limited purposes

▶ adequate, relevant and not excessive

▶ accurate

▶ kept for no longer than is necessary

▶ processed in line with your rights

▶ secure

▶ not transferred to countries without adequate protection.

OVER TO YOU!

Find out more about the Data Protection Act 1998 and write some notes that can be used for revision purposes.

▼ PRESENT A POSITIVE IMAGE TO CUSTOMERS

You will form your opinion of an organisation within minutes of making contact, either by telephone or face-to-face. The manner in which you are received will immediately colour your experience.

Try to remember the last time you made a purchase at a shop. Was the assistant helpful or completely uninterested? If he or she tried to help, you will probably feel positive towards that organisation, even if you were not able to make your purchase.

If a customer perceives that they have received a high level of customer service, they will be far more likely to use your organisation again. Building good relationships with your customers is essential if you are to gain their loyalty. Forming a good relationship with a customer does not have to take a great deal of time or expense. Remembering the customer's name and using it appropriately is an example of how a good customer relationship can be built.

Even if there is a problem with the service transaction, for example the goods the customer bought were faulty, it is still possible to build a good relationship. This is because the way in which your organisation handles the problem will be the deciding factor for the customer.

In order to give a positive image you should remember the following.

- **Keep your work area tidy and organised:** File papers away regularly and remove coffee cups and food wrappers as soon as you have finished with them. A disorganised and untidy desk will give the wrong impression of both the organisation and yourself.

- **Your appearance should also be neat and tidy:** You should wear appropriate clothes to the office; avoid high fashion or clothes that expose bare flesh. Even if you have not got much money to spend on clothes you can ensure that your clothes are spotlessly clean and pressed. Shoes should also be clean and suitable for your work.

- **Be friendly and cheerful at work:** There is nothing worse than walking into an organisation to be greeted by a miserable or moaning receptionist. A friendly smile and a pleasant greeting will work wonders.

- **Use an appropriate style, tone and language:** When you are dealing with customers remember to use an appropriate style, tone and language. You should greet and speak to customers in a more formal manner; do not make jokes or use slang. Use the standard company greeting. Be aware of your tone, try to be friendly and welcoming and, of course, watch your language.

- **Use appropriate body language:** It is important that your body language reflects what you are actually saying. Your body language can say a great deal about you and therefore you should ensure that it gives a positive image. You should try to keep your back straight because walking, sitting or standing tall will look positive as well as giving you confidence. Do not slouch or hunch over your desk because this gives a very negative image. Do make eye contact with your customer, although be careful not to turn this into a stare. Where appropriate 'reflect' the customer's body language, for example by nodding your agreement.

- **Be cheerful on the telephone:** Try to answer the phone with a 'smile' in your voice. Answer the telephone promptly and use the standard company greeting.

- **When dealing with a customer, stop what you are doing:** This may sound obvious, but many people do not do this. It gives the wrong impression to customers as it makes them feel as though they are unimportant or a nuisance. It also prevents you from focusing on their needs and wants.

- **Don't keep customers waiting:** If you are unavoidably delayed, apologise immediately. It should go without saying that you should never continue a personal conversation either with a colleague or on the telephone if you have a customer waiting. If you have a queue forming, then apologise and ask for help. If you have arranged to meet a customer, always ensure you are on time.

- **If you can't help a customer yourself, find someone who can:** Similarly, if you cannot answer a customer's question immediately, go and ask for help. Do not make up the information.

- **Keep your promises:** If you have agreed to do something for a customer, whether it is to provide information or to call him or her on a certain day, ensure that you do so. If for any reason it is impossible for you to do this, either call the customer to explain what has happened or, if you are absent from work, ask a colleague to do so.

- **Use the customer's name:** If you know the customer's name, use it. Be careful not to overdo it. An acknowledgement such as 'Good morning, Mrs Cruz' will make the customer feel valued.

- **Show a determination to help:** If a customer has a problem, complaint or query, show that you are determined to help. This may mean passing the customer to someone else if you have not got all the answers or it may mean dealing with the whole transaction yourself. Never say, 'I don't know' and leave it at that. Be honest, tell the customer that you don't know the answer, but also tell them you will find out.

- **Show loyalty to your organisation and colleagues:** If you have a customer who is unhappy with the service he or she has received it is easy to agree with them, particularly if you think they have been badly treated, but never comment on the work of others in a negative manner. If a colleague has forgotten to do something, don't say 'Oh, I expect he forgot to ring you' as this will make the customer feel unimportant. Instead say something along the lines of 'I expect there is a reason why he hasn't been able to call. I'll find out for you.'

- **Be decisive:** Take action where necessary or, if you cannot answer the question, find someone who can. Don't dither, appear vague or blame your colleagues.

- **Be flexible:** By being able to adapt to different situations quickly to meet different needs, you will be providing a high level of care. Remember that being flexible does not mean making promises that you cannot keep or exceeding your limit of authority.

If you can do all of the things listed above, not only will you present a positive image, but you will also be building a good relationship with your customer. This is important as it will help the customer remain loyal to your organisation.

▼ USE AN APPROPRIATE TONE AND MANNER

Using an appropriate tone and manner is essential when working with customers. If a customer is upset or angry, the wrong tone or an uncaring manner can inflame the situation. If, however, you can adopt a soothing tone and a positive attitude you may well be able to resolve the situation.

Dealing with customers politely and confidently

How we feel will affect our manner. For example, if you are tired and fed up, you will probably look bored and disinterested. However, if you are enjoying time with friends, you will appear happy and interested. The manner you adopt when dealing with customers will influence the success of the customer transaction. Therefore you should adopt a positive, friendly and interested manner in all of your customer dealings, even if they are angry or upset with you. The following will help you deal with customers politely and confidently:

- **Always appear interested:** If a customer is upset or angry, adopt a caring and soothing manner, although be careful not to patronise the customer in any way. Do not 'talk down' to anyone: this is very off-putting.

- **Be friendly and approachable:** A friendly and approachable manner will help any customer service transaction. However, you must avoid becoming too friendly or over-familiar with your customers, particularly if they are external customers. Keep your conversations business-like and don't venture into personal areas. It is not considered correct to use terms of endearment such as 'love' when addressing customers.

- **Use appropriate language:** It is obvious that you should not swear or use slang expressions; however, remember that if you are using technical jargon or business terms, your customer may not understand what you are saying. Try to pitch your language to your customer. If you are speaking to senior management or colleagues, it can be safely assumed that they will understand 'jargon'. When speaking to external customers, tactfully check their understanding and give explanations of any technical terms or abbreviations if appropriate.

- **Be confident:** Customers will find your confidence reassuring and will respond to this. Even if you cannot help them, an assertive 'I'll find out and let you know at once' shows a level of confidence. The customer will feel reassured that someone is going to help.

- **Be knowledgeable:** It does help if you have made yourself aware of basic facts about your organisation and know the answers to common queries. This will save you and the customer a great deal of time, will make you look efficient and will reflect well on the organisation.

- **Remain calm:** Even if your customer is angry or abusive, never respond in the same way. No matter how angry they are with you, you should never lose your temper. If you cannot cope with their anger, excuse yourself for a minute or two until you calm down. If a customer becomes abusive, ask for help from your supervisor or another colleague.

- **Don't be over-confident:** Do be careful not to appear over-confident or, even worse, arrogant. Your customer may be feeling nervous and an over-confident approach may make the situation worse.

- **Be polite:** It should go without saying that you should always be polite when dealing with customers. Small pleasantries such as remembering to say 'please' and 'thank you' are essential. Remember to use the customer's name and, at the end of the conversation, thank them, even if they have made a complaint.

Taking complaints seriously

If a customer has a complaint of any kind, the first thing they want is to be taken seriously. Often the customer will be behaving reasonably until they feel that they are not being taken seriously and then they become angry. In order to avoid this situation, treat the customer as you would like to be treated. Below are some rules:

- adopt an interested manner and attitude

- never laugh at the customer, even if you think the complaint is ridiculous

- do not dismiss their complaint as nonsense

- find out as soon as possible what it is the customer wants from the organisation. This will save lots of time in the long run and makes the complaint easier to deal with

- show that you are willing to help the customer

- use an appropriate tone and language when speaking to the customer. For example, if a customer is upset, do not make light-hearted remarks, as this will make him or her feel they are not been taken seriously

- if you need to clarify the situation by asking for further information, do so tactfully

- if you need to involve another colleague, then explain the situation tactfully, using an appropriate tone and manner. This is particularly important if you have to speak to your colleague in front of the customer

- present a professional image of your organisation, yourself and your colleagues by being loyal and positive.

OVER TO YOU!

In pairs, carry out a short role play between a customer service assistant and an angry customer. Afterwards, discuss how you each felt. Did the customer feel that he or she was being taken seriously? What was the manner and attitude of the customer service assistant? Swap roles and repeat the role play.

▼ INTERACT EFFECTIVELY WITH CUSTOMERS

You have learned how to adopt a positive image in order to deal with customers effectively. Now you need to ensure that you are well equipped to handle different situations.

It is vital to remember that communication is a two-way process – this means actively listening. Remember the following when speaking to a customer either by telephone or face-to-face.

- **Don't interrupt** or second guess what the customer is going to say. Not only is this rude, but it means that you are not listening correctly.

- **Respond appropriately:** This means that you should say the right thing at the right time, using the appropriate body language.

- **Check your customer's understanding:** Use careful questioning and summarising to check that the communication has been received and understood correctly. Once your customer has finished speaking, summarise the information back to the customer to check that you have understood correctly. When you have finished giving information, use tactful questioning to check that he or she has understood what you have said.

- **Plan what you are going to say before you say it:** Give yourself and your customer time to make an appropriate response. Be aware of the impact that your words might have on the customer and the situation. If there are pauses when the customer is thinking of a response, do not hurry them along or show irritation.

- **Be aware of your customer's feelings:** If you are dealing with a customer face-to-face, it will be easy to read their body language and respond appropriately. You should also be aware of non-verbal signals from your customer when speaking on the telephone. These might include pauses, sighing or shuffling of papers.

- **Ensure satisfaction:** After you have checked your customer's understanding of the situation and summarised the main points of the conversation, check that they are satisfied before you finish the communication.

- **Follow up the communication:** Don't forget to keep any promises that you have made. If you have had to refer the customer to a colleague, check later that they have carried out the action.

Planning your communication

Make sure that you understand what the communication is about before you start. This sounds obvious, but often communication problems are caused by not being sure of the situation. Gather together as much information as you can so that you are able to plan the communication effectively. You will then be prepared and confident, which in turn will aid the communication process. If you plan carefully, you will also have sufficient information to assist your customer.

Think about what you are going to say. This will avoid long pauses or vague ramblings. This is particularly important if you are dealing with a customer complaint. Write notes to assist you.

Concentrate on the communication. Do not try to do two things at once. If you are using the telephone, do not do anything except make notes. Don't gaze around the room or try to read a document. If you are dealing with a customer face-to-face, don't fiddle with items on your desk, doodle on your notepad or shuffle about.

Find somewhere quiet for your conversation. This can be difficult if you work in a large, noisy open-plan office. Choose a quiet moment such as during the lunch period or first thing in the morning or find a quiet area. This will also help you avoid becoming distracted by watching your colleagues or trying to listen to their conversations at the same time.

Listen to your customers

If you do not listen to your customers, you will not be able to communicate satisfactorily. Keep in mind the following when listening to your customers.

- Use your active listening skills as described on page 114 to ensure that you hear what your customer is saying.

- Check your understanding by using reflective questioning.

- Summarise the points of a conversation to ensure your understanding.

- Ensure you use appropriate body language. This will reassure your customer that you are listening and will help you concentrate on the conversation.

- If a customer makes a suggestion relating to their problem or query, take it into consideration, it may be just the solution you are looking for. If a customer makes a more general suggestion regarding the organisation, then politely tell them that you will pass it on to the relevant person, and do so.

- Encourage your customer to make suggestions. This is particularly relevant if the customer is complaining. A complaint will be dealt with much more efficiently and effectively if both sides know what the customer wants in the way of a solution. Once you have found out what the customer expects you to do about a problem, it is quite straightforward. You will either be able to comply with their request or hand it on to another person.

▶ No matter how angry the customer becomes never lose your temper and try to conceal your own anger. You excuse yourself to give yourself chance to cool down or consult another colleague. Always ask for help if a customer becomes abusive.

Recognising a customer's special requirements

The law dictates that customers, and particularly those with a disability, are treated fairly, equally and with special consideration for their needs. Your organisation will have measures in place to ensure that there is no discrimination of staff or customers and you will need to be aware of, and be able to follow, these procedures.

Disability discrimination laws ensure that organisations make specific provision for disabled customers to access their goods and services. These relate to provision of information in large print, Braille or recorded on tape for those that have sight or hearing difficulties and the improvement of access for those with mobility problems.

Customers may have various special requirements and it is up to you to recognise them and take them into consideration. You should have procedures that will help you with some requirements, but you will need to have the confidence to deal with these requirements in a positive manner. Some of the customers with special requirements you may come across include those who:

▶ have physical disabilities or impairments

▶ are unable to speak English well

▶ have a particular requirement linked to their culture and/or religious beliefs

▶ have an individual or unusual request

▶ have personal circumstances that require understanding or consideration.

Physical impairment or disability

People with these requirements may need assistance with one or more of the following:

▶ access

▶ printed information

▶ help in an emergency.

In order to assist, you can do the following.

▶ **Be aware of the facilities provided by your organisation:** These might include toilets for the disabled, ramps for wheelchairs, large print or recorded information. Know how to access these facilities.

▶ **Be sensitive when offering assistance:** Tactfully offer people help with heavy doors, completing forms, etc.

▶ **Allow additional time:** It may take longer for someone to read information, walk along a corridor or get papers ready, so do not be impatient.

Language difficulties

For those with poor English skills, trying to communicate can be very frustrating. Be aware of and sensitive towards the following.

▶ Difficulty understanding verbal information. If you find it difficult to understand what the customer is saying, then it is equally likely they will find it difficult to understand you.

▶ Difficulties with completing forms or reading printed information.

You can assist people with these requirements by doing the following.

▶ Be aware of any organisational procedures or facilities. Your organisation may be able to provide printed information in other languages or there may be staff who speak other languages. If so, know how to access these facilities.

▶ Offer assistance in completing forms. If the customer has difficulty reading the information, offer to read it to them.

▶ Speak slowly so that they have time to process what you are saying.

▶ Use appropriate language. Use simple English words that are commonly used and easy to understand. If you have to use any technical language, be sure to explain clearly what you mean. Use short sentences.

▶ Listen carefully. You will need to use active listening skills to ensure that you are concentrating fully on the customer.

▶ Repeat back what you hear in order to ensure understanding.

▶ Use sign language and gestures to aid communication.

Cultural or religious beliefs

If your organisation regularly deals with customers from different cultures or with different beliefs, there may be procedures in place or assistance available to help you communicate effectively.

Be aware that people may have one or more of the special requirements shown below:

▶ different expectations

▶ different needs

▶ different interpretation of body language

▶ different food requirements

▶ different clothing.

It helps if you are aware of any cultural differences. You can also:

▶ learn about these cultural differences so you know how to respond

▶ make sure that you are fully aware of any organisational procedures or facilities

▶ be sensitive to different needs

▶ be aware of your body language

▶ if in doubt, ask a more senior colleague.

Personal circumstances

Some of your customers may have particular personal circumstances that will affect their behaviour and needs. They may have a shorter fuse and become impatient or irritable quickly. In order to assist these customers:

▶ prioritise urgent requests

▶ keep the customer informed of your progress

▶ be sensitive to mood changes

▶ stay calm.

Individual requirements

Occasionally you may find a customer makes a request that you have not previously encountered. When this happens it can be difficult to know how to approach the request. You should deal with this type of problem by:

▶ remaining positive

▶ make detailed notes of the request so that it can be passed on to the appropriate person

▶ never agree to or refuse the request outright. Tell the customer that you will investigate the possibilities of granting the request and get back to them

▶ ask for assistance from a more senior colleague.

If you take on board the hints given above, you will be better prepared for any situation you may encounter.

OVER TO YOU!

In small groups, research the facilities and assistance provided by your organisation to those with special requirements. Discuss your findings with the class.

▼ IDENTIFY CUSTOMER NEEDS

Every customer will have a different expectation of your organisation even if on the surface they appear to want the same thing. Remember, it is the experience each customer has when dealing with your organisation that will form their opinion of the service they have received and their overall opinion of the organisation. This is why it is so important to be absolutely sure that you understand what it is the customer wants or needs before you can deal with them efficiently and effectively.

Asking for clarification, summarising and reflective questioning have all been discussed on page 115, but below are a few more hints for ensuring that you can identify the customer's needs.

Ask for information

You may need to ask customers for further information in order to ensure their needs are met correctly. You should remember that you are finding out what it is the customer wants, not leading an interrogation. It will help if you plan the questions in advance so you will be able to structure the interview. Given below are some guidelines that might help you.

▶ Tell the customer that you need to ask him or her a few questions in order to provide a high level of service. This will prepare them in advance.

▶ Ask one question at a time and make sure your customer understands the question.

▶ Ask questions in a logical order.

▶ Where possible interview your customer in a quiet area where you cannot be overheard. This is particularly important if you are asking for personal information.

▶ Ask questions tactfully and, if you are asking for personal information, be prepared to explain why you need the information.

▶ Use pauses in the conversation and be aware of your tone so that you don't sound threatening.

▶ Avoid inappropriate personal questions, such as asking a customer why they cannot keep an appointment.

▶ Ask open questions, that is questions requiring more than a yes or no answer, in order to get a full response. Use words such as 'why', 'what', 'who' and 'when'.

▶ If you are not sure of the answer, or did not get sufficient information from the first answer, then use a follow-up question to clarify.

▶ Don't frown or look shocked when you receive answers. You are there to obtain information, not to judge.

▶ Write down answers so that you do not have to ask the customer again.

Ask for information in writing

If the customer has a complicated complaint involving lots of dates and different responses or a request for information that has many parts, ask them to make a few notes for you to use, outlining key points and dates. Explain to the customer that by doing this you will be able to provide a much better level of service. This approach may be quicker than having lengthy conversations on the telephone or having to interview a person face-to-face.

Provide information for the customer

If the customer is not sure about the service they require, then help them to decide by giving them information about your organisation. You may find that one or more of the following will help.

▶ Talk through the problem and decide who is the best person for the customer to speak to. For example, if the customer has a problem with a statement or invoice, someone in finance should be able to help.

▶ Have a ready supply of information on the goods and services your organisation provides.

- Be prepared to find information either from the computer or the organisation's files. Ensure that you are not handing out confidential information.

- Give the customer contact names and telephone numbers of colleagues who may be able to help.

- If you are providing complex information, put it in writing as well so that the customer can refer to it later.

Verify the requirements with the customer

Once you feel that you know what it is that the customer wants, you should verify the requirements with the customer to be absolutely sure that you both have the same understanding. This final check will ensure that you can assist the customer in the correct way and will prevent you from wasting time. It will also ensure that the customer is not presented with incorrect information, which in the case of a complaint will inflame the situation further.

In order to verify the requirements, summarise your understanding of their requirements back to the customer and ask him or her if you are correct. Check any dates or information that you have written down so that you will be working with accurate information.

OVER TO YOU!

Work in pairs with one person acting the part of a customer asking for information, the other taking the part of the assistant identifying the customer's needs. Discuss how each of you felt during the interview. Swop roles and repeat the process.

▼ CONVEY INFORMATION TO CUSTOMERS CLEARLY AND ACCURATELY

It is essential that any information you give to a customer is clear, accurate and up to date. If it is not, you are in danger of:

- wasting your own time and that of the customer

- creating a dissatisfied customer who might become angry

- costing your organisation or your customer money

- facing disciplinary proceedings.

You can make sure that the information you provide is accurate and up to date by doing the following.

- Make sure the information you provide is relevant to the customer's needs and requirements. If you have correctly assessed the customer's needs (as described on pages 118–120), it will be easy for you to ensure that the information is relevant. If in any doubt, check your understanding of the problem with the customer.

- Give the customer sufficient information to work with. Think about his or her requirements and try to anticipate any further information they might need in relation to their problem or query. Do not, however, give the customer a great deal of unnecessary information that they have to plough through to get to the relevant facts.

▶ Check your facts. Do not rely on your memory when giving out facts and figures. Look them up in your records and make sure you write down any information accurately.

▶ If you have to ask a colleague for information, make sure you write this down, rather than relying on memory. Check your understanding with your colleague to ensure that you do not misinterpret what they have said.

▶ When writing down dates, figures and telephone numbers, repeat them back to the person to ensure that you have recorded them correctly. Check unusual or difficult spellings with the customer, particularly in name and address details.

▶ Provide information as promptly as possible. This will prevent time being wasted and will help reduce problems.

▶ Make sure that the information you provide is complete. This will prevent customers from having to contact you for further details.

▶ Write clearly so that others can read your notes.

▶ Make sure that you do not give out confidential or sensitive information.

Depending on your job role and level, there will be certain actions that you may not take. For example, you may be allowed access to certain files, but it is very unlikely you would be allowed access to all the financial records of the company. There may be limits imposed on the following:

▶ making telephone calls

▶ relaying information

▶ access to certain information

▶ access to resources

▶ authorisation of expenses.

If you are in any doubt as to your authority, then ask. Never authorise anything that might cost the organisation money without getting prior permission. This is particularly important when you are dealing with customers. If a customer has a complaint and wishes to receive compensation, you should not agree unless you have checked with your manager or supervisor.

You should also be aware of the limit of your authority when giving information to customers. You should never give out confidential information. You should also be aware of giving customers information that is sensitive. For example:

▶ do not give information on discussions that have taken place within your organisation

▶ never discuss internal matters that are not directly relevant to the transaction with the customer

▶ never discuss one customer in front of another

▶ never speculate about the reaction or response of another member of staff to a situation

▶ watch what you are saying over the telephone or to a colleague when you are within earshot of a customer

▶ if you are in any doubt about whether you should disclose information, check first.

Discuss with your group whether the following would be confidential or sensitive information and should be given to a customer. If you decide the information should not be passed on, discuss how you would deal with the situation.

▶ Janet, who had previously been dealing with the customer, is off work following the break up of her relationship.

▶ Tom, the manager, said that if the customer made enough fuss, he would pay up to £100 in compensation.

▶ Mrs Patel, another customer, bought the same washing machine and was very pleased with it.

▶ The company made its biggest annual profit last year, 25 per cent up on its previous profits.

▼ CONVEY INFORMATION TO COLLEAGUES CLEARLY AND ACCURATELY

It is equally important to ensure that the information you pass to colleagues is clear and accurate. If you have to hand over a customer request or complaint to another colleague, ensure that you do the following.

▶ Include all the relevant details. If you have kept notes during your dealings with the customer, check through them to ensure that they are clear and readable before passing them on. It may be wise to keep a copy for yourself in case you need to discuss the matter at a later date.

▶ Check your colleague's understanding. As with customers, use a mixture of reflective questioning and summarising to ensure that your colleague understands the situation.

▶ Ensure that your colleague knows what you have promised. If you have told a customer that a colleague will call later the same day or within a certain timescale, make sure that you explain this clearly to your colleague. Similarly, if you have promised to take a particular action, make sure your colleague is aware of this.

These simple guidelines will ensure a smooth handover of the transaction, which will enable your colleague to provide a high level of customer service. They will also prevent the customer from having to start the transaction all over again, which can be very annoying and time consuming for all concerned.

▼ BUILD EFFECTIVE WORKING RELATIONSHIPS

In order to provide a high level of customer service, it is necessary for you to take a proactive approach in building effective working relationships with your customers. A good relationship will be one in which the customer perceives that they are satisfied.

Here are some ways in which you can help build effective working relationships and provide customer satisfaction:

▷ Try to be PERFECT:

- **p**rofessional

- **e**fficient

- **r**eliable

- **f**riendly

- **e**xpert

- **c**aring

- **t**rustworthy.

▷ If you see a customer looking around, don't wait for them to approach you, approach them first and ask if you can help.

▷ Ensure that your greeting and your farewell give the right impression. Look friendly, helpful and interested and ensure that your body language is saying the same thing. When you say goodbye, thank the customer. This will make them feel valued, even if they have only delivered a parcel to your organisation.

▲ Figure 2.5 Make the customer feel valued

▷ If a customer needs advice, then give it. You may be able to provide a customer with information on the goods and services your organisation provides, various procedures for making complaints or the names and telephone numbers of colleagues who can help. Do not, however, give your personal opinions and make sure you do not give out confidential information.

▷ Offer additional support where possible. This might take the form of finding out extra information or asking a colleague to contact the customer. If you offer these services, the customer will feel valued.

▷ Ask for feedback. Before the customer leaves check that they are satisfied with the level of service you have provided. Record their comments and pass them on to your supervisor or manager.

Recording customer feedback

Many organisations will have procedures for reporting customer feedback as it is important for them to know what their customers are thinking. This will allow an organisation to improve its goods, services or level of customer service to meet or exceed customers' expectations. It is therefore important that you record any feedback you receive, whether it is in the form of an enquiry, complaint or suggestion.

Some organisations hold this type of information on a computer database that allows you to record details about individual customers. This might show the purchases they have made, together with any queries or complaints. Each record takes the form of a 'case history' so if you call up a particular customer on screen you will be able to see all of their transactions with the company. There will also be a comments section where complaints and actions can be listed. This is particularly useful for organisations that have a call centre as the person answering the call will immediately know what has happened without the customer having to repeat all the details.

Customer requests for goods or services that are not currently stocked can also be logged and reviewed on a regular basis. As soon as the organisation feels that it would be cost effective to offer such goods or services, it can do so and then inform the customers of its action. The organisation can also evaluate its current product range to check that it is in line with customer requirements.

Customer feedback should be logged and recorded. Any suggestions that a customer might make should be recorded and passed to the relevant person. If a customer pays the organisation a compliment this should also be passed on; it is good for morale to hear that the organisation is meeting customer expectations.

If you are recording customer information you need to ensure that you obtain all the relevant details from the customer. If you are using a computer database, this will be straightforward as you can ask the customer for details according to the fields that are provided.

If you have to handwrite the information, make sure you include the following:

▶ the current date

▶ the customer's name and address; do not forget the postcode and check any unusual spellings

▶ telephone number, including area code

▶ customer reference number (or if new, allocate a customer number)

▶ order details

▶ the nature of the enquiry

▶ the action that was taken or the information that was provided. If the query was passed to a colleague, the name of the colleague and the date it was passed on.

▼ IDENTIFY PROBLEMS AND SUGGEST SOLUTIONS

Occasionally no matter how hard an organisation tries, it will inevitably make mistakes or the level of service will not match the customer's expectations. This is when complaints are made.

Most complaints can easily be resolved without fuss or upset and if an organisation can meet a customer's expectations while resolving the problem, the customer will still feel they have received a reasonable level of service.

When you are dealing with a customer complaint, it is essential that you do the following.

▶ **Have the right attitude:** If a customer is already making a complaint, they will be sensitive towards your attitude. If they perceive that you have been rude or off-hand, this will only inflame the situation. Remember to be caring, sympathetic and apologetic.

▶ **Adopt the correct approach:** Be confident, sure of your facts and don't make any promises that you cannot keep. Be knowledgeable about the products or services your organisation offers and about the structure of the organisation. Make sure you know who to deal with within the organisation and have their names and contact details to hand.

▶ **Acknowledge the complaint:** You should apologise to the customer because they are feeling they have not received a high level of service. You should not, however, admit liability. Therefore, a few well-chosen words such as 'I am sorry you are unhappy with our product (or service)' will soothe the customer without admitting that your organisation, product or service is at fault.

▶ **Follow organisational procedures:** The organisation may have procedures in place to deal with customer complaints. Make sure that you know whether this is the case and if so, familiarise yourself with them. Record the complaint in line with the procedures as soon as you have finished your interview with the customer. This will ensure that the information is accurate.

▶ **Know your limits:** You should know what your limits are in two respects. The first is the offer that you can make to the customer in terms of refund or compensation. Never exceed your limit of authority or offer the customer any form of compensation without checking first with your supervisor. The second limit is the amount of help, information or advice that you can give according to your knowledge and job role. If you do not know an answer or if the complaint is too serious for you to deal with, pass it on to a more senior colleague as promptly as possible.

▶ **Use questioning techniques:** Questioning skills have already been discussed (on page 119). If you use these techniques well, you will quickly get to the root of the problem, making it easier to calm the customer and provide assistance.

▶ **Ask the customer for a solution:** What would the customer like you do to about the problem? They may just want a simple refund or exchange. Some customers just require an explanation as to why their goods didn't arrive on time. It will save a great deal of time if you ask the customer what they would like because you can then either comply with their request or negotiate another settlement.

▶ **Keep the customer informed at all times:** Many complaints originate because the customer has received a poor service. It may be that they have been kept waiting or a promised delivery or action has not happened. In this instance keep the customer informed about what you are going to do and the progress you are making.

▶ **Follow up the complaint:** If you have had to pass on the complaint to a colleague or if you have had to take action, you should always follow up the complaint to ensure that the customer has received a satisfactory outcome. Make a note in your diary or on your electronic organiser to remind yourself to do this.

It is also essential that you do not do the following.

▶ **Do not argue with the customer:** This will only make a poor situation worse. Remain calm, listen and establish the facts. If the customer is rude or abusive, ask a more senior colleague for help.

- **Never be rude:** It can be difficult not to answer back, particularly if the customer is very angry. If you are face-to-face with a customer who is getting very upset, try to take them somewhere quiet and out of the public view so that you can assist them correctly.

- **Do not keep talking or interrupting:** Allow the customer to have their say, otherwise they will become more frustrated and upset. Do not interrupt at any point. You will need to ensure that your body language reflects that you are listening to the customer, otherwise they may misinterpret the silence as being aggressive.

If you can follow these guidelines, you should be able to resolve the customer complaint and still maintain a good working relationship.

▼ CHECK CUSTOMERS' REQUIREMENTS ARE MET, IDENTIFY FOLLOW-UP ACTION

Customer relationships can be maintained and improved by a good after-care service. This might take the form of contacting the customer after a transaction to see if they have been satisfied with the product and with the service they received. Organisations do this because:

- it exceeds the customer expectation

- it provides feedback for improving products and services.

When dealing with a complaint, you must ensure you follow it up in several ways.

- **Ensure that the customer is satisfied with the proposed solution:** In order to do this you should use summarising to ensure that the customer is clear about the offer and is happy to accept it. Use reflective questioning to clarify the customer's understanding.

- **Ensure that the agreed solution is carried out:** It is not enough to promise a solution to a problem, you have to ensure that it happens. It is often the failure to deliver the solution that causes the real customer complaints. Make notes in your diary or organiser to check on the progress of a complaint. If you have passed it on to a colleague or have asked for goods to be sent, then tactfully check that they have dealt with the customer as agreed. If there is likely to be a delay for any reason, for example if you are waiting for goods to arrive or for an answer to a query, keep the customer informed.

- **Ensure that the customer is satisfied with the outcome:** A follow up call once the situation has been resolved will help maintain good working relationships.

- **Ensure that the details of the transaction are recorded according to organisational procedures:** You must do this as soon as you have completed the transaction.

These guidelines will help you to provide a level of service that exceeds customers' expectations and will therefore be perceived as a high level of customer service. This will in turn encourage customer loyalty.

Assessment requirement 2

The assessment of this element will take place by observation. You are required to take part in two separate customer service transactions, both witnessed by your tutor or supervisor. A witness statement will be completed for both transactions and your tutor or supervisor will comment on your effectiveness in dealing with the customer.

Reviewing the organisation of business activities

Introduction

This unit is all about the ways in which organisations operate and the role of administration in those environments. At the end of the unit you will be able to do the following.

▶ Analyse and describe the different forms of business organisation

▶ Review and analyse the structure of business organisations

▶ Identify and evaluate effective working practices

▶ Review the factors that affect workplace conditions

The information in this unit will give you a thorough knowledge of how businesses are formed and structured, and how they operate and are administered. You will learn how to work effectively, efficiently and safely.

The assessment for this unit is by a 3-hour written examination. Each area of the syllabus is examined separately with a short scenario leading into the questions. The key to success is applying your knowledge in order to relate your answers to the scenarios.

▼ ANALYSE AND DESCRIBE THE DIFFERENT FORMS OF BUSINESS ORGANISATION

This section relates to the different types of business formation. You will learn about the following:

The private sector

▶ sole traders and partnerships

▶ private and public limited companies

▶ multinational companies/global business

▶ charities

▶ franchise operations.

The public sector

▶ public corporations

▶ government departments

▶ quangos/watchdog bodies.

You will also learn how organisations grow and expand and how they must plan in order for their organisation to succeed.

The private sector

The term 'private sector' refers to any business or organisation that is owned by private individuals. These can range from very small businesses owned and run by one person to the very large organisations such as Marks & Spencer or McDonald's, which are owned by many different people.

Cathy Richmond has always dreamed of owning her own business. She is in her late twenties and has had a variety of jobs since leaving full-time education. These have included administration officer, finance officer, retail assistant and catering assistant. Cathy feels she has a good all-round knowledge of the commercial world and is well placed to run a small business.

Cathy has recently completed a jewellery designing course. She found she really enjoyed the work and discovered that she has a real talent for designing and making jewellery. She would like to start her own business making and designing jewellery and selling it by mail order using the Internet. Cathy decides to call her business Richmond Jewels.

Once she made this decision she telephoned her local business advisory centre and made an appointment to see an adviser. The adviser gave her lots of information about becoming a sole trader. Below is a summary of the information Cathy was given:

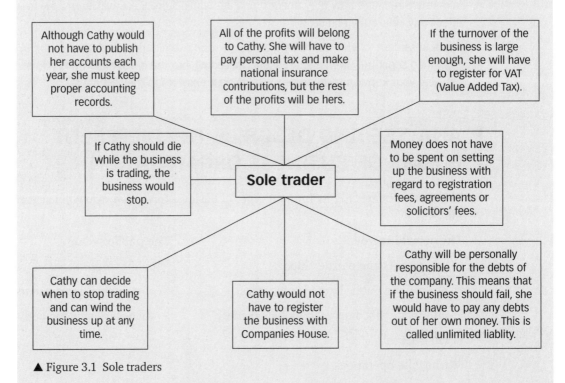

▲ Figure 3.1 Sole traders

From this Cathy realises it would be easy to set up her new business as a sole trader as she would not have to complete a lot of paperwork or register her new business with any legal body. The business advisory service did tell her that she would have to inform the Inland Revenue and the National Insurance Contributions Agency so that her personal tax and national insurance details could be updated.

Cathy has also been offered a job as a jewellery designer at a large jewellery workshop. She draws up a list of advantages and disadvantages of becoming a sole trader and being employed (see Table 3.1).

Table 3.1 Cathy's comparison of sole trading and employment

Sole trader: advantages

Freedom to make own decisions

Can control direction of business

Choose working hours to suit

Keep all (if any) profits

Challenge of working for self

Involved in all aspects of business

Can make jewellery to own designs and specifications

Employment: advantages

Only have to work set hours

No worries about the business when off duty

Do not have to keep accounts or do other administrative work

Tax and national insurance: automatically deducted from pay

Will receive benefits such as holiday pay, sickness entitlement, maternity leave

Some job security

Sole trader: disadvantages

Entire responsibility for business

Responsible for all paperwork including accounts.

Must keep on top of workload

May have to employ staff and then be responsible for them

Ensure business operates within law

May have to work long hours

Financially responsible if business fails

No job security

If jewellery doesn't sell, no money comes in

No holiday or sickness entitlement

No other benefits such as pension plan

Employment: disadvantages

Have to work the hours that the employer sets

Have little control over designs

Have no control over how business runs

May be made redundant

It would seem from the list that there is little to recommend owning your own business. However, many people enjoy the challenge of running their own company and the rewards can often be great, both in terms of finance and self satisfaction.

OVER TO YOU!

1. Sole traders run the risk of losing their home and other belongings if the business fails. What is the name for this risk?

2. State three reasons why Cathy might want to become a sole trader rather than work for a major jewellery designer.

3. Give three disadvantages of becoming a sole trader.

4. What must Cathy do in order to ensure that her business is set up according to legal requirements?

Callum and Anya met at university while studying furniture restoration. They have now graduated and are planning their future career. They have decided to set up a small workshop and provide a restoration service with a small antiques shop. The business will be called Restoration Antiques.

They looked at a number of ways of opening the business, but decided that a partnership would best suit their needs. Here is an outline of the legislation that surrounds partnerships.

Partnership legislation

1 Partnerships do not have to register with any regulatory authority.

2 It is not necessary to draw up a formal agreement in order to start a partnership.

3 Partners do not need to have an equal share in the business; the share can be divided in any way.

4 Liability is still unlimited, but would be divided between the partners according to the share they have in the business.

5 A Deed of Partnership can be drawn up, which would be a legally binding document. This would set out the salary, share of profits and name of the firm. The liability of each partner would also be set out in this document.

6 Although partnerships do not have to sign a Deed of Partnership or register with Companies House, all partnerships are governed by the Partnerships Act of 1890. This assumes that all partners are equal and have equal liability for the debts of the business.

7 It is possible to become a limited partnership under the Limited Partnership Act 1907. However, there must be at least one partner with unlimited liability. The other limited partners can be sleeping partners. This means that they cannot take an active part in the business and would be just investors in it.

8 The maximum number of partners in a partnership is 20.

9 The financial accounts of the business are private and do not have to be published.

10 If one of the partners should die or wish to leave the business, the partnership is considered to be ended.

▲ Figure 3.2 Partnership legislation

Callum has some savings that he is going to use to start the business. Anya doesn't have any money to contribute and so the shares are to be divided at 70 per cent to Callum and 30 per cent to Anya to reflect this. This doesn't mean that Callum will receive 70 per cent of the money that the business takes or will earn more than Anya. This can be decided between them and may reflect the amount of work each does towards the running of the business. It does mean, however, that if they decide to sell or close the business Callum will be entitled to 70 per cent of any money whereas Anya will only receive 30 per cent.

This sounds fair to both Callum and Anya; however, Callum must also realise that if the business should fail, he will lose the most. As he will own 70 per cent of the shares of the business, 70 per cent of the debts will be his responsibility.

Other ways in which Callum and Anya could start the business would be for one of them to be a sole trader and just employ the other, or they could start a private limited company (Ltd).

They draw up a list of advantages and disadvantages of becoming a partnership (see Table 3.2).

Table 3.2 Advantages and disadvantages of partnerships

Advantages of partnerships	Disadvantages of partnerships
The responsibility is shared.	Profits will be shared.
The decision making is shared.	Neither partner has full control over the business.
Someone available to cover holidays, sickness, etc.	One partner may decide to leave after a while and will need to be bought out if the business is to continue.
Usually all partners will invest some money into the business.	
Two sets of ideas are coming into the business.	One partner may decide that the business should be run in a different way or have different aims.
Two sets of skills are coming into the business.	It will be important for the partners to get on with each other, working on an equal basis.
Each could specialise in certain aspects of the business.	If one partner does anything wrong or illegal both partners are responsible.
	If one partner should die, then his or her estate is entitled to be paid the share of the business. The remaining partner would have to find the funds to pay this amount or wind the business up.

Callum and Anya decide to start their business as a partnership and immediately employ three staff. Two staff members will run the antiques shop and the third will assist Callum and Anya in the workshop.

OVER TO YOU!

1. Callum and Anya have decided to operate as a partnership. Give two advantages to becoming a partnership rather than Callum operating as a sole trader with Anya as his employee.

2. State two disadvantages to Callum of having Anya as a partner.

3. Explain why Callum should insist that a Deed of Partnership is drawn up before starting the business.

4. Give two disadvantages to Anya of becoming a partner in Restoration Antiques.

Patrick is an executive of a company that manufactures children's clothing. However, in recent years he has become disillusioned with the company and wants to work for himself. His friend, Imran, is a senior accountant with a large company and he would also like to change his job. Patrick is very interested in starting a company that will manufacture fashion clothing for sale to a target market of females aged 18–25. His experience in the clothing business will be very useful and Imran's financial expertise will help ensure that the business stays on track.

Both Patrick and Imran have substantial savings and they have talked to various banks and other lending agencies. They have the funds in place to start their business. They now need to decide how to operate it. It would be easy to set up a partnership, but they both feel that they would prefer to own a limited company.

They have researched private limited companies and have found that the company is seen as a legal entity. This means that the company exists in its own right and not through the shareholders.

The owners are shareholders, i.e. each owns a share of the company. This amount can vary and additional shareholders can be added at any point. There is no maximum number of shareholders. The shareholders do not have to work for the business, although they do have to be invited to become shareholders by the board of directors. The issue of shares is private, hence the name private limited company. Given below is an outline of the legal requirements of starting a private limited company.

Starting a private limited company

1 Limited companies must produce two documents, **Articles of Association** and **Memorandum of Association**.

2 There must be a minimum of two members of the company, each owning shares. There is no upper limit to the number of people who can own shares in the company.

3 The details, including the Articles and Memorandum of Association must be registered with the **Registrar of Companies**. There is a fee to register a limited company.

4 Once the details of the company have been accepted by the Registrar, a **Certificate of Incorporation** will be issued. This allows the company to begin trading.

5 Private limited companies must send full copies of their accounts to Companies House each year. These can be viewed by members of the public upon receipt of an application and a small fee.

▲ Figure 3.3 Starting a private limited company

Registrar of Companies

The Registrar of Companies at Companies House ensures that all private and public limited companies are registered or incorporated and therefore licensed to trade. This means that in order to add the letters Ltd or plc to a business name, an organisation must register. Then the organisation must abide by certain regulations, provide copies of accounts each year and adopt a formal Memorandum and Articles of Association. Companies House also ensures that accurate, appropriate information about all registered organisations is available to the public.

Memorandum of Association

This document sets out the constitution and various details such as the name of the company, the name and address of the registered office, the objectives of the company and the scope of its activities, the liability of its shareholders, the amount of capital that will be raised and the number of shares to be issued.

Articles of Association

This deals with the internal running of the company and includes details such as the timing and frequency of company meetings, the procedures for appointing directors and the limit of their responsibilities, the arrangements for auditing company accounts and the rights of the shareholders, depending on the type of share they hold.

Although all of this sounds complicated, you can choose to adopt the standard Memorandum and Articles that are put together by Companies House, just filling in the relevant details.

Patrick and Imran draw up a list of advantages and disadvantages for both partnerships and private limited companies to see which type of organisation might best suit their needs (see Table 3.3)

Table 3.3 Comparison of partnerships and private limited companies

Partnership: advantages

Easy to set up: no legal requirements.

Accounts can remain private.

Can add partners if necessary.

Cheap to set up; do not have to register anywhere, just inform the Inland Revenue.

Annual accounts are cheaper as they do not have to be as detailed as a private limited company's accounts.

Private limited company: advantages

The company is a legal entity; this means the company exists in its own right.

The liability is limited; this means that if the business becomes bankrupt the owners will lose only the amount originally invested in the company.

At present there are tax advantages for companies that partnerships do not receive.

Additional shareholders can be added to the company at any time.

If a shareholder dies, the company can still operate.

Shares can be issued in different ways: some provide shares of the profit, others do not.

Control of the company cannot be lost to outsiders as shares can only be sold to new members if all shareholders agree.

It can be easier to obtain external funding.

Partnership: disadvantages

If one of the partners decides to leave the business, the other has to buy their share.

If one of the partners dies, the business has to be wound up.

Liability is unlimited; this means that the owners are responsible for all debts of the company and could lose their personal belongings in order to pay any debts.

The partners in a partnership are the company and so they are personally liable for accidents, fraud, tax responsibilities, etc.

Private limited company: disadvantages

More expensive to set up and administer in terms of legal requirements.

Accounts must be submitted to Companies House each year, where they are published for all to see.

If a shareholder decides to leave, the shares must be purchased from them.

The amount of capital that can be raised by the issue of shares is restricted in that members of the public cannot buy shares.

If a shareholder decides to sell their shares it may take time to find a buyer because all existing shareholders must agree the sale.

Although initially it is less expensive to set up a partnership, Imran and Patrick feel that the initial investment to set up a private limited company is worthwhile as they will receive tax benefits and be protected by limited liability. They decide to go ahead with their new business venture and call it I and P Designs (IPD) Ltd.

CASE STUDY 3.4 – Preston Hotels PLC (a public limited company)

Harry Preston is the chairman of a private limited company called Preston Hotels Ltd. The company owns a chain of 50 luxury hotels and is very successful. The board of directors would like to expand the company and have been given the opportunity of buying a small chain of hotels that would fit into their existing portfolio very well.

The purchase of these hotels would be very expensive. The board of directors have considered various finance options, but have decided that the best way forward would be to form a public limited company (plc). This means that they will be able to raise capital by selling shares in the company to members of the public. They discuss this option with their bank and business advisers. The following information helps them to make their decision.

Features of a public limited company

1 Capital can be raised by selling shares to members of the public through the **Stock Exchange**.

2 As well as the Memorandum of Association and Articles of Association, a **Statutory Declaration** must be provided. This states that all the requirements of the Company Acts have been met.

3 It is usual for a **Prospectus** to be issued, which sets out the aims of the company and is used as advertising material in order to encourage the public to purchase shares in the company.

4 It is expensive to set up a private limited company as solicitors must be paid to verify the contents of the prospectus.

5 The company may use the services of a financial institution, such as a bank, to process share applications.

6 Share issues: when a number of shares are released to be sold to the public, they must be **underwritten**. This means that the company must insure itself against the possibility of some shares remaining unsold. The underwriter agrees to purchase the unsold shares for a fee.

7 There must be a minimum of £50,000 share capital.

8 The public limited company cannot begin trading until it has received at least 25 per cent payment for the shares that it has issued. Once this money has been received, a **Trading Certificate** is issued and the company can begin trading on the Stock Exchange.

9 The company will incur expenses in producing material and prospectuses in order to attract shareholders.

10 There must be a minimum of two members and at least two directors.

11 plcs must submit their accounts to the Registrar seven months after the end of the accounting period, while private limited companies have 12 months.

▲ Figure 3.4 Features of a public limited company

Harry and the rest of the directors are sure that there will be many people willing to invest their money in buying shares of Preston Hotels. It is a very well-known hotel chain and has an excellent reputation. People will know that the company is doing well and will feel that their money is safe. The extra advertising and promotion that would accompany a move towards becoming a plc would mean that the company receives a great deal of public interest, which in turn would be good for the business generally.

After due consideration and many meetings of the board, Preston Hotels decide to start the process of floating the company on the Stock Exchange.

OVER TO YOU!

1 Give three reasons why Preston Hotels would want to become a public limited company.

2 What are the legal requirements of becoming a public limited company?

3 State the minimum number of directors required to run a public limited company.

CASE STUDY 3.5 – Phoenix Enterprises plc (a multinational conglomerate company)

Phoenix Enterprises plc was founded over 30 years ago by Alexander Levitski. He had been working at a factory that manufactured toys for large department stores. When this factory became bankrupt, he bought the business and started selling directly to the public from a factory shop. When this proved successful, he opened small specialist shops throughout the UK. During the 1970s, Alexander investigated the possibility of having the toys made outside the UK. He began by buying in stock made in Southeast Asia and took advantage of the low labour costs to make his business more profitable.

During the 1980s, Alexander and his board of directors decided to float the business on the Stock Exchange. They agreed that the money raised would be used to set up factories of their own in Southeast Asia, thus increasing their profits further. As a result, Phoenix Enterprises became a very successful multinational company.

During the early 1990s, Phoenix Enterprises plc suffered a decline in turnover and profits. The toy sector was very competitive and the profit margin was becoming smaller and smaller. The board decided to look at other ventures that might be successful and saw an opportunity to manufacture and supply mobile phones. Phoenix is now a brand leader in mobile phones and accessories throughout the world. It has kept the toy side of its business and feels that it is now better placed to face the future because it has diversified. It is, however, always looking for new opportunities that will add value to the company's portfolio. By diversifying in this way it has become a conglomerate company.

Table 3.4 Advantages and disadvantages of multinationals and conglomerates

Advantages of being a multinational or conglomerate

▶ Can take advantage of tax breaks, loans, development grants, etc. wherever they are being offered

▶ Benefits from economies of scale

▶ Spreads risk; if one area of the business is doing badly, a more successful area will help keep the business afloat

▶ Can control the costs of distribution, etc. allowing large profit margins

▶ Assuming that the multinational company has been registered in the UK, they have the same set up, advantages and disadvantages as any other private limited company

▶ Can take advantage of low labour or material costs in various parts of the world

Disadvantages of being a multinational or conglomerate

▶ Must abide by the law of each country in which it operates; this increases the administrative load and can mean staff are treated differently according to where they work

▶ Expensive to operate

OVER TO YOU!

1 Explain the difference between a multinational and a conglomerate.

2 Give three reasons why an organisation would want to diversify.

3 State three advantages of being a multinational company.

Emily Craddock has been a breeder and trainer of labrador dogs for many years. During this time, people have often asked her to look after stray or unwanted labrador dogs. She has been very happy to do this and once the dogs are fit, she tries to rehome them.

She now finds that there are more and more unwanted dogs being brought to her kennels. The burden of feeding these animals, together with associated veterinary bills, is costing more than she can afford. Often local people give her dog food, but this contribution is not enough to pay for all the animals she looks after. Emily now thinks that she may have to give up breeding dogs and turn her kennels into a rescue centre. She has researched registering as a charity so that she would be able to do some fund raising for the centre. Given below is the information she found.

Registering as a charity

1 A charity must have exclusively charitable purposes. This means it cannot have some charitable activities and some profit-making activities.

2 The extent of political or campaigning activities is restricted.

3 Strict rules apply to trading by charities.

4 **Trustees** (i.e. those who run the charity) are not allowed to receive financial benefits from their charity unless these have been specifically authorised by the governing document of the charity or by the Charities Commission. This includes salaries and the rule also applies to spouses, relatives and partners of trustees.

5 Trustees are, however, allowed out-of–pocket expenses for purposes such as travel.

6 Charity law imposes financial-reporting obligations. These vary with the size of the charity.

7 A charity must register with the Charities Commission if it has an income of £1000 or more; if it uses or occupies land or buildings; or if it has assets that constitute permanent endowment (for example, if the charity receives a large sum of money).

8 In order to call itself a charity, its purposes must be exclusively charitable. These aims are usually set out in the governing document. Charitable purposes can be grouped under four broad headings:

   a the relief of financial hardship

   b the advancement of education

   c the advancement of religion

   d other purposes for the benefit of the community.

9 If the trustees of the charity act lawfully and in accordance with the governing document, any liabilities they might incur can be met out of the charity's resources. However, if they are in breach of trust, the liabilities may have to be met out of their own resources. As trustees act jointly, this liability may extend to all trustees if one has acted unlawfully.

▲ Figure 3.5 Registering as a charity

From this, Emily can see that her existing business as a breeder of labrador dogs would conflict with the interests of the charity. Her own personal income would be lost and it would appear that she would have to apply for permission to be paid an income from the charity as trustee.

However, the benefits of registering as a charity would be:

▶ the rescue centre would not normally have to pay income or corporation tax, capital gains tax or stamp duty, and gifts to charities are free of inheritance tax

▶ the charity would not have to pay more than 20 per cent of normal business rates on the buildings they use and occupy to further their charitable purposes

▶ it may be possible to get special VAT treatment

▶ As a charity Emily would be able to raise funds from the public, grant-making trusts and local government more easily than she might as a non-charitable body

▶ Emily and her fellow trustees would be able to give the public the assurance that the charity was being monitored and advised by the Charities Commission

▶ the trustees would be able to seek help and advice from the Charities Commission.

Emily cannot make this decision alone. She gathers all the information together and has a family meeting to discuss the best course of action for her and her family.

OVER TO YOU!

1 State three benefits of becoming a registered charity.

2 State two disadvantages to Emily of registering as a charity.

3 Explain the process of registering a charity.

4 Explain the liability of trustees of a registered charity.

CASE STUDY 3.7 – Global Trading (a franchise)

Rachel and Tahmina have operated a partnership business selling fashion and home accessories such as jewellery, cushions and trinket boxes with an ethnic theme. The business, named Global Trading, has proved to be very successful. The partnership currently owns four shops and would like to open many more. However, Rachel and Tahmina have agreed that a rapid expansion is not possible as they do not have the capital to open a large number of shops. They are also concerned that the amount of time and effort it takes to open a new shop detracts from the running of the business.

They have looked at a number of options, including taking on extra partners and becoming a private limited company. However, they attended the National Franchise Exhibition in London and felt that franchising might be a good option for them. They read the information they received at the exhibition and made a list of the features of franchising.

Features of franchising

▶ Franchising is a method of business whereby the **franchisor** (that is, the seller of the business opportunity), sells the **franchisee** (the buyer of the business opportunity) the right to trade under the name of that business (in this case, Global Trading).

▶ The franchisor usually provides the following: training to help set up and run the business, a corporate logo, mission statement and company ethos.

▶ The business is usually tried and tested, making it a safer bet for the franchisee.

▶ If the franchise business is a retail business, the franchisor usually supplies the goods to the franchisee and controls the type of stock that may be sold.

▶ The corporate image must be used in the franchisee's business. This means that any shop fittings must fit into the corporate image so that all stores look the same. These are usually supplied by the franchisor (at an extra cost).

▶ The franchisor retains control over the business, including its direction and expansion. The franchisee is tied into a contract that states that it must abide by the franchisor's rules; these may include certain standards regarding the quality of service required to uphold the brand image.

▶ As well as the branding, franchisors often sell territorial rights. This means that it is agreed by the parties that, within a certain area, only a restricted number of people will be able to open a branch or offer the service.

▶ It is possible for the franchisor to charge an ongoing fee based on a percentage of the sales or profits of the business.

▶ Franchisors do not only sell retail companies; it is possible to franchise services, processes or even products.

▲ Figure 3.6 Features of franchising

Rachel and Tahmina feel that this might be the way to develop their business quickly. They draw up a list of advantages and disadvantages of becoming a franchisor.

Table 3.5 Advantages and disadvantages of becoming a franchisor

Advantages of becoming a franchisor	Disadvantages of becoming a franchisor
Able to grow the business without having to find all of the necessary capital.	To set up a franchising package will take time and money.
Can remain in control of the direction of the business.	Initially, it may be difficult to find people willing to become franchisees.
Can set company objectives, ethos, etc.	A poor franchisee can ruin the reputation of the business.
Will increase income as franchisees pay a share of their income to the company.	
Will be able to sell their goods at a small mark up, which will increase profits.	Increased administration in looking after the needs of the franchisees.
May be able to achieve rapid growth of the business.	May not attract franchisees in the locations where they are most wanted.

Table 3.5 Continued

Advantages of becoming a franchisor	Disadvantages of becoming a franchisor
Will be able to buy goods in much bigger bulk and will therefore be able to demand larger discounts, again increasing profits.	The rapid expansion of the business may cause problems in terms of trying to run it efficiently and effectively.
Will be able to select the franchisees.	Increase responsibility of the business.
Will increase the assets of the business.	
Will increase the value of the business.	

Rachel and Tahmina see that they will have to consider this method of raising money very carefully. However, they also see that rapid expansion could be possible by franchising. The risk to their personal investment would be lessened, which of course is another advantage.

OVER TO YOU!

1. Give three advantages of becoming a franchisor rather than remaining a partnership.

2. What will happen to the liability of Rachel and Tahmina if they become franchisors?

3. State three ways Global Trading will benefit financially from becoming a franchisor.

CASE STUDY 3.8 – Paper Work (a franchise company)

Max has just been made redundant from a large manufacturing company. He had been a member of the senior management team for more than 15 years. Max received a substantial redundancy package and is now wondering what to do next. He does not want to work for another company and feels that he would enjoy the challenge of running his own business. However, as he has family commitments, he doesn't want to take a large risk. He researches buying a franchise in Paper Work, a company that provides administrative services to small businesses and the public. The company offers document preparation, photocopying, faxing, bookkeeping, mailing and other administrative services. Max draws up a list of the advantages and disadvantages of becoming a franchisee (see Table 3.6).

Max feels that there are many advantages to becoming an franchisee, but some of the disadvantages could be far reaching, for example the consequences of the franchisor losing the company's good reputation. He decides that he is very interested in starting the Paper Work business, as currently there are no similar facilities in his area. However, he is not willing to risk all of his redundancy payment on the business so he makes an appointment to see his bank's business adviser to find out whether the bank will lend him any money to help finance the purchase of the franchise.

Table 3.6 Advantages and disadvantages of becoming a franchisee

Advantages of becoming a franchisee

Franchisees invest in a business that has been tried and tested and so often the risk is less.

The experience and knowledge of the franchisor means that the franchisee is less likely to make mistakes.

The administration of setting up a business is less difficult as the franchisor should help with this process.

The franchisor may offer training and support.

The business should enjoy a good reputation and already be well known and respected.

Franchisees should benefit from the advertising and marketing undertaken by the franchisor.

Many banks and financial institutions recognise the benefits of franchising and are more prepared to lend money to inexperienced business people if they are purchasing a franchise.

As the franchisee does not necessarily need experience in the chosen area, it allows them to explore new avenues of business.

As the franchisee will own their own business, they will enjoy the rewards of self-employment.

Disadvantages of becoming a franchisee

A percentage of the income or profit has to be paid to the franchisor.

The initial investment can be costly.

The business may be restricted in terms of choice of supplier, employment policy, ethos, direction, etc.

The failure of the franchisor can mean that the franchisee's business also fails.

If the franchisor sells the business, this may not be beneficial to the franchisee.

The reputation of the business relies on everyone involved in the company, including the other franchisees and franchisor.

It may not be possible to resell the franchise.

It may not be possible to expand the business easily or at all.

OVER TO YOU!

1 State two advantages to Max in purchasing a franchise business.

2 Explain why Max thinks running a franchise business poses less risk to him and his family than becoming a sole trader.

3 How could Max expand his franchise business?

The public sector

The term 'public sector' refers to any service or industry that is owned by the state. Public sector organisations fall into three main categories.

▶ **Service providers:** As the name suggests, these organisations provide a service to the population. Examples include the National Health Service, the armed forces and the courts of law.

▶ **Government departments:** These devise and implement the policies needed to organise the infrastructure of the country. Examples include the Treasury, and the departments of Culture, Media and Sport, Transport, and Education.

▶ **Trading bodies:** These organisations operate in the same way as private sector businesses because they sell goods and services to the public. However, they differ from companies within the private sector as they are non-profit-making and owned, controlled and regulated by central government. Examples of these include the Bank of England, the Royal Mail and the BBC.

The main aim of a public sector organisation is to provide a service to the whole population. The policy of the organisation is decided by central government who own, control and regulate it. A public corporation is set up by an Act of Parliament and although it is owned and controlled by central government, it has a separate legal identity.

There used also to be many public sector industries (called nationalised industries) in existence. However, since the 1970s many have been privatised, i.e. transferred or sold into the private sector. Examples of these include British Gas, British Steel, British Airways and British Telecom.

Public sector organisations are funded in the following ways.

▶ **By direct taxation:** the Treasury will allocate funds from taxes to the corporation.

▶ **By indirect taxation:** for example, each household that owns a television set must buy a television licence every year. The Treasury collects this money and it is given to the BBC as part of its funding.

▶ **Some public corporations sell** their goods and services to help fund themselves. For example, the BBC sells its programmes to other countries and television networks. The fees they receive for this are put back into the corporation. Another example are the charges made for postage, which are used to support the Royal Mail.

▶ **Government subsidy:** in some cases it is not possible for the organisation to survive by other methods of funding alone. Where the service is essential to the country's well-being, the government will provide funds in the form of a subsidy. This means that the organisation does not have to repay the money.

Generally, public sector organisations are expected to meet strict financial targets and to at least, break even. In order to do this, some organisations such as the National Health Service have had to introduce charges to the public. For example, although the majority of health care is provided free of charge, the public now has to make a contribution to National Health dental or eye care.

Central government controls the public corporation by appointing a minister who is responsible for the general policy of the corporation. The appointed minister will:

▶ influence the selection of the chairperson and board of directors, who are responsible for running the corporation on a day-to-day basis

▷ liaise with the Treasury to ensure that sufficient funds are in place

▷ answer questions in parliament that relate to the performance of the corporation.

A Select Committee and/or Consultative Committee monitors and investigates any irregularities or complaints about the public corporation. Consumer councils, set up by groups of consumers, will also monitor the activities of the corporation.

Watchdogs

These are formed to ensure that consumers' interests are protected. OFCOM (Office of Communications) is one example. It was set up in December 2003 and replaced OFTEL (Office of Telecommunications). Its main purpose is to ensure that consumers receive the best quality, choice and value for money for all communications and broadcasting services. OFCOM is run by a director general and its functions include:

▷ to balance the promotion of choice and competition with duties to foster plurality and informed citizenship, protect viewers, listeners and customers and promote cultural diversity

▷ to serve the interests of the citizen-consumer as the communications industry enters the digital age

▷ to support the need for innovators, creators and investors to flourish within markets driven by full and fair competition between all providers

▷ to encourage the evolution of electronic media and communications networks to the greater benefit of all who live in the United Kingdom.

Some advantages and disadvantages of public sector organisations are shown in Table 3.7.

Table 3.7 Advantages and disadvantages of public sector organisations

Advantages of public sector organisations	Disadvantages of public sector organisations
Essential services such as the health service and transport are guaranteed, controlled and accessible to all.	The organisations tend to be very bureaucratic.
Essential supplies such as water and energy can be guaranteed, controlled and accessible to all.	Most large public sector organisations have a monopoly; this means there is no competition.
Jobs are usually protected, which reduces unemployment throughout the country.	Inefficiency can occur because of diseconomies of scale.
Everyone shares in the profit made by public sector organisations as the profit is put back into ensuring the services and supplies are provided and maintained.	There is a lack of incentive to employees to perform as there is no competition.
Planning can be co-ordinated through central control.	Losses are met by the taxpayer.
Duplication of services is eliminated.	Political interference may affect the organisation.
	Accountability causes problems as the organisation is owned by the state.
	Taxes are higher in order to pay for these services.

Quangos

Central government does not always have the expertise or resources to carry out all the services it provides and so specialist bodies undertake this work for them. These are called quangos (quasi-autonomous national government organisations). Generally their role is to allocate government funds to various projects and bodies and to promote and represent their members' interests.

Sport England is an example of a quango. It is responsible for providing the strategic lead for sport in England, in order to deliver the Government's sporting objectives. It develops the framework for the country's sporting infrastructure and distributes National Lottery funding to where the money will deliver most value for sport.

Other examples of quangos include the Arts Council, the Higher Education Funding Council and the Further Education Funding Council.

Local government

Local government is also responsible for providing services to the public. Divided into geographical areas, local government is run by local authorities (also known as councils). Examples of the services provided by local government include:

- education
- emergency services
- police
- refuse collection
- maintenance of parks.

Local authorities work within the powers set out in various Acts of Parliament. Some of the functions undertaken are mandatory, which means that the local authority must, by law, do what is required. Other functions are discretionary, which means that the authority may provide the service if it wishes. Central government ministers have powers over local authorities with regard to certain services, to ensure that there is uniformity in standards and to protect the rights of individual citizens. If a local authority exceeds its statutory powers, it is regarded as acting outside the law and could be challenged in court.

Elected local councillors agree and oversee the implementation of policy. As with members of parliament, local councillors are usually aligned to a political party and are elected by the public. The political party that has the most seats and therefore most councillors takes control of the local authority and the decisions will be made with the party's political policies and beliefs in mind. The body of councillors that make these decisions is known as the council.

A chief executive, who is a paid employee, manages the day-to-day running of a local authority. The chief executive and his or her team prepare policies and budgets to propose to the council. The council will then either approve the policies and budgets or ask for amendments. Once approval has been obtained, the chief executive is responsible for ensuring policy is implemented.

Local government expenditure accounts for about 25 per cent of public spending. It is financed in the following ways:

- direct taxation, for example council tax on domestic and business premises

▶ indirect taxation through grants and borrowing from central government

▶ sale of goods and services. Examples of these are local leisure centres, fees for disposing of business waste, building inspections and car parking fees.

OVER TO YOU!

1 Briefly explain the purpose of a quango.

2 State three ways in which local authorities are funded.

3 State the three main categories of public sector organisations.

4 Give two examples of public corporations.

5 State two ways in which public sector organisations are funded.

6 What is the purpose of a government watchdog?

Acquisition of finance

In order to run a business successfully, it is necessary to have sufficient finance in place. This is not just the amount of money you need to actually start the business, but also what is needed to keep it running while it becomes self-sufficient. For some companies, particularly those that require a large initial investment, this may take several years.

Many people use their life savings to start their business, while others start with very little money and borrow what they need. There are advantages and disadvantages to both methods. Most businesses use a combination of methods for funding. Some of the most common methods of financing a business are given in Table 3.8 on pages 146–147. Look at these before answering these 'Over to You!' questions.

OVER TO YOU!

Suggest suitable methods for funding the start up of the following:

▶ franchise

▶ sole trader

▶ public limited company.

Discuss your answers with your tutor.

OVER TO YOU!

Preston Hotels (case study 3.4) will need to show growth in order to attract investors. List three ways in which they could achieve this within their existing business.

Table 3.8 Acquiring finance

METHOD	SUITABLE FOR	DESCRIPTION AND RISKS
Personal savings	All types of business	In order to start anything other than a very small business, you will need substantial savings. You will be risking all you have in order to start your venture and will have nothing to fall back on should it fail.
Borrowing from friends/family	Sole traders, partnerships, limited companies	The biggest risk to borrowing from friends and family is that you may fall out. However, friends and family may agree to lend money at a lower rate of interest than formal lending organisations and may also agree to an extended repayment timescale. Problems occur if the business fails, as obviously the borrowed money will also be lost.
Bank loans	All businesses	Banks will offer loans to all types of business start-ups and existing businesses. However, they are not always flexible in the repayment terms and more often than not will require some security. This means they need to be assured that the business will be able to repay the loan. This security could be taken against company assets, e.g. stock, premises, vehicles. In the case of a start-up business they may require the owner to use their personal assets, e.g. savings.
Government grants and loans	All businesses	There is a range of government grants and loans available to all types of business. However, there are usually restrictions on the type of business that can apply for the loan or grant and this often depends on the area in which you wish to start the business. The advantages are that grants can be given without the need for repayment and loans are offered at preferential rates and conditions.
Trusts	Depends on the Trust's aims, but could be for people aged under 30, disabled people, long-term unemployed, etc.	Trusts, such as The Prince's Trust, will give grants and advice to people who would like to start their own business. Each Trust will have its own aims and eligibility criteria, together with methods of repayment. Very useful method of raising finance if you meet the criteria.
Additional partner(s)	Partnerships	A partnership can raise funds by taking on an additional partner who pays for a share in the business. Advantages include having

Table 3.8 Continued

METHOD	SUITABLE FOR	DESCRIPTION AND RISKS
		additional labour, skills and ideas as well as the finance. Disadvantages include losing some control.
Business angel	All businesses, particularly start-ups with a finance requirement of around £250,000 or less	The terms of borrowing can vary from borrowing money at a higher rate than banks to giving a share in the company to the investor. This can be a good way of financing a business if you are unable to raise money in the more traditional ways. Business angel loans are normally unsecured; this means the borrower does not have to risk their own savings or property. The risk to the business angel is high, but they do receive tax benefits for this type of investment and the rewards can be great.
Venture capitalist	All businesses that require finance of over £250,000	Venture capitalists are very similar to business angels, although they tend to deal with much larger start-ups or companies. A venture capitalist can be a sole investor, group of investors or specialist companies that operate purely to invest in other businesses. Again, the repayment terms are high, usually a share in the company, and the risks to the investor are large.
Selling shares privately	Private limited companies	Private limited companies can sell shares to selected individuals in order to raise finance. These individuals will then own a share of the company and will be entitled to dividends, etc. There is no guarantee of repayment and if the business fails, the investors will lose their money. The disadvantage to the borrower is that they are losing a part of the business and, depending on the agreement made with the investors, could also lose some control of the business.
Selling shares on the Stock Exchange	Public limited companies	A company can float on the Stock Exchange in order to raise finance. This is a good way to raise capital; however, there are risks involved. These can affect the Stock Market as a whole, for example, if there is a lack of confidence in the British economy, British stocks may lose value. This will have a direct effect on the company's accounts and the public's perception of the company.

Growing the business

Most businesses need to grow in order to achieve or maintain success. For example, Cathy, the sole trader in case study 3.1, would need to grow her business from the small number of orders she receives in the first few months to a level where the business not only supports itself, but provides her with a reasonable income. When a business enjoys growth, it usually means that it has increased some or all of the following.

▶ **Economies of scale:** These relate to the cost per unit, sale or order. For example, a mail order company selling gifts will have certain costs that remain the same no matter how many items it sells. These fixed costs include rent of premises, the cost of heating and lighting the premises, business rates, publicity and promotional material, catalogues, photography or printing. Once the cost of all these items has been covered the business starts to make a profit. Therefore, the more items that are sold, the less expensive each sale becomes. Stock is not included in this list because unless you have sold your stock you do not need to buy more – it is a variable cost. Staff are another variable cost. If the mail order company was not successful, it would reduce the number of staff it employed.

▶ **Profitability:** This can be achieved by increasing the price of the goods or services, by reducing overheads and/or by economies of scale.

▶ **Range:** By offering new products or services, a company may be able to achieve growth.

▶ **Turnover:** The money received from selling goods or services is called turnover. This does not relate to profitability because although a company's turnover may be high, the cost of selling the goods or service could also be high, making the business not very profitable. However, businesses are often rated by their turnover and so a company that increases its turnover would be considered to have achieved growth.

In a successful business, growth should happen annually. A business should expect its sales to increase year on year and if this does not happen it will lose some of its profitability. If this carries on year after year, the business could be forced to stop trading as it would not have sufficient funds to carry on.

Even if a company did not wish to become bigger or more profitable, it would still need to plan for growth each year in order to keep up with inflation.

Expanding the business

Expansion is different from growth. It involves making the business bigger, for instance by opening new branches or outlets or by offering more goods and services.

Many businesses wish to expand for some or all of the following reasons:

▶ to increase their share of the market

▶ to make more profit

▶ to enjoy economies of scale

▶ to make their business more secure

▶ to enable them to employ more staff.

Expanding a business can be done in many ways including the following.

▶ **Opening more outlets:** Shops, restaurants, cafés and wholesale outlets can open more outlets or move to bigger premises so that they can expand their range of goods.

- **Taking on more staff:** Just taking on more staff doesn't always expand a business, but firms of consultants and other professionals such as solicitors, accountants, insurance brokers, dental surgeons and vets could expand their businesses by employing other professionals to join the practice. This would enable the business to expand as they could take on more customers.

- **Franchising:** This is a form of expansion as the number of outlets will increase. By doing this, the payment made by the franchisees will increase the company's turnover and if the franchisor is supplying goods, it will be able to enjoy larger economies of scale.

- **Increasing the goods or services on offer:** For example, a company that manufactures carpets could expand by opening a showroom and selling direct to the public. Alternatively, a shop that sells clothing could expand its range to include accessories such as bags and jewellery.

- **By taking on new partners or shareholders:** Although this act in itself will not expand the business, the resulting investment from the new partner or shareholders would allow the company to expand through funding changes such as an increased range of services, a move to better premises, etc.

- **Merging or taking over other companies:** This allows rapid expansion as the business will immediately benefit from the sales and turnover of the existing company. It can be a very expensive way of expanding.

In order to expand successfully, a business would need to plan carefully the way in which the expansion is to take place. Areas that would need to be considered include the following.

- **The overall cost of expansion:** Opening new shops, moving to bigger premises or buying in more stock will cost a considerable amount of money. Businesses need to ensure that their current financial position will allow for these extra costs to be met.

- **Customer needs:** There would be no point, for example, in opening three new shops in the same town unless there are sufficient numbers of new customers that would support them.

- **Competition:** Again, there needs to be enough customers to support the expansion. For example, if a competitor is enjoying a high level of success in a particular town, it may not be sensible to open a branch of the business in that area as customer loyalty will reduce the chances of success.

- **Timescale:** It is important for businesses to plan the timescale of their expansion carefully. Many companies have failed because they have expanded too rapidly and the increase in business has not been sufficient to pay for the increase in expenses.

Not all businesses wish to expand. There is always a degree of risk that has to be faced with expansion. Sometimes the cost of expanding successfully is just too high. Other companies do not wish to increase their workload or staffing levels. These companies will need to ensure that their annual growth allows them to keep their business at the level at which they are comfortable.

OVER TO YOU!

Global Trading (case study 3.7) wish to expand through franchising the business. Discuss two other ways in which Global Trading could expand without using the franchising option.

Diversification

Diversification is when a company changes or adds to the range of goods and services it offers. True diversification occurs when the change is radical. For example, a company that sells clothing and decides to add fashion accessories to its range is not truly diversifying, it is just expanding its range. However, a clothing company that decides to sell freezers could be said to have diversified.

Some companies diversify into many different areas. For example, Virgin is a company that has diversified from selling music to operating trains, aircraft and financial services.

There are both advantages and disadvantages to diversification (see Table 3.9).

Table 3.9 Advantages and disadvantages of diversification

Advantages of diversification	Disadvantages of diversification
▶ The risks of the business are spread: if one market fails, the other will help support the business.	▶ Company resources will need to be diverted to launch the new side of the business.
▶ Businesses are more secure when markets change.	▶ If the new business fails, resources will have been wasted.
▶ New markets will provide challenge and change, which often result in renewed enthusiasm and effort.	▶ The effects that the new business might have on existing business need to be considered.
	▶ The business may grow too fast and suffer diseconomies of scale.

Mergers

A merger takes place when two or more companies join together to make one larger company. There are two ways in which this can take place:

▶ two (or more) firms agree to merge to form a larger company

▶ the stronger company buys a weaker firm for its assets and knowledge. The aim is to purchase the weaker company for a sum that is lower than the total value of the company's assets. The stronger company sells off the parts that are valuable and closes down those that are not profitable. This is called asset stripping.

A merger can be classed in the following ways:

▶ horizontal

▶ vertical

▶ lateral

▶ conglomerate.

Table 3.10 shows the various classifications of mergers, based on a jewellery wholesaler business called Gems.

Table 3.10 Types of merger

Type of merger	Description	Example
Horizontal	The type of business is the same and they are at the same stage of production.	Gems merges with a smaller company.
Vertical (backwards)	The type of business is the same, but at a previous stage of production.	Gems merges with a jewellery maker.
Vertical (forwards)	The type of business is the same, but at the next stage of production.	Gems merges with a jewellery retailer.
Lateral	The type of business is different, but has common areas, i.e. production techniques, materials, distribution channels, technology.	Gems merges with a clothing wholesaler.
Conglomerate	The type of business and production are different.	Gems merges with a kitchenware manufacturer.

A merger can give the newly formed company the following benefits:

▶ economies of scale

▶ reduced fixed costs

▶ reduced competition

▶ larger market share

▶ sharing of assets

▶ more efficient operation

▶ the potential to diversify

▶ reduced costs of raw materials (in a backward vertical merge).

Mergers are not always popular. The shareholders of the weaker company may be concerned that their investment is not safe. The government has put in place regulators such as the Department of Trade and Industry and the Monopolies and Mergers Commission to look at proposed mergers to ensure that customers will not be disadvantaged. This is because large companies that merge may become a monopoly. A monopoly is currently defined in the UK as any business with over 25 per cent of the market.

Monopolies can charge very high fees for their goods and/or services as they have little competition and the customer has little choice. Ensuring that there is competition in the economy is also an important consideration before the regulator can agree that the merger can take place.

It often happens that when news of a proposed merger reaches the public, other companies will also make a bid for the weaker company. This can mean that the weaker company changes hands for far more money that it is worth, which will appeal to the existing shareholders because their profits will be much larger. However, some shareholders will oppose the highest bid because they fear that the new company will not provide the future growth and investment to ensure the company's success in the longer term.

Demergers

A demerger is when a company splits its business activities into two or more parts. A company may achieve this by either selling part of its business or by operating the various parts as independent organisations. Conglomerates are more likely to demerger because their business interests will cover more than one market and so it is easier to split the organisation. An organisation may choose to demerger for one or more of the following reasons.

▶ **Specialisation:** A company may decide to concentrate on one area of the business.

▶ **To raise funds:** If a company sells off part of its assets, the resulting cash can be invested in other areas of the business.

▶ **To avoid rising costs.**

▶ **To increase efficiency:** Larger businesses can become very inefficient with too many layers of staff and management.

▶ **To increase the organisation's value:** Generally two smaller companies will have a higher value than one large company.

▶ **To ensure success:** If an organisation sees a fall in one of the markets in which they operate, separating the activities will help ensure the continued success of the other areas.

Takeovers

A takeover will occur when a company purchases 51 per cent (or more) of another company's shares in order to take control of the business. This can either be a forced or hostile takeover, when the weaker company does not wish to be taken over, or a friendly takeover, when the weaker company invites the stronger company to do so.

There are legal restrictions to this practice. Once a company has purchased only 3 per cent of the shares of another company, it has to declare this to the Stock Market. This will then alert shareholders to the possibility of a takeover. Takeovers are also subject to investigation by the Monopolies and Mergers Commission.

Takeovers can be very costly as the legal and administrative costs can be very high. The share price of a company that is the subject of an attempted takeover often rises as investors take advantage of the fact that the shares are in demand. This can result in the actual cost of the takeover becoming too high to be of value to the company attempting the takeover bid.

OVER TO YOU!

1 Explain the difference between a takeover and a merger.

2 Explain the difference between growth and expansion.

3 Give two reasons why a company might wish to demerger.

4 Explain the difference between a company expanding its range and diversifying.

5 Briefly explain the meaning of the term 'monopoly'.

6 State three benefits to a company of merging with a smaller company.

▼ EXPLAIN THE NEED FOR AN ORGANISATION TO MAKE CLEAR ITS AIMS AND OBJECTIVES

Almost without exception, businesses have a clear aim: to make money. However, in order to make money successfully, businesses need to set aims and objectives. These will set out what it is the business wants to achieve and how it will go about achieving it.

Aims

Aims are the long-term intentions of a business. For example, a company may decide that one of its long-term aims is to own 15 shops at the end of five years. This aim will help set the objectives because these are the short-term targets, which can be measured. So, the company's objectives for the next year might be to open three shops in order to help reach their stated long-term goal. At the end of the following year the directors will be able to look back to see if they met their objectives and how the success or failure of this will affect the company's aims.

CASE STUDY 3.3 – IPD Ltd

Patrick and Imran have set up their company and are now manufacturing fashion clothing. Their long-term aims are as follows:

▶ to become a market leader in innovative fashion clothing

▶ to substantially reduce the borrowing of the company within three years

▶ to maximise the profitability of the company.

Objectives

As you have just seen, the objectives are the short-term targets that can be measured to assess progress within a business. There are four levels of objective and these are:

▶ corporate

▶ strategic

▶ tactical

▶ operational.

Corporate objectives

These directly relate to the long-term aims of the company. Some management consultants feel that corporate objectives should be set for each of the following areas:

▶ profitability

▶ market standing

▶ physical and financial resources

▶ managerial performance

- worker performance
- public responsibility
- productivity
- innovation.

If an organisation was to set objectives in all of those areas, its entire organisation should be focused on meeting the long-term aims. Many companies use the SMART rule when setting objectives. This stands for:

- **s**pecific
- **m**easurable
- **a**ttainable
- **r**ealistic (or **r**elevant)
- **t**ime-specific.

How ever the organisation decides to set its objectives, they should be clear to all who read them. It is also extremely important that an organisation reviews its objectives on a regular basis so that they can see:

- if the objectives needs amendment because of external factors, such as recession, change in consumer needs, increase in the price of resources, changing markets, etc.
- the progress made by the organisation in meeting the objectives
- if the timescale of meeting the objectives needs to be altered
- that the objectives are still realistic
- if the objectives are still in line with the organisation's long-term aims.

CASE STUDY 3.3 – IPD Ltd

As IPD Ltd is a new business, the corporate objectives must be based on what Patrick and Imran hope to achieve with their company. Their corporate objectives are as follows:

- to show a profit within two years
- to reduce the borrowing of the company by 15 per cent within three years
- to be recognised as a manufacturer of high quality, innovative fashion clothing
- to use the best quality materials available within their financial budgets
- to keep costs and overheads under strict control
- the management of the company will constantly strive to provide the best possible service within the budget and resources
- the staff of the company will constantly strive to meet deadlines, work within budgets and provide the best possible service both to external and internal customers
- the company will source their materials from fair trade organisations whenever possible.

OVER TO YOU!

Draw up the corporate objectives you think that Phoenix Enterprises (case study 3.5) might have.

Strategic objectives

These relate to finance, markets, products and production. They will set out how to achieve the corporate objectives. For example, Patrick and Imran have set the following strategic objectives :

- to reduce borrowing by 5 per cent each year
- to increase profits by 25 per cent year on year for three years
- to achieve sales of £3.5 million within five years.

From this you can see that Patrick and Imran have looked at their corporate objectives and have then set the strategic objectives that will enable the corporate objectives to be met.

OVER TO YOU!

Using the corporate objectives you drew up for Phoenix Enterprises plc in the exercise on page 154, write the strategic objectives that will ensure that the corporate objectives can be met.

Tactical objectives

Tactical objectives are written for the short term. They are broken into targets for the various departments or functions of a business. For example, the human resources department might be given the tactical objective of reducing absenteeism by 5 per cent within six months. The finance department could be given the objective of producing the profit and loss account within one month of the company's financial year-end.

Although tactical objectives might not relate directly to the strategic and corporate objectives, the overall tactical objectives of a company, when joined together, will help ensure that the strategic and corporate objectives are met.

CASE STUDY 3.3 – IPD Ltd

As IPD Ltd is a new company, the tactical objectives will be quite general until the directors see how the business operates. The tactical objectives Patrick and Imran have set their various departments include the following:

- sales: to achieve sales worth £500,000 in the first year of business
- research and design: to design four full collections of fashion clothing within the first year of business.

OVER TO YOU!

Using the corporate and strategic objectives, devise tactical objectives for the following departments of Phoenix Enterprises plc (case study 3.5):

- human resources
- finance
- sales.

Operational objectives

These short-term objectives are given to groups of workers or even individuals. They relate more to the day-to-day activities and can be used to deal with problem areas as they arise.

Business strategy

A business will need to prepare plans for meeting its aims and objectives and to ensure continued success. These plans are known as a business strategy. There are a number of elements that make up a business strategy and these include:

▷ **the mission;** the main purpose of the business, which is in line with the expectations or values of the stakeholders

▷ **the vision or strategic intent;** the aspirations of the organisation, what it really wants to achieve

▷ **goals;** what it is actually aiming to achieve

▷ **objectives;** how the goal or aim is going to be achieved

▷ **core competences;** the skills, resources and other elements that make up the competitive advantage over other similar companies

▷ **strategies;** the long-term direction of the company

▷ **the strategic architecture;** the resources, processes and skills required to put the strategies into effect

▷ **control;** the monitoring of the plan and objectives to measure the effectiveness of the strategies.

OVER TO YOU!

Write a list of six objectives Preston Hotels might devise for the company. Discuss your answers with your tutor.

Cathy has made the decision to start her own business. She now needs to work out exactly what she wants from her business in the future. She may decide that her business idea is fine and that she does not want the responsibility of running a larger operation. Alternatively she may wish to expand her business in the future and perhaps employ other designers and manufacturers to broaden the range.

Although Cathy hasn't even started her business, she needs to have a strategic plan for the company. This will be useful as it will help her to focus on the business in the following ways:

▶ to see where she wants to be within a given timescale, for example five or ten years

▶ to see what needs to be achieved in order to reach her goals

▶ to keep the business focused on the long-term aims

▶ so that people she deals with, for example finance lenders or suppliers, will have an idea of where the company is heading

▶ so that she can get the resources in place to achieve her goals

▶ to monitor her progress

▶ to measure her success.

It is important to be realistic and to update the aims and objectives on a regular basis, otherwise she may lose out on opportunities that arise.

After looking at the various options and researching her market carefully, Cathy has drawn up the following long term objectives:

▶ to expand the choice of jewellery items to ten new ranges each year

▶ to employ a number of new and fashionable designers to keep ahead of the competition

▶ to open three retail shops in major shopping centres within a five-year period

▶ to maintain the high quality of the jewellery.

You can see that these are quite ambitious aims and Cathy will need to work hard to achieve them. She will also need to develop good business skills in order to keep her company running while she puts these plans into action. Cathy realises that she will need to update these aims on a regular basis.

CASE STUDY 3.4 – Preston Hotels

The board of Preston Hotels Ltd has now started the process of becoming a plc. As part of the financial plan and prospectus for investors the board must set out the aims and objectives of the PLC. The reasons for setting out the objectives are the same as for Richmond Jewels with the following additions:

▶ to show investors where the company is heading

▶ to show investors that the business is a good and safe investment

▶ to include in the prospectus.

CASE STUDY 3.6 – Craddock Dog Sanctuary

Emily and her family have decided that she should run a charity in order to continue helping the unwanted animals. They feel that the charity should extend its help to all dogs and not just labradors. Emily must set out the purposes of the charity in order to be registered with the Charities Commission. By setting out the purposes, Emily will then be able to see what the objectives are. The purposes of the charity must fall into one of the broad categories set out by the Charities Commission. As there is no specific outline for providing sanctuary for animals, Emily will have to ensure that her purposes and objectives fit one or more of the outlines.

The purposes of the Craddock Dog Sanctuary are:

▶ to relieve the suffering of dogs in need of care and attention and to provide and maintain a rescue home for the reception, care and treatment of such dogs for the benefit of the public

▶ to promote humane behaviour towards dogs by providing appropriate care, protection, treatment and security for those in need of care and attention by reason of sickness, maltreatment, poor circumstances or ill usage, and to educate the public in matters relating to animal welfare in general and the prevention of cruelty to dogs in particular.

OVER TO YOU!

Explain why it is important for Emily to clearly explain the aims and objectives of the charity. Write five objectives you think she might include.

Mission statement

As well as setting out aims and objectives, companies often write and publish a mission statement. This is seen as very important by many organisations. It gives the entire business a focus and sets out its aims and objectives for all to see. The role of the mission statement is to:

▶ act as the main focus for the business

▶ help set objectives

▶ show customers, stakeholders and staff the ethos of the business, its aims and objectives and the way in which it intends to achieve these.

A good mission statement will also describe the business's products and market, and reflect the values of the senior management team.

It should contain the following:

▶ an insight into the organisation

▶ how it differs from its competitors

▶ the broad purposes of the organisation; what it does

▶ business objectives for the future; what it intends to do and become

- how it will meet customer needs
- guidance for the behaviour of the people who work in the business.

The art of writing a good mission statement is to ensure that it is relevant, that progress can be measured against it and that it inspires the people who read it.

OVER TO YOU!

Global Trading (case study 3.7) will need to have an informative and well-designed mission statement if it is to attract franchisees to its business. Write a mission statement it could use.

Company policy

Every company will have a number of different policies in place. These may relate to any or all of the following:

- staff employment
- customer service
- rules and regulations
- health and safety
- equal opportunities.

Some of the policies, such as health and safety and equal opportunities are required by law. Other policies are devised in accordance with the company's beliefs, values and plans. The strategic plan will affect a company's policies in that the aims and objectives will be the driving force of a business. This in turn will affect the way in which the company goes about its activities and the ethos behind the business.

The culture of a business

The activities, values and beliefs of a company will affect the culture of the business. For example, you would expect a business that runs a children's nursery to have a caring culture, one in which the welfare of the child is of equal, if not greater importance than the making of money. Obviously any owner of a business would need to make a profit, but for some companies this is paramount, for others it is of less importance.

The culture of a business is not solely dependent on how much money the company wants to make. The aims and objectives will also affect the culture. For example, if an organisation has decided that it must double in size within two years, you might expect it to have an aggressive management style. Staff will need to work tirelessly and take a hard sell approach in order to help the company achieve its aim. A different type of organisation might have set its aims at providing the best possible customer service. The aggressive, hard sell approach would not be appropriate for this company's aims.

Every organisation has a responsibility to others. This includes the staff, the customers, the public and the environment. Some of these responsibilities are now governed by law. For example, an organisation cannot sack a member of its staff without a valid reason, nor can it dump poisonous waste into rivers. Many organisations go much further than just complying with the law in their business dealings. Some organisations provide a very high level of welfare for their staff, including free health care or counselling services, extensive training programmes and other benefits. Other organisations make great efforts to treat suppliers of goods fairly by paying a fair rate for their labours and ensuring that contracts are kept. A large number of organisations are now ensuring that their activities do not harm the environment and are constantly researching 'green' ways of producing goods and dealing with waste. All of these factors will affect the culture of the business.

A big part of being successful at work is finding employment with a company whose culture suits you. If your beliefs and values are very different from those of the company for which you work, you may find that you do not enjoy your job very much.

OVER TO YOU!

1. Emily plans to have staff to help her at the dog sanctuary (case study 3.6). Some will be paid employees, others volunteers. Discuss in a group the business culture of the dog sanctuary.

2. How will the culture of the organisation as portrayed by the mission statement be affected by Preston Hotels' plans to become a public limited company (case study 3.4)? Discuss this with your tutor group.

▼ EVALUATE THE IMPACT OF EXTERNAL FACTORS WHEN DETERMINING OBJECTIVES AND STRATEGIES

As well as deciding on the business idea, finding finance and planning what is wanted from a business, it is also extremely important to consider external factors that might affect it. A careful and considered analysis of external factors will help to determine whether the business is likely to be successful and what its success might be threatened by.

PEST analysis

This is used to consider the possible **p**olitical, **e**conomic, **s**ocial and **t**echnological influences (PEST) on a business. It is a very useful tool when planning business activities and development as it will show the external factors that could influence the business. Table 3.11 shows some of the factors that need to be assessed and the possible effects they could have on an organisation.

Table 3.11 External factors that affect business organisations

Area	Factor	Possible effect
Political	Fiscal policy	Rate of personal tax increases or decreases, affecting customer spending. Rate of business tax increases or decreases, affecting profitability. Investors may receive less return on their money. Prices will need to rise, affecting customer spending as they will purchase less. An increase in the rate of VAT not only increases the price of the goods and restricts consumer spending, but also increases an organisation's overheads as the tax has to be paid on the raw materials or goods they buy in.
	Monetary policy	Interest rates rise; an organisation's borrowing will be more expensive, therefore the company becomes less profitable. Personal borrowing becomes more expensive and consumers will reduce the amount they borrow and therefore spend.
	Legislation	This could cost the business money and time in adapting current working practices or introducing new practices. Increasing the minimum wage could mean that staff are more expensive to hire.
	Political relations with other countries	If the government imposes trading restrictions with other countries, this would have an effect. Acts of terrorism reduce the number of tourists to the UK, which in turn reduces spending. Obtaining goods from suppliers may also become difficult.

Table 3.11 Continued

Area	Factor	Possible effect
Economic	The base interest rate may increase/ decrease	Any increases or decreases affect consumer spending. They also have an effect on the company as any borrowing that might be in place will cost more (or less).
	The cost of living may rise	When the cost of living rises, people have less money to spend on luxuries such as jewellery, eating out, holidays.
	The level of employment	If there is a high level of unemployment in the area in which the business operates, labour will be cheap and it will be easy to find skilled and committed staff. If employment in the locality is high, the organisation may have to offer higher salaries.
Social	Demand increases or falls	Any increase or fall in the demand for the goods and/or services supplied by a company will have an effect.
	The location of a business	If the goods and/or services are supplied direct to the public, the organisation must be in a good location for its market. If the business is in an area where there is high employment, it may need to pay more than the minimum wage to attract staff.
	Seasonality	Will customers want the goods or services all year round? If not, the feasibility of the business will depend on whether sufficient money can be made within the season to support the business all year.
	Competitors	It is important to keep up to date with the activities of competitors. This includes trends in fashion, pricing and customer service.
Technological	New products and/or services	A company will need to ensure that its products and/or services are kept up to date and in line with customers' wants. Those offered by competitors will need to be matched or improved upon.
	Working patterns and processes	Changes to these could be brought about by legislation, e.g. the Working Hours Directive, or by changes to the way in which work is undertaken, e.g. new machinery or equipment.
	New technology	It is important to keep up to date with new technology to see if there are any real benefits in purchasing new equipment.

OVER TO YOU!

Table 3.11 gives only a few examples of items that could be included in a PEST analysis. In groups, think of at least four more for each category. Present your ideas to the rest of the class.

Cathy does a PEST analysis to see what external factors could affect her business. Table 3.12 shows what she included.

Table 3.12 A PEST analysis for Richmond Jewels

Political
- ▶ Central government may increase the rate of taxation paid on personal income.
- ▶ Local government may increase business rates.
- ▶ Central government may increase VAT on luxury items; this would mean the prices would have to rise.

Social
- ▶ Is there sufficient demand to ensure a reasonable number of customers?
- ▶ Will people be prepared to pay a reasonable amount for a good quality product?
- ▶ Will customers require jewellery all year round or are the sales just at Christmas time?
- ▶ Jewellery designs can be very fashionable; how would I keep up with the latest designs without having too much stock?
- ▶ If I need to employ staff, what would I need to pay in order to attract the best?
- ▶ Are there any other jewellery designers living in this area?

Economic
- ▶ The cost of living may rise and discourage people from buying jewellery.
- ▶ The cost of equipment and supplies may rise, making the jewellery more expensive.
- ▶ If I need to employ staff and the minimum wage rises, this will affect the profitability of the business.
- ▶ Are any of the businesses in the area likely to close or make staff redundant?
- ▶ Are new businesses likely to open?
- ▶ What is the competition and how would this affect my business?

Technical
- ▶ How close is my nearest supplier?
- ▶ If the nearest supplier is unreliable, how will I be able to get supplies on a regular basis?
- ▶ Will I need to continually invest in new equipment? How reliant will I be on equipment?

As well as a PEST analysis, Cathy also draws up a SWOT analysis. This stands for **strengths**, **weaknesses**, **opportunities** and **threats**. The analysis can also be used for external factors, but it is a very useful tool for analysing the strengths and weakness of a company or even yourself.

Table 3.13 on page 164 shows Cathy's SWOT analysis.

Table 3.13 A SWOT analysis for Richmond Jewels

Strengths
- I am prepared to work hard to ensure the business is a success.
- I have the necessary skills in order to cope with the work.
- At the moment I don't need to earn a great deal of money in order to pay my living expenses.
- I have a talent for designing.

Opportunities
- My jewellery designs are unique and fashionable.
- There are not many jewellery retailers currently on the Internet.

Weaknesses
- As a sole trader I have to make all my own decisions, sometimes in areas I don't know a great deal about.
- I don't always cope well under pressure.

Threats
- Jewellery retailers may open and I could lose business.
- If I can't keep up with the demand for stock, I will lose business.
- If fashion changes quickly, I may be left with stock I cannot sell.

From this analysis, Cathy will be in a much better position to decide whether her new venture will be successful.

OVER TO YOU!

1 Assuming that you are taking a course of study, draw up a SWOT analysis to show your strengths and weaknesses, opportunities and threats. Discuss your findings with your tutor or colleagues.

2 Draw up a PEST analysis for Max who is deciding whether to purchase a Paper Work franchise (case study 3.8).

▼ REVIEW AND ANALYSE THE STRUCTURE OF BUSINESS ORGANISATIONS

Functional areas of business organisations

A business, even a very small one, will undertake a large number of activities in order to keep running. Table 3.14 shows the various functional areas of most businesses, the objectives of each area and the activities carried out. Not all businesses will need to have all of these function areas; it depends on the goods and/or services they provide. In some organisations function areas such as sales and marketing may well be combined, as would warehouse and despatch.

Table 3.14 Functional departments

Function area	Objectives	Activities
Administration	To ensure that the general administration of the business is dealt with efficiently and effectively.	Filing. Photocopying. Routine letter writing. Taking routine telephone calls. Providing reception, switchboard and postal services.
Finance	To ensure that the business has sufficient funds to operate. To ensure that budgets are set and maintained. To organise payment for staff in terms of salaries, pensions and benefits. To pay suppliers. To invoice customers and ensure that payment is received. To project profit and loss and report to directors. To prepare end of year accounts.	Paying invoices. Raising invoices. Projecting cashflow. Setting budgets. Monitoring budgets. Bookkeeping. Projecting profit and loss. Paying salaries. Controlling credit. Dealing with expenses. Reconciling bankings. Making investments. Assisting in acquiring finance.
Human Resources	To ensure that staffing levels are correct and maintained. To provide a welfare service to staff. To negotiate with staff regarding changes to terms and conditions. To organise staff training and development. To liaise with trade unions. To ensure that the company works within current employment legislation. To deal with grievance and disciplinary procedures.	Dealing with the recruitment process. Dealing with grievance or disciplinary issues. Providing a welfare service to staff. Organising staff training and development. Consulting with staff over changes to terms and conditions. Organising redundancy payments and packages. Providing advice on current employment legislation.
Purchasing	To ensure sufficient supply of goods as requested. To negotiate favourable purchasing terms from suppliers. To research the best products for the company. May also oversee stock control.	Liaising with suppliers. Raising orders. Negotiating favourable terms i.e. for bulk buying. Ensuring receipt of goods purchased.
Production	To manufacture goods to consistent, stated quality standards. To manufacture goods within reasonable timescales. To minimise wastage.	Manufacturing goods. Setting quality control standards. Checking of goods for quality.
Despatch	To send goods to customers within reasonable timescales.	Collating orders. Preparing parcels. Preparing despatch documentation. Organising postal collections.

Table 3.14 Continued

Function area	Objectives	Activities
Research and development	To ensure that the company keeps up to date with new techniques, equipment and materials. To design new products. To provide costings for new products. To research customer opinions and develop goods in line with customer wants.	Researching new techniques, materials and equipment. Keeping up to date with latest advances. Using findings of market research to develop new products or improve existing products. Working out the cost of any development.
Sales	To sell goods and services to external customers. To negotiate terms and conditions of sale. To maintain good customer relations. To keep customers informed about products, offers and service. To provide a good customer service.	Meeting customers. Negotiating with customers. Raising sales documentation. Maintaining sales records. Maintaining customer records. Sending information to customers.
Warehouse	To store goods safely and securely and in line with health and safety regulations. To maintain good condition of stock. Keep up-to-date records of stock levels.	Storing stock. Maintaining good condition of stock. Keeping and maintaining records. Provide up-to-date information to other departments on stock levels/shortages.
Marketing	To promote the company. To promote the goods and services offered by the company. To ensure customer recognition of the brand. To research customer wants, needs, expectations and satisfaction. To research most productive methods of advertising. To ensure and maintain good reputation of company. To promote customer awareness.	Devising and implementing advertising campaigns and strategies. Undertaking customer research, analyse findings and prepare reports. Researching competitors activities. Researching advertising methods.

Depending on the company's size and activities, you may also find the functional areas shown in Table 3.15.

Table 3.15 Additional functional departments

Legal	To ensure that the organisation operates within the law. To advise on legal matters.	Preparing legal documents including contracts, tenders, agreement and leases. Interpreting legal documents received by the company. Researching new Acts and regulations and ensuring organisation updates policies and practices accordingly.
IT	To provide and maintain communication systems throughout the organisation. To keep up to date with the latest technology and report to senior management.	Setting up equipment. Maintaining equipment. Troubleshooting problems. Ensuring confidentiality. Preventing viruses and network hacking. Researching and reporting on latest technology. Preparing user manuals. Undertaking training.
Customer service	To provide an excellent standard of customer service to all customers.	Preparing customer service policy. Dealing with customers and ensuring customer satisfaction. Keeping up to date with the levels of service provided by competitors.
Call centre	To provide an efficient and effective communication system for customers.	Dealing with customers by telephone.
Design	To design and develop packaging, brochures, leaflets and other marketing literature.	Designing packaging and other materials. Dealing with printing of materials. Organising estimates for printing and materials. Selecting suitable suppliers.

Agents, consultants and other service providers

The majority of companies do not need to employ experts such as solicitors and financial advisers on a full-time basis. However, they may need to use their services from time to time. In this case, the business will use the services of an agent or consultant. These can include experts on business matters who would cost far too much to keep on the company's payroll and would in fact be underemployed. Their expertise can assist businesses on matters such as management, advertising, company structure, recruitment, legal and/or financial matters and so have an important part to play in the success of a business.

Other service providers that are important to businesses are banks, financial institutions, insurance companies, accountants, auditors, recruitment agencies, cleaners, catering providers and webpage designers.

The advantages to a business of employing a consultant on a temporary basis can include the following.

▶ The business does not have to employ consultants and is therefore not responsible for their tax and national insurance contributions, holiday and sickness pay and other responsibilities that are incurred when employing staff.

▶ A consultant will normally be an expert in a particular field.

- A consultant should have up-to-date knowledge and technical expertise.

- A consultant should have experience of the same or similar problems or events. This is particularly useful if a company is setting up a new system or thinking of diversifying into new areas.

- Usually you can buy as much or as little of their time as you require (or can afford).

- They should remain unbiased. This is particularly important if, for example, a company was hiring the consultant's services to advise it on a major restructure.

- They will be discreet and maintain confidentiality. This could be very important if, for example, a company wished to reduce the number of staff.

OVER TO YOU!

1. Cathy's main business is to design and sell jewellery over the Internet (case study 3.1). Make a list of the functional activities she will undertake on a day-to-day basis.

2. Preston Hotels (case study 3.4) will need to use several outside agents and consultants to help them prepare for floating their business on the Stock Exchange. Make of list of those they might employ and give reasons why they would need them.

How an organisation is structured to meet its objectives

The structure of a business relates to the way in which it is organised in terms of the following:

- the relationships between staff in terms of responsibility and authority

- the decision-making process

- communication channels

- dividing up the work.

Although there are a number of broad structures commonly used in organisations, each business will be different because of the following factors:

- the size of the organisation

- the nature of its work

- the product and/or service it offers

- the number of outlets

- its geographical location

- the ethos of the directors

- its strategic plan and objectives.

Some of the most commonly used structures are explained in the next sections.

Functional areas

Patrick and Imran are planning how to organise their business. They want to structure the company by functional area. This means that there will be separate areas for the various activities. The functional areas they have agreed upon are:

▶ production

▶ finance

▶ warehouse

▶ despatch

▶ purchasing

▶ human resources

▶ administration

▶ sales and marketing.

Initially, Patrick will take care of the marketing of the business and other managerial tasks. Imran will be overseeing the financial matters of the company. This structure is common for many organisations. The advantages of structuring an organisation by function are as follows:

▶ staff are trained in one area and become specialised

▶ you know who to go to with a particular problem.

However, one of the problems with this structure is that it can be difficult for the areas to interact with each other, sometimes resulting in friction and little co-operation between staff.

Geographical areas

Preston Hotels do not use functional areas to structure their business. As they have a number of hotels throughout the UK they have a geographical structure. This means that the work is divided into areas of the country, such as the south west or midlands. This structure is often used by companies that have business world wide.

Process areas

Some organisations divide the work by process. Each part of the process is a separate department. For example, in a printing company there would be the following departments: design, typesetting, paper purchasing, printing and binding.

Product areas

Product areas are where the work is organised according to the product. For example a retail company could have departments for fashion, accessories, home furnishings and so on. This could also be a good way to structure an organisation that provides a number of services.

Project areas

These are similar to product areas. The organisation is structured into project teams or groups and each works on a separate event or project. This structure would work for a company that organises conferences, for example. Each team would have one or more projects to work on.

Customer areas

An organisation that deals with both the public and other businesses could use this structure with a separate area for each.

OVER TO YOU!

Suggest how Callum and Anya might structure their new business (case study 3.2). Discuss your ideas with your tutor.

Centralised services

Some companies centralise their administration functions. This means that all activities such as filing, photocopying, document production, purchasing and mail handling are dealt with by one section. This can be a very efficient way of working, however there are also disadvantages. Table 3.16 lists the advantages and disadvantages of centralising services.

Interaction of the functional areas

The most important part of any structure is the interaction between the various departments and areas. All departments will need to work, liaise and co-operate with each other, often on a daily basis. For example, the financial department will need to process payments and issue invoices for work carried out by the sales, marketing and purchasing departments. They will also pay the salaries of all the staff, after being informed of the rates by human resources.

Work can only be carried out efficiently and effectively if staff co-operate with each other. It should be remembered that staff are all working for the same aim – to complete their work to the best of their ability in an efficient and effective manner.

Table 3.16 Advantages and disadvantages of centralised services

Advantages of centralised services	Disadvantages of centralised services
▶ Staff become specialised in their area.	▶ Staff morale can be low as there is little variety in the work.
▶ It can be more economic for the company as staff become very efficient at their work.	▶ The service may be inflexible in that it might be difficult to get work done in an emergency.
▶ It is also economic because, for example a filing clerk would not need to earn as much as a general administrator.	▶ The workload may be very heavy, causing staff to feel under pressure.
▶ Training is easy and economical.	▶ There may be duplication when other departments do the work themselves in order to get things done more quickly.
▶ Staff know where to get things done.	▶ If the work is highly technical, there may be more errors (for example, the data input clerk may not understand some of the terms used).
▶ If purchasing is centralised, the organisation may benefit from economies of scale, i.e. buying larger amounts at a time to benefit from greater discounts.	▶ If errors are made, it can be time-consuming to get work corrected.
▶ Procedures can be easily set up and standardised.	▶ In order to request work, there may be paperwork to complete that is time-consuming and adds to the administrative load.
▶ Equipment costs can be kept to a minimum.	▶ If staff feel they are under pressure, they may become less helpful when dealing with requests, causing friction in the workplace.
▶ Equipment that has an impact on health and safety in terms of noise levels, cable management and ergonomics can be kept to one part of the building.	
▶ Duplication of work can be avoided.	
▶ Quality control; it is much easier to control the quality of the work.	
▶ The service is easier to manage and supervise.	

OVER TO YOU!

1 State two advantages to the organisation of having centralised services.

2 Give three examples of possible interaction between the sales and marketing departments.

3 State two advantages to staff of having centralised services.

The internal management structure of a business

Any organisation, even the smallest, will need to have a structure. This is so that staff working for the organisation know who they should report to, who they are in charge of and who is in charge of them. Without a proper structure, it would be difficult to ensure that the work is carried out efficiently and effectively.

Most organisations will have a structure based on one of a few standard models. You will recognise these models from the way in which your school, college or organisation works.

The structure of an organisation can be seen by its organisation chart. This usually gives the following information:

▶ job titles of employees

▶ formal relationships between employees

▶ the departments within the organisation.

The chart should be read from top to bottom with the most senior members of staff and those with the most authority at the top, and the staff with the least amount of authority at the bottom. Remember:

▶ responsibility flows downwards

▶ accountability flows upwards.

CASE STUDY 3.2 – Restoration Antiques

Callum and Anya have employed three staff. This is how their organisation chart would look:

▲ Figure 3.8 Organisation chart for Restoration Antiques

From this you will see that Callum and Anya have equal authority and responsibility in the business and work at an equal level. Satish, Lucy and Angus all work on the same level. You will also see that Callum and Anya are jointly responsible for the staff.

If Callum was to run the restoration side of the business while Anya took full control of the antiques shop, the organisation chart might look like this:

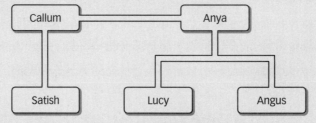

▲ Figure 3.9 New organisation chart for Restoration Antiques

You easily see where the responsibility and accountability lies from the new organisation chart. In Figure 3.9 Callum is responsible for Satish and Satish is accountable to Callum. In the same way Anya is responsible for Lucy and Angus, and they are accountable to her.

Formal relationships

The formal relationship between staff in an organisation is shown by responsibility, accountability and authority. For example, the relationship between Lucy and Anya in Figure 3.8 is that Lucy is accountable to Anya and Anya is responsible for Lucy. Obviously this chart is very simple and as Anya is a director, it would be expected that she has responsibility for Lucy. However, in larger organisations with a number of staff the formal relationship between various jobs would need to be clearly shown.

Responsibility

All employees have responsibility to perform the work that is required of them and to act in a certain way. This is fully covered on page 211. However, as it is not possible for one person to be responsible for everything that happens within an organisation, work must be delegated. Therefore, senior members of staff are also responsible for the staff working below them. They must ensure that the work is carried out satisfactorily and that their staff are competent. Because of this, they also need to have authority.

Authority

Senior members of staff will need to be given the power to make decisions, delegate work and oversee the work of staff below them.

Accountability

Accountability flows upwards and from Figure 3.9 we can see that Lucy and Angus are accountable to Anya. This means that they must report to Anya about work-related matters. You are usually accountable to your **line manager**, the next person up in the chart, identified by the line that connects your job role to theirs.

Chain of command

The chain of command shows the flow of responsibility and accountability throughout the organisation as each level is responsible for the level below and accountable to the level above.

Generally as a business grows, the levels of staff increase. This is because staff will become more specialised and more levels of responsibility and authority will be required. This is known as a hierarchy.

Hierarchical or pyramid structures

If Restoration Antiques (case study 3.2) expanded, the organisation chart might change to the model shown in Figure 3.10 on page 174.

You can see that two extra levels of management have been added to the restoration side of the business. The staff at the bottom of the chart are much further away from Callum and Anya, who now oversee the business as a whole and have delegated their specific areas to managers. If the business expanded further, the chart could have even more levels added to it.

This structure is also known as a pyramid structure and can be seen in Figure 3.11.

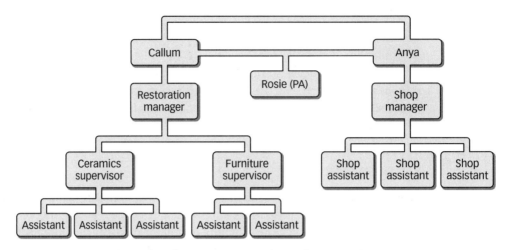

▲ Figure 3.10 Organisation chart for Restoration Antiques after expansion

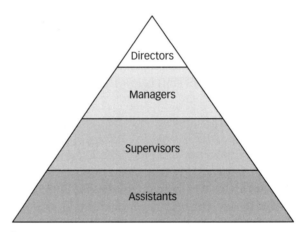

▲ Figure 3.11 Pyramid structure

If you add more levels to the pyramid then the structure will become taller, fewer levels and the structure is flatter. The general rule is the higher the level, the fewer the staff, so the very top layer will consist of the managing director (MD) and the very bottom layer will be the general workforce, i.e. those with no specific responsibility for other members of staff.

The structure of the company will not only be determined by the number of layers of management, but also by the following.

▶ **The type of work the organisation undertakes:** You could have a large number of employees who carry out the same type of work. In this case there would be no need for many levels of management.

▶ **The decision-making process:** Some companies are keen to involve their staff in the decision-making process and give their employees responsibilities and the authority to make some decisions.

Span of control

The span of control is the number of workers a manager or supervisor have direct responsibility for. If you look at Figure 3.10 you will see that the restoration manager's span of control is two members of staff – the ceramics and furniture supervisors.

Generally in a hierarchical structure, the span of control is narrow at the top and becomes wider through the levels. This is because there are fewer members of senior management than of the general workforce.

Delayering

As an organisation grows it is easy to add layers of management to the structure. However, this is often unnecessary, it just adds to the payroll and overheads, but does not increase profitability. When this happens an organisation might decide to restructure and remove one or more layers of management. This is called delayering.

When delayering takes place the organisation's structure changes in the following ways:

▶ it becomes a flatter structure

▶ the span of control of the remaining managers becomes wider.

Matrix structure

This structure is often used in organisations in which people need to work on specific projects. Staff from various departments with particular expertise will form a team to complete a specific project. Once the project has been completed, the team will be disbanded.

Depending on the way in which the company operates, it is possible that at any given time a member of staff will be accountable to two or more managers. Team leaders or project managers might be appointed for a particular project, but once it has finished they lose their managerial status.

This structure is useful to an organisation because it helps motivation and morale as staff have the opportunity to meet and work with people from different areas. Staff are able to use the opportunity to broaden their own work experience.

Functional relationships

Functional relationships within an organisation are based on specialisation. For example, the finance manager of a company will run his or her own department, but will also be responsible for the finances throughout the entire organisation.

This means that on matters of finance, the managers of other departments will need to co-operate and liaise closely with the finance manager. The role of the finance manager will often be that of adviser, giving advice on matters of finance. However, when necessary he or she will have authority over the other managers, for example in setting up financial procedures.

Most companies will need a mixture of line and functional relationships in order to work efficiently and effectively. Other formal relationships found in the workplace include lateral and staff relationships.

CASE STUDY 3.3 – IPD Ltd

Patrick and Imran have decided that they would like to add fashion accessories to their range. They set up a team to work on this project. The team is shown in Figure 3.12.

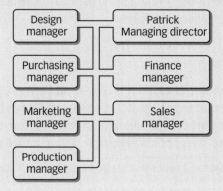

▲ Figure 3.12 Project team for fashion accessories

The team will work together to look at the feasibility of producing this new range. The reporting lines will need to be made clear from the outset and, although Imran is the financial director of the company, he will be working at an equal level to other staff for this project. This means that the functional relationship usually found at IPD Ltd has changed temporarily.

Lateral relationships

This is where staff of equal status and authority work together and have the same line manager. For example, the shop assistants of Restoration Antiques have a lateral relationship (see Figure 3.10). They report to the same manager and have the same level of authority. However, they also have a formal relationship with each other as they are expected to work together and co-operate with each other while carrying out their duties.

Lateral relationships do not only occur where staff are doing the same job. The two supervisors at Restoration Antiques also have a lateral relationship as they both report to the same line manager and have equal levels of responsibility and authority.

Staff relationships

A staff relationship relates to an advisory or support relationship that exists between two job roles. If you look at Figure 3.10, you will see that Callum and Anya have a personal assistant, Rosie, working for them. This role involves supporting Callum and Anya by providing administrative services. Rosie does not have any formal authority and she is not responsible for any staff.

Informal relationships

As well as formal relationships, staff will also form their own informal relationships with others in the organisation. This may be encouraged by management in the form of organised social events or the setting up of a social club. Staff will also form their own friendships and these can have both positive and negative effects on an organisation. The positive benefits are that staff will enjoy their work and be more motivated. Their enthusiasm will also bring in new ideas and a positive attitude to their work. The negative affects may include staff dissatisfaction and becoming disruptive to the flow of work.

The role of senior management

The chairperson

The most senior member of staff in any organisation is the chairperson, as it is he or she who chairs the board of directors. This might be a specific role; most plcs have a chairperson as well as a managing director. However, in smaller companies the roles are often combined. A sole trader is also the chairperson for his or her company.

The managing director

The managing director will also be a member of the board of directors. He or she will head the board of directors and lead the business in line with the organisation's aims and objectives. Another name for the managing director is chief executive.

Executive and non-executive directors

Executive directors are those who are employed by the company. They usually have responsibility for a specific area of the company, for example human resources or production.

Non-executive directors are invited to become a director by the board. The reason for this may be because they have a particular expertise that would be useful to the organisation and they can ensure that the organisation is run with the shareholder's interests in mind.

Appointing the directors

In a private limited company (Ltd.) the chairperson, managing director and directors tend to be shareholders, often those who initially formed the company. However, there may also be non-shareholding directors who have been appointed by the board.

In a public limited company (plc) the shareholders elect the directors at the Annual General Meeting (AGM). This does not mean that anyone can become a director. The board must approve the nominations before votes are cast.

In theory the board of directors should elect the managing director. Legally, there is no distinction between the various directors and this includes the managing director. Therefore legally, the finance director of a company would be responsible for all areas of the business, not just finance. However, many companies allocate specific areas of responsibility to individual directors according to their expertise (see Table 3.17).

Table 3.17 Roles and responsibilities of senior management

Job title	Role	Responsibilities
Chairperson	Chair the board of directors	Lead the senior management team. Advise the managing director. To be involved in public relations for the company. To network with other high level executives. Ensure board meetings and the AGM are held in line with legal requirements.
Managing director	Manage the company	Set policy. Devise corporate and strategic objectives. Oversee the implementation of the corporate and strategic objectives. Act as the link between board of directors and the rest of organisation. Monitor the finances of the organisation. Ensure that there are sufficient financial resources to implement the strategic plan. Ensure that there are sufficient resources, e.g. equipment, staff, materials. Ensure that the structure of the organisation is efficient and effective. Devise and implement restructuring plans as and when required. Ensure monitoring of strategic plan. Motivate staff. Delegate work to other directors. If the organisation does not have a chairperson, to take on this role and responsibilities. Look after the interests of shareholders. Ensure that the organisation complies with legal requirements and regulations.
Directors	Assist managing director in running the company	Assist in devising policy. Devise corporate and strategic objectives. Implement corporate and strategic objectives. Agree major decisions (e.g. takeovers, acquiring major assets. Authorise major expenditure. Write and agree annual report to shareholders. Be responsible for employees in their own specialist areas (e.g. human resources director would be responsible for the employees, finances and other related matters within the department). Report to the rest of the board regarding their specialist area. Comply with legal requirements and regulations.

The role of operational managers in implementing policy

The term 'operational managers' can refer to either the middle management, i.e. those between the directors and the first line managers, or to the first line of management itself.

Middle managers

The middle management of a company will usually head a department and assist the directors in the following ways:

- ▶ devise a strategy for translating the strategic and corporate objectives into operational objectives, i.e. planning the actual work to be done
- ▶ delegate work to supervisors or first line management
- ▶ co-ordinate and monitor the work of staff below them
- ▶ co-ordinate and monitor progress of operational objectives
- ▶ report to senior management on progress
- ▶ liaise with senior management on new projects, ideas, etc. which in turn will help senior management when devising objectives and strategic plans
- ▶ act as a link between senior management and supervisors.

It is this level of management that is usually removed when a company de-layers.

First line managers

This level of management can also be called team leaders or supervisors. Their role is much more 'hands on' as they will be dealing with the mechanics of the work, whether it is administrative or technical. Their responsibilities are as follows:

- ▶ direct the workforce on a daily basis
- ▶ co-ordinate the work to be carried out by the workforce
- ▶ solve problems encountered by their staff
- ▶ liaise with and report to middle management
- ▶ motivate staff.

The planning process

We have looked at the various strategic plans and objectives that need to be in place in order to focus an organisation to meet its aims. In order to ensure that an organisation works efficiently and effectively, the work needs to be planned and monitored.

In the previous section we discussed the role and responsibilities of management. Their responsibilities with regard to planning are as follows.

▶ **Directors: strategic planning.** Directors, including the managing director, are responsible for devising the long-term strategic planning for the organisation.

▶ **Middle management: tactical planning.** Middle management undertakes the medium-term tactical planning. This involves organising the resources and activities that will assist the organisation in meeting its objectives.

▶ **First line management: operational planning.** This is short-term planning and will involve organising and co-ordinating the various activities that must be carried out on a day-to-day basis.

OVER TO YOU!

Using Figure 3.10 as the current organisational structure for Restoration Antiques, state who would be responsible for the planning of the following:

▶ the direction of the company for the next five years

▶ a new shop display

▶ the purchase of new, larger premises

▶ the distribution of work in the restoration section

▶ training of shop staff

▶ the expansion of the restoration section.

Importance of planning

The idea of sitting down and planning work can be very tedious. Think about how you felt when you had to plan an essay or piece of coursework. Did you feel it was a waste of time drawing up a plan? If you did, think about the success of your work. Did the work turn out as well as you expected or did you find out at the end that it could have been better?

Planning is important for the following reasons:

▶ you will be clear about what you want to achieve

▶ you will be able to work out the resources necessary to carry out the work

▶ targets and deadlines will be easy to set

- the quality of the work can be decided on before starting

- nothing will be forgotten

- it is easier to see where problems might occur and plan for them

- it is easier to change or amend a plan if the need arises

- it is much easier to control and monitor a plan

- tracking work is simple

- it is easier to communicate your ideas and wants to others involved in the work

- you will be able to set the criteria for measuring the success of the work.

Process of planning

Drawing up a plan that is logical, well ordered and realistic is quite a skill. It requires far more than just writing down everything that needs to be done. A successful plan will need to consider the following.

- **Objectives:** The first thing to consider when drawing up plans is the objectives of the plan. What are you trying to achieve? If you are not sure about what you are doing, the plans you devise will not work.

- **Targets:** It is important to set targets so that you can keep on track, remain motivated and have something tangible to work towards.

- **Deadlines:** Deadlines are needed in order to keep the work moving along. If deadlines are not set, then there will be no urgency to complete the work. It is very important that the deadlines set are realistic. It is very demoralising working to a deadline that cannot be achieved.

You need to work out all the steps that will have to be taken in order to meet the targets and achieve the objectives. The following will have to be considered:

- the activities that need to be undertaken

- the order in which the activities need to be completed

- the information that is available to you, including previous experience of similar tasks

- the resources required, including equipment, materials, funding and staff

- delegating work to others

- timescales for each part of the plan; these must be realistic

- methods of working to be used

- how information will be communicated to others

- the quality of the work

- any factors that might affect the success of the plan, including those outside your organisation or control

- procedures for monitoring and controlling progress

- flexibility in case plans need to be amended.

Contingency planning

The best laid plans can sometimes go wrong. Having to make a change to the plan does not necessarily mean a disaster. It is very useful when drawing up a plan to look at the areas that could go wrong or may need amending. For example, if you were organising an outdoor event for your company, it would be sensible to have an alternative plan in case of bad weather. By doing this, it is easier to avoid or prevent problems.

Sometimes, however, events happen that you could not have planned for in advance. For example, if the company that was printing your brochure suffered a fire at its premises, this would disrupt your plans. In this instance, it would not have been practical to have another firm of printers waiting in case there was a fire at the appointed company.

The key to dealing with contingencies is to remain as flexible as possible. Always allow an extra day or so for receiving work back from others and try to think of alternative options in case key activities go wrong. If a change does occur, think positively. Respond to the change as a challenge and try to find areas where you can amend and adapt activities to get the plan back on track.

Control, monitoring and evaluation

The plan must have some kind of control and monitoring attached to it, otherwise you will not know how you are progressing. This is particularly the case when you are delegating work to others.

You will need to monitor the following:

▶ that your aims are achievable

▶ that the plan is realistic

▶ that the timescales are realistic

▶ that the resources and equipment are ready when required

▶ that others complete their work on time

▶ that the quality of the work is up to standard.

Evaluating your plan is very useful. You will see the strengths and weaknesses of the plan, the way in which people worked and how people reacted to problems and changes. From this you will learn how to improve performance in the future and will be able to use the information to help set future objectives.

Communication

The key to success when planning is how you communicate your needs and wants to others. It is important when giving information to others that your instructions are clear and unambiguous. Confidentiality is also an important consideration when planning a project. It may not be appropriate, for example, to give out details of the cost of the project or how much new business the project is expected to bring into the organisation. If in any doubt, you should always consult your line manager.

It is equally important that everyone who is working with your plan knows the procedures for reporting back to you. This procedure should be clearly established before you start work.

Consequences of failure

If you do not plan correctly, you must be prepared for failure. Unfortunately the consequences of not being properly prepared can be far reaching. The effects that failure might have include:

- holding up other people's work
- work not being completed on time
- work being forgotten or duplicated
- staff not knowing what to do
- overspending
- inaccurate information being used for decision making and other purposes
- an adverse effect on the organisation's reputation
- the loss of business
- the loss of your own job.

Using planning and control aids

In order to help with the planning process, there are a number of aids that can be used (see Table 3.18).

Table 3.18 Types of planning aid

Aid	Purpose
Diaries	Keeping track of appointments, deadlines, etc.
Planners	These can be used for project planning, holiday rotas, etc. Wall-mounted year planners are useful for all types of planning.
Forms	These can be used to make lists or for project management.
Checklists/ activities on plans	Very useful for planning all types of events and activities. All the activities that need to be completed are listed. A column that can be used for comments or signatures when work is completed provides an easy visual aid for keeping track of progress.
Reminder systems	This can be used as a brought forward system whereby notes or documents to be completed or checked in the future can be stored. You must, however, remember to look at these systems on a regular basis.
Electronic planning aids	These can range from specialist or technical project management software to hand-held personal organisers.
Schedules	A schedule can be used to plan any activity or event, which can be listed in order of completion, with deadlines added to show the timescale for each part.
Critical path analysis	This is used for the planning of more formal projects, e.g. construction work. The planning is much more detailed and specific to the type of activity being undertaken. Specialist computer software can be purchased for different types of project.

Given below are a number of activities that need to be planned. For each one, suggest the most appropriate form of planning aid:

▶ a meeting to be arranged for three regional managers

▶ sending customers a renewal notice for an insurance policy

▶ organising the mailing of a new brochure

▶ organising a conference.

The importance of prioritising work

It is not enough just to plan your work, you need to be able to order the work so that urgent items are dealt with first. This can be tricky as everyone who asks you to complete work for them always thinks that their work is the most important and urgent.

The difference between urgency and importance

It is easy to judge urgent work by its deadline. The closer to the deadline, the more urgent the work. Important work may include work for which you are personally responsible or will have serious consequences if not completed.

As a general guide, Table 3.19 defines the order in which tasks should be completed.

Table 3.19 Task order

Order	Category	Type of work
First	Urgent and important	Tasks that are crucial to the overall job.
Second	Urgent and important	Tasks that others need you to complete before they can start their own work.
Third	Urgent	Tasks that are very close to their deadline (or are overdue).
Fourth	Urgent	Tasks that may need time to sort out. This might be because others are involved or research needs to be undertaken.
Fifth	Important	Tasks that must be carried out, but are not necessarily or currently urgent (filing should be included in this category).
Sixth	Routine	These might include routine tidying, sorting of files, clearing out old paperwork, etc.

Taking account of routine work

Don't forget that if you ignore routine work for too long it will eventually become both important and urgent! Try to get into the habit of filing documents away immediately you have finished with them. Spend five minutes each morning and evening organising your desk and replenishing stationery items. This will help to ensure that you have the maximum time available for working on the urgent tasks.

If at all possible, book out a few hours or half a day, once a week or fortnight to clear all the routine work. This will help ensure that you keep on top of your workload and will enable you to work more efficiently and effectively.

Taking account of commitments

It is important that when prioritising your work you remember your responsibilities and commitments. For example, if you have agreed to help a colleague, but before you do so you are given other work, you will have to consider your commitment when devising your plan.

If you are responsible for something such as ordering the stationery supplies each week, you must ensure that this is completed, even if you have been given other urgent and important work to do.

It can be difficult to prioritise work correctly. If you make lists of tasks that have to be completed and prioritised according to Table 3.19, you will have a good basis from which to work. Experience will teach you how to prioritise correctly within your own workplace.

Monitoring work

It is a good idea to keep a list of tasks that must be completed and update this each morning before starting work. This way you will see any work that has been left for a while or that is now becoming urgent. Tick off work once it has been completed and write a fresh list the following morning.

Contingencies and the need for flexibility

Occasionally you may be working on a task that is both urgent and important when your supervisor arrives with work that has to take priority. This can make you feel anxious and worried. How can you deal with this situation?

There is no magical solution to this type of problem and sometimes it will mean that you have no alternative, but to put aside your work and complete the task you have been given. Below are some ideas that might help you to avoid more serious consequences.

▶ Keep a list of tasks to be done so that nothing is forgotten. This should help prevent routine work becoming urgent.

▶ Spend a few minutes each day on routine and non-urgent work so that you do not build up too much of a backlog.

▶ If you are working on something urgent, let your colleagues know that you cannot be disturbed. If at all possible, either switch your phone to voicemail or divert your calls to a colleague (after asking their permission first, of course).

- If it is impossible for you to meet a deadline because of unexpected work or emergencies, let the person concerned know as soon as possible. This will allow them some time to make alternative arrangements. Although your colleague or manager may be annoyed, you will have to face the music at some point and with advance warning an acceptable solution may be found.

- If you find that your workload is so heavy that you are never in a position to deal with non-urgent or routine work, do tell your supervisor or manager. Unless you work particularly slowly or spend too much time gossiping, your workload is too much. Your supervisor or manager will be able to help you either by suggesting different working practices or by removing some of your excess workload.

Communicating changes

- It is extremely important to keep everyone informed of any changes that need to be made. It is a good idea to put the amendments in writing so that the recipient has a clear record. This will help avoid any problems later on.

OVER TO YOU!

Camilla, the PA to Harry Preston (case study 3.4) has the following tasks to complete. Write a list putting the tasks in order of priority.

▶ Draft a reply to a letter from an angry customer.

▶ Prepare some sales figures for a meeting to be held next week.

▶ Organise lunch at a restaurant in Bath where Harry will be meeting some business clients tomorrow. He would like lunch to be at 12.30 pm.

▶ Ring Simon in accounts to see if he has prepared the budgets you requested two weeks ago. You need the figures for a meeting early tomorrow morning.

Factors that affect the efficiency of the workplace

Sometimes, no matter how organised you are, things happen that prevent you from working as efficiently and effectively as you might like. Some of these factors might be unavoidable and include:

- distractions such as being given an important task at the last minute

- interruptions from colleagues and/or visitors

- unexpected telephone calls

- a problem with the workflow, for example colleagues not completing their work on time and therefore holding up your work

- problems with the work itself; you cannot complete the work because of an external factor, for example your suppliers have not completed their work on time or the hotel you wished to use is booked.

It might be the case that you have caused the inefficiency through any of the following:

- inefficient working practices

- not having all the necessary resources and information before starting a task
- not following instructions correctly
- not understanding instructions
- spending unnecessary time on a task.

Receiving instructions

It is important that you fully understand what is expected of you when given a task to do. Sometimes it all seems very clear when the person giving the instructions is speaking to you, but afterwards you may find that this is not the case. In order to ensure that you understand what to do, try the following.

- Stop what you are doing and listen very carefully to what is being said. This may seem obvious, but often our attention is distracted while we are listening. To listen properly you need to give the speaker your full attention. This means making eye contact and concentrating on what is being said.

- Make notes. Write down the key points so that you will have a useful reference guide once you start the task. Make sure that your notes will be understood later on by jotting down the key points, preferably in a logical order.

- Check your understanding of the instructions. Use techniques such as repeating back to the speaker, in your own words, what is required. This will give him or her the opportunity to correct you if necessary.

- Ask questions. This will ensure that you understand what is expected of you and again, if you are on the wrong track, give an opportunity for you to be corrected.

- Ask if there are any similar examples of work available for you to look at. This can be very helpful to ensure that you include all the necessary elements in your own work and may give you a starting or reference point.

- Ask how and when you can contact the person concerned in case if you need to clarify any points later on.

- Agree a realistic completion time for the work.

- As soon as you have finished speaking to the person concerned, look through your notes, adding anything that may help you later on.

- Make a note of the task and its deadline in your schedule or 'to do' list.

Dealing with distractions

Some distractions are unavoidable; however, spending too much time gossiping to a work colleague or looking at irrelevant sites on the Internet are avoidable. Do not forget that when you are enjoying a chat with a colleague you are also stopping them from working. The following hints will help you deal with distractions tactfully.

- If you need to concentrate on a task, tell your colleagues. They will then give you the time you need to complete your work.

- If you are asked to take on extra work when you have a deadline to meet, tactfully explain the situation to your supervisor. This will allow him or her to make alternative arrangements if necessary. This is a far more efficient way of dealing with the problem, because if you just take on the extra work and then fail to complete it on time you will look inefficient.

- If possible, switch your phone to voicemail or divert your calls to a colleague.

- Allow yourself a short break every so often. This will help your concentration when you return to your task.

- If people continue to interrupt you, politely tell them that you cannot speak to them now, but will get back to them once you have completed your task. If the interruption is caused by your boss, you may have to accept the interruption and make up the time later.

- If at all possible, take your work to a 'quiet area' or separate office. However, you should check with your supervisor before leaving your desk.

- If casual visitors arrive, politely ask them to make an appointment to see you at a more convenient time. Alternatively, arrange a time when you could telephone them. Remember email is a very quick and convenient method of communication.

- Do not encourage personal calls from friends during the working day. Not only does this waste time, but it is obvious to all concerned, especially your boss.

- If you have personal distractions, such as a problem at home, share this with your supervisor or boss. They may be able to suggest ways in which you can be supported.

Managing time effectively

We all waste time occasionally and it is very easy to do so in the workplace when there are colleagues to chat to. However, when you have deadlines to meet and urgent work to complete, it is essential that time is used as efficiently as possible.

The following hints and tips will help you to keep on top of your workload and ensure that tasks are completed in the correct order.

- Make a 'to do' list each morning so that you can see what needs completing urgently and the tasks that can wait. Revise this each day to prevent non-urgent tasks becoming urgent.

- Do important and urgent tasks at the start of the day. This will give you a little time for contingencies and emergencies.

- Organise your workspace and keep often used resources close to hand. This will aid an efficient workflow.

- Plan your work before you start. This will help ensure that you have all the information and resources to hand. It will also help ensure that you do not forget anything and prevent mistakes.

- Plan to do work in batches, for example photocopying or faxing. This will save time.

- Once you have started a task, keep working on it until you have finished, even if it is boring or difficult. Once completed, you will feel a real sense of achievement and be motivated to start another task.

- Don't put off jobs that are difficult or boring. They won't go away and you will become demotivated. The thought of doing the work is usually far more difficult than actually doing it.

Communicating clearly with others

It is much better to tell your colleagues why you are not able to chat than to just ignore them. Similarly, if you are struggling to complete all your work on time, tell your boss or supervisor. They will be able to help you with your time management or if necessary organise some help.

Given below are some hints on dealing with communicating changes to others.

▷ If you have to make a change or cannot meet a deadline, tell others as soon as you know. This will allow for alternative arrangements to be made. If at all possible, negotiate an extension to your deadline. Generally colleagues will be sympathetic to this if you can give a new, firm date for the work to be completed.

▷ Remember to tell everyone who might be affected.

▷ You should be polite and diplomatic when telling others of changes. Do not put blame on others or make flimsy excuses. Tell people the facts and remember to thank them for understanding, this may help defuse any irritation.

▷ If you are unable to meet many of your deadlines, you probably need some help either with your workload or the way in which you work. List all the tasks you have to complete, together with the deadline dates, and ask your supervisor or boss to discuss them with you. You will find that he or she is much more reasonable if you take this proactive approach than if you constantly fail to meet deadlines with no explanation.

OVER TO YOU!

1. David has been given some work to do by his line manager, Sandy. State three ways in which David can ensure that he has understood the instructions

2. David has some urgent work that must be completed before lunch. State three ways in which he can avoid disruptions.

3. David may not be able to complete his work on time. Briefly explain the measures he should take to deal with this problem.

4. Sandy thinks that David should manage his time more effectively. State four ways in which he could improve his time management.

Organising the work area effectively

The state of your desk will tell others quite a bit about you and the way in which you approach your work. A disorganised desk with piles of paper gives the wrong message to others. Even if you do know where everything is kept, you will give the impression of inefficiency. A tidy desk will give the right impression and will help you to work efficiently and effectively.

You may feel that you are too busy to keep your desk tidy or file papers away once you have finished with them. However, doing these things will help you work efficiently. If you can put your hands on what you need straightaway, you will save lots of time, feel confident that you know where everything is and create the right impression to others.

Table 3.20 on page 190 gives some simple rules for keeping your work area organised.

Table 3.20 Organising your work space effectively

Storage	This is one of the most important aids to keeping your desk tidy. Ensure that you have sufficient storage for all your papers, equipment and resources. Use desk tidies, filing cabinets and box files to keep everything in order. Labelling files and folders will ensure that you know the contents at a glance. Use folders for current work and have in and out trays. This means that when new work arrives you will have a place for it. If necessary, ask your boss if you can purchase extra storage items.
Filing	Many people find filing very tedious; however, it is a necessary evil in the workplace. It is much quicker and less tedious if you file papers away immediately you have finished with them. There is nothing worse than a large pile of papers waiting to be filed. If you file papers immediately you will benefit in several ways: you will always be able to find things quickly, your workspace will be tidy and you really will save lots of time.
Resources	Keep a small supply of paper, envelopes, compliment slips, etc. close to hand. This will save you having to get up every few minutes to fetch stationery. Be careful not to become a hoarder though; too much stationery will clutter up your workspace.
Equipment	Small pieces of equipment such as a hole punch, stapler, etc. should be kept in the top drawer of your desk for easy access. Remember to replace the piece of equipment after use. This will ensure that you always know where things are.
Working practices	Regularly tidy your desk and throw away things that you no longer use or that are broken. Do not, however, throw away papers that may be important; check with your supervisor first. If possible archive papers in box files or archive files. When possible, work on one task at a time and then clear away all papers and documents relating to that task before starting another. Do not clutter your desk with personal items and photographs. Spend a few minutes each evening filing papers and putting things away. This is a good way to wind down before leaving the office and makes your arrival the next day much more pleasant.

Reducing waste in the office

The amount of waste paper to be found in any office is staggering. This is costly to both the company and the environment. You will need to be able to recognise the activities where it is possible to waste large amounts of paper and be able to take preventative measures to ensure that this does not happen.

Table 3.21 gives some of the activities that can cause wastage and solutions to overcome this problem.

Table 3.21 Avoiding wastage in the office

Activity	Solutions
Photocopying	Check the settings on the photocopier are correct before pressing the copy button. Photocopy one sheet to check it is acceptable before making multiple copies. Check the work for errors and omissions before copying. Ensure that there is plenty of paper in the copier before starting; low amounts of paper often cause paper jams. Check the toner is full before starting a large photocopying run. Don't make more copies that you actually need. Keep the glass of the photocopier clean. When possible, photocopy on both sides of the paper.
Printing	Try a test print before making multiple copies. Where possible use print preview to ensure that the document is correct. Use the spell and grammar checking tools to ensure that your work is correct. Ensure that the toner and paper supplies are full before printing a number of copies. Use draft print for internal documents where possible. Print only the required number; do not be tempted to take extra copies.
Emails	Don't be tempted to print a hard copy of every email you receive. Use email to send messages to colleagues wherever possible. Send draft documents to colleagues by email when possible.
General	Take extra care when stapling and collating documents; a missing or crumpled page will make the whole set unusable. Use the correct type of paper for the job. Encourage your company to buy the correct type for your printer. This will reduce jamming and the overall appearance will be better. Store paper correctly: flat and out of direct sunlight or damp conditions. Rotate your stock of paper so that the oldest is used first. Replace the tops of pens, correcting fluids and highlighters.
Recycling	Encourage your company to send away used toner and ink cartridges for refilling; this is a cheaper option as well as being environmentally friendly. Reuse envelopes for internal use. Use wasted or out-of-date printed paper as scrap pads. Remove transparent folders and wallets when archiving documents for reuse. Reuse box and level-arch files when archiving documents. Shred waste paper and use for packaging. Any excess can be put out for the recycling collection.

OVER TO YOU!

1 State four ways in which you can recycle items in the office.

2 State four ways in which you can keep your work area tidy.

3 State three measures you can take to avoid wastage.

Improving your performance in the workplace

Some companies are committed to providing training opportunities for staff, allowing them to develop skills and abilities. Other companies do little in the way of promoting learning and improvement.

Even if the company you are working for does not provide training or development opportunities, there are a number of ways in which you can assist your own learning and self-development. There are a number of benefits from taking the time to learn new skills and improve your performance at work. You will find that work is more enjoyable and interesting, you will be more confident and, of course, you may be able to find a better job or put yourself forward for promotion.

Obtaining feedback

It is always a good boost to your confidence to hear that you are doing a good job. However, not all bosses and supervisors bother to say if you are doing well; the only feedback you will get is when something has gone wrong. If you don't receive feedback on a regular basis, ask your supervisor to spend some time going through your work with you. Other ways in which you can obtain feedback on your performance include the following.

▶ **Colleagues:** Politely ask colleagues if they could spare you some time to go through your work with you.

▶ **Customers:** You will receive indirect feedback from your customers, especially if something has gone wrong. However, occasionally a customer will tell you that you have done a good job.

▶ **Appraisals:** Many companies operate an appraisal system, which gives you and your supervisor an opportunity to review your work in a structured format.

▶ **Indirect feedback:** Watch and listen to the reactions of others to you and your work. This will give you an indication of how well you are doing.

▶ **Reviewing your own work:** By checking your own work for errors and omissions on a regular basis you can see how well you are progressing. This is a worthwhile method of obtaining feedback as it will show up your strengths and weaknesses.

Setting targets to improve performance

Just as companies set targets for improvement, so can you. By setting targets you can give yourself a series of short-term objectives to achieve. This will help you to remain realistic and even optimistic about what you can achieve and the timescale in which you can complete it.

You should decide on your long-term plan – what you would like to achieve or do in a few years' time. Once you have decided this, you can set your short-term objectives, which will help you achieve your aim.

Many people and companies use the SMART principle for setting targets and objectives.

▶ **Specific:** Keep your objectives specific so that you know exactly what you are aiming for. For example, you could set yourself the target of learning to drive a car within the next six months.

▶ **Measurable:** Your objectives should include a way of measuring success. If we take the goal of 'learning to drive within the next six months', the way in which you can measure success would be by passing your driving test.

▶ **Achievable:** The targets you set should be achievable. If you are specific about what you want to achieve, it should be easy to check that it is also achievable. To learn to drive a car within six months is achievable. However, if you set yourself the target of getting a much better job next year, without being more specific, it may be difficult to achieve.

▶ **Relevant:** Your targets should be relevant to your long-term plan. For example, if your long-term plan is to study for a degree in chemistry, there would be no point in having a short-term aim of taking more word processing examinations.

▶ **Time-based:** This relates to the timescale for each of your objectives. It is important that these are realistic. If the time allowance is too short, you will be disappointed and demotivated when you do not achieve your targets. If the time allowance is too long, you may become bored and lose interest.

Identifying opportunities for training

Try to take advantage of any training that is offered to you, particularly if the company you are working for has agreed to pay for it. If you do not work for a company that offers training, you can obtain training in a number of ways, some of them free of charge.

Table 3.22 shows a number of ways in which you can obtain training.

Table 3.22 Training opportunities

In-house training	Your company will arrange for you to attend an organised workshop or session within the company. You could be trained on the job with someone showing you what to do. Ask a colleague to train you to do work that you are not usually expected to undertake. If possible, ask someone if you can shadow them for a day. This means that you will watch them to see how they deal with their work. Job rotation is another good way of getting in-house training. With this method you would exchange jobs with a colleague for a short period of time. This may give you a wide variety of skills. Offer to help colleagues when possible; this is an easy way to learn new skills.
External training	These courses might also be organised and paid for by your company. Evening classes can be attended to improve skills. Correspondence courses are available which can be worked on in your own time. The Open University and Learn Direct offer a wide range of courses for those who wish to study from home. E-learning is now available, whereby you can train by using interactive computer packages.

Importance of self-assessment

It is important to be realistic about your strengths and weaknesses. This will help you set targets for yourself in terms of what you will be able to achieve and what you need to improve on.

A SWOT analysis is a very useful way of looking at your strengths and weaknesses.

Table 3.23 A SWOT analysis

Strengths Have good communication skills. Have excellent IT skills. Can take criticism and advice from others. Good at numerical work. Quick to learn.

Opportunities Company offers free training. Have time to attend courses out of work. Colleagues are helpful and will teach me new skills.

Weaknesses Spelling needs improving. Not very patient. Not very tactful. Concentration could be improved.

Threats Social life may stop me from studying.

Table 3.23 shows a basic SWOT analysis, but should give you an idea of how to go about completing one. List your strengths and weaknesses. Be honest with yourself about your skills and abilities, and then think about the opportunities you have that will help you with your self development. Once you have completed this, then think about things that may stand in your way and list them as threats.

The completed SWOT analysis should give you some idea of the areas you would like to develop or improve and the obstacles that may stand in your way.

Importance of regular reviews at work

We have looked at how you can obtain feedback on your achievements at work; however, it also is important to have reviews with your supervisor or line manager on a regular basis.

Many companies use an appraisal system to review the performance of members of staff. This may take place once or twice a year. It is an official and formal method of reviewing your performance and should be taken seriously by both parties.

The appraisal system normally follows the following procedure.

▶ Advance notice will be given of the appraisal and a date and time agreed with your manager.

▶ You should be given a document outlining the procedure together with a form to fill in. Complete this very carefully as this is your opportunity to give your views on your performance. Be honest with yourself; an appraisal form that states you are 'very good' at everything does not lend itself to constructive discussion. There should be a section on the form that allows you to state any further training or development you would like to have.

▶ At the meeting you should work through the completed form with your reviewer. As the meeting is private you will have the opportunity to speak frankly about your performance at work, your personal aims and plans and the development you require.

At the end of the meeting you should agree on an action plan for your personal development with your reviewer. This will be used as the basis for your next discussion.

The appraisal meeting should be a positive experience; it is not an opportunity for your boss to criticise you unduly or tell you off. However, a frank discussion about your performance will touch on your weaknesses and you must be prepared for this.

OVER TO YOU!

1 List three ways in which you can obtain feedback regarding your performance at work.

2 State two areas you should consider when undertaking self-assessment.

3 State two benefits of having a regular appraisal with your line manager.

4 List three ways in which you can undertake training in the workplace.

▼ REVIEW THE FACTORS THAT AFFECT WORKPLACE CONDITIONS

Office layout and ergonomics

The layout and condition of the office will affect work in a number of ways. These include:

- the efficiency of the workflow; if the layout is poor, it will take longer to complete tasks
- the morale of the staff; if you work in dark and cramped surroundings, you may find that your morale is low
- the motivation of the staff; if working conditions are poor, you will not feel particularly motivated
- the health of the staff; there are many factors that affect your health in the workplace.

The way in which the office is laid out will have a great effect on the workflow. For example, if the only photocopier is two floors away from your desk, you will spend a great deal of time getting to and from it. This will make the workflow inefficient.

Ergonomics is the way in which work performance is affected by the work systems. This means that when looking at the workplace from an ergonomic point of view, the following would need to be considered:

- the physical, mental and social capabilities and limitations of the staff
- the actual job and related tasks, and the safety and efficiency of the way in which the tasks are currently performed
- the layout of the office and the possible effects on the individual, for example incorrect seating, which could give back problems or cause safety problems
- the restrictions (if any) the current layout poses to the individual
- any legal regulations relating to health and safety.

The way in which tasks are completed should have a great impact on the way in which the office is designed. Some of the factors that should be taken in to account include:

▶ access to equipment; this should be situated close to the main users. However, health and safety issues must also be taken into account

▶ working groups; if staff regularly work together on tasks, it makes sense for their workstations to be close to each other. This also applies to supervision of staff

▶ resources; as with equipment, staff need to be able to access resources easily.

Unfortunately, not all offices are well designed and spacious. A large number of workplaces are situated in old buildings with many small rooms that do not lend themselves to modern working. However, if the layout has been carefully designed, it is possible to work efficiently and effectively in these buildings.

Most companies prefer to have open-plan offices where staff work in large groups. There are advantages to this layout as the staff can easily be supervised. There are other cost savings in that equipment is easily accessible and you do not need so much of it. However, noise is one of the biggest disadvantages of open plan offices and this can lead to further problems. A well-designed open-plan layout will have separate areas for different purposes and these might include the following.

▶ **Reception:** This can be created with screens and chairs provided for visitors. This looks much more efficient and professional than meeting clients in the middle of a busy room.

▶ **Working areas:** Some open plan offices have cubicles, built with acoustic screens, which help contain noise and allow staff to work with a small degree of privacy.

▶ **Confidentiality:** It can be difficult to speak in confidence in an open-plan office. It may be that you have a client to speak with or you may just wish to talk to your line manager about a particular problem. When designing an office layout there should be an area available where confidential meetings can take place. If at all possible, a small, separate office should be kept for this purpose. If this is not possible, acoustic screens will allow some privacy.

▶ **Quiet rooms/meeting areas:** A well-designed office will allow space for 'quiet areas'. These are areas where staff can work without interruption and away from the noise of the general office. Some offices keep a separate office for this purpose. If the company hosts a large number of meetings, it is essential that a room is set aside for this purpose. It is just not possible to conduct effective meetings in the corridor or the middle of a large open-plan office.

▶ **Staff area:** A rest area for staff, away from the main working area, will allow some respite from work and is important if staff are to work effectively all day.

▶ **Equipment area:** Large and noisy pieces of equipment should be kept away from the main working area for several reasons. It will help with the noise levels, allow safe working and be easily accessible for all staff.

Hot desking

Many staff spend the majority of their time working away from the office. The cost to the company of each member of staff having a permanent workspace in the office can be large. A solution to this problem has been found in the 'hot desking' concept. This provides a number of workstations that have been set aside for staff to use when they are working at the office. The workstations do not 'belong' to any one person. This cuts down on the amount of office space required and therefore has cost savings.

Environmental conditions

One of the largest factors that will affect the layout of the office and its efficiency are the environmental conditions. If the office block is modern, light and spacious, designing an efficient and safety-conscious layout will be relatively easy. However, if the office is situated in an old building that is dark and full of corridors, it will take considerable imagination and ingenuity to design an efficient, safe and effective workplace. The environmental conditions that must be considered include those shown in Table 3.24.

Table 3.24 Environmental factors affecting the workplace

Lighting	It is important that the lighting is correct to avoid eye strain and headaches. You cannot work safely if the lighting is too dark or too bright. The lighting should be positioned so that the light reflects correctly on desks, equipment and walkways. Where possible, workers should have access to natural light, so desks should be positioned by a window.
Heating	If the temperature of the room is too hot, workers will feel tired and lethargic. If the temperature of the room is too cold, workers will not be able to concentrate. The temperature of the work area must be a minimum of 16°C.
Ventilation	There must be sufficient fresh air circulating in the building, preferably provided by an efficient air-conditioning system. If the workplace is stuffy, then workers will feel tired and lethargic. If there is no fresh air circulating the office, the workers are more likely to catch any airborne illnesses within the office. Fumes from equipment can cause illness.
Décor	Dull or very dark colours can be demotivating for staff. Bright, fresh colours give a feeling of spaciousness and light. A non-reflective paint finish can help with problems caused by glare from computers. Different colours can affect people's moods in different ways. Fresh décor in relaxing colours will have a positive effect on morale, motivation and job satisfaction.
Workstations	A minimum of 11 cubic metres for each person who occupies a workstation must be allowed. If possible, ergonomically designed desks should be provided.
Noise control	Offices can be very noisy places. An overload of noise can have a significant effect on the performance of staff. Too much noise can increase stress levels. Acoustic screens can help reduce noise, as can correct positioning of equipment.
General	Flooring must be in good condition and not show any signs of wear and tear. Handrails must be provided for stairways. Sufficient toilets must be provided, as must washing facilities. A supply of drinking water must be available.

OVER TO YOU!

1 State three advantages of an open-plan office to the company.

2 State three advantages of an open-plan office to the staff.

3 List four ways in which noise can be controlled in an open-plan office.

4 Briefly explain what is meant by workflow.

5 Briefly explain the meaning of ergonomics.

OVER TO YOU!

Patrick and Imran have rented purpose-built premises for their manufacturing company (case study 3.3). There is a large open-plan office situated away from the machinery.

Write a short report outlining the factors that should be taken into consideration when designing the layout of this new office.

▼ IDENTIFY AND EVALUATE THE FACTORS AFFECTING JOB SATISFACTION, MOTIVATION AND MORALE

The most important resource a company has is its staff. A well-motivated workforce will be productive, project a good company image and help the company meet its objectives. Most people enjoy being employed and take pride in their work. Although salary is important this isn't the only motivation for people to go to work.

Needs of people at work

The most important need is, of course, financial. However, money is not the only consideration when people are looking for work (see Table 3.25).

Table 3.25 Needs of people at work

Social needs	Employment provides social interaction.
Fulfilment	Most people enjoy taking on and completing a task. Employment that offers this opportunity can be very rewarding.
Development	Generally, people enjoy learning new skills and developing their own abilities. Employment can provide excellent opportunities for learning.
Recognition	If your work is done in an environment where praise, thanks and encouragement are part of the management culture, you will enjoy your work much more.

Table 3.26 shows that financial reward of a salary also fulfils several needs.

Table 3.26 The benefits of a salary

Wage required for	Secondary factor
purchasing food	survival
paying rent or mortgage	security
paying household bills such as gas and electricity	comfort
paying for a hobby or relaxation, such as visiting the cinema or going to a nightclub	fulfilment
paying for the future, for example a holiday or a course of study	development

Organisation culture and management style

The way in which people are managed and supervised at work will determine the overall job satisfaction and motivation. An autocratic style of management that closely supervises staff, gives little responsibility and does not allow staff any input into the decision-making process may demotivate them. A more participative style of management will allow staff to become involved in decision making, give responsibility to them and the communication system will be effective both upwards and downwards.

There are many theorists who have looked at management style and the effect that it has on job satisfaction, motivation and productivity.

McGregor's Theory X and Theory Y

Douglas McGregor interviewed a large number of managers and supervisors and felt that he could classify them into two distinct groups: the Theory X managers and the Theory Y managers. The classification is made using the prior assumptions that the managers held regarding the attitudes of staff towards their work. Table 3.27 shows the differences between the two types of manager.

Table 3.27 Theory X and Theory Y managers

Theory X managers	believe that people do not like work, will try to avoid it, lack ambition, are lazy, unimaginative and resistant to change. Closely supervise their staff and use threats and incentives to ensure that staff work as required
Theory Y managers	believe that, given the right conditions, people generally enjoy work and want to realise their own potential. Believe that people will be self-motivated and will work harder if they are given responsibility and their involvement is welcomed

Obviously, not everyone fits neatly into one of these categories, but may lean more towards being an X or a Y manager. This will have an impact on the way in which staff are motivated and encouraged in the workplace.

Tannenbaum and Schmidt continuum

This is a model that shows the relationship between the level of freedom that a manager chooses to give a team and the level of authority used by the manager. In theory, as a team's freedom is increased, so the authority required by the manager decreases. This model encourages managers to develop their team and to delegate responsibility, allowing the team to make decisions according to its abilities (see Figure 3.13).

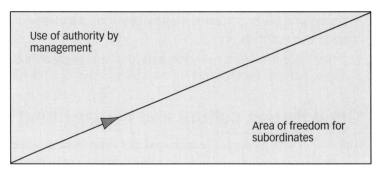

▲ Figure 3.13 Relationship between freedom and authority

This works well in theory, but managers must be aware that even if they have delegated almost all of the work, responsibility and decision making, they are ultimately responsible for the success or failure of the team.

From this it can be seen that the way in which people are managed and the culture of the organisation will have an impact on the motivation of the staff.

Motivation and job satisfaction

Motivation is a very personal issue. What motivates one person, may not motivate another. The earning of a salary is an important motivator for working, but there are many other factors that can be considered. It is important to remember that motivation can come from negative factors as well as positive ones. For example, the threat of losing your job and income may well motivate you to work harder.

It makes sense for organisations to take into account the factors that help motivate staff so that they become committed to working towards meeting the organisation's objectives. Some companies do this by providing lots of fringe benefits such as financial bonuses, company cars and discounted goods, while others to do by the way they treat staff.

Maslow's hierarchy of needs

There are many theories regarding motivational factors; one of the most widely recognised is that of Abraham Maslow. Maslow was a psychologist and he felt that human needs could be explained by a series of levels. As one level of needs becomes fulfilled then the next level of need becomes the most important. This can be seen in Figure 3.14.

▲ Figure 3.14 Maslow's hierarchy of needs

1 **Physiological needs:** All human beings need to have the basic facilities of food, water, clothing, shelter and sleep. These will be our first and highest priority needs.

2 **Safety and security needs:** After our basic needs have been met, we look for safety and security. We need a safe place to live and some kind of security, usually employment.

3 **Acceptance and social needs:** As human beings we like to have the company of others. We also need to feel as though we belong. We can satisfy these needs partly through employment.

4 **Esteem needs:** We all like to feel as though we are appreciated. If we have the respect of others, our self-esteem will be high. This can be achieved through status and prestige, among other factors.

5 **Self-realisation:** After all our basic needs have been met, we are ready and able to accept challenges and show our creative sides. We will be able to continue our personal development and achieve personal growth.

Maslow argues that the first two needs, which are classified as 'lower' needs, must be satisfied before we can move on to the 'higher' level needs. However, not everyone accepts this theory because people do not always move through the steps in the same order. Maslow's theory does not take into account that different people have different priorities.

Herzberg's two-factor theory

Frederick Herzberg took a different approach to finding out about human motivation. He conducted surveys into the factors that gave people job satisfaction. He discovered that some factors actively cause satisfaction, while others caused dissatisfaction if they were not present. This meant that job satisfaction was not a direct opposite of job dissatisfaction.

From this he concluded that there are two types of factor, those that cause satisfaction (motivators) and those that cause dissatisfaction, which he named hygiene factors.

▶ Motivators actively cause job satisfaction and these relate to the content of the job, achievement, recognition, responsibility, advancement and personal growth.

▶ Hygiene factors do not lead to actual satisfaction, but cause dissatisfaction if not present. They relate to the job context and include company policy and administration, supervision, working conditions, salary, relationships with supervisors, colleagues and subordinates and personal life.

The key point about Herzberg's theory is that just by dealing with the hygiene factors you will not make staff more satisfied, but will prevent them from becoming dissatisfied. For example, if staff are given a financial bonus it will not make them any more satisfied with their work, but will prevent them from becoming more dissatisfied with their job.

Hygiene factors satisfy the 'lower' needs as described by Maslow. However, this satisfaction is only temporary. For example, the staff that received a financial bonus will eventually forget this factor and will start to look for other improvements.

Motivators satisfy the 'higher' needs and will encourage staff to take on more responsibility, work harder and co-operate with others. These effects are positive and can be long term.

Other motivation theories

Many other studies have been conducted into people's needs. Table 3.28 on the following page gives an outline of some of the most widely recognised.

There are many other theorists on this topic, but we can see that the basic theory is that motivating staff is good for business and the individual. This is because motivated staff are more likely to:

▶ be more productive; this is good for business as it can result in higher profits

▶ stay with the company; this brings benefits to the company as they will have experienced staff and recruitment savings are made

▶ provide a high level of customer service; this is extremely valuable to any business.

The majority of the theorists also reach the same conclusions when discussing how people are motivated at work. Organisations that wish to motivate their staff may use some of the ways shown in Table 3.29 (page 204) to achieve a high level of motivation.

There are also financial motivators and these must be taken into consideration. The most interesting and challenging of jobs will still not meet an employee's needs if it does not pay a wage sufficient to pay their bills (see Table 3.30 on page 205).

As well as these motivational factors, there are also factors which actively demotivate staff (see Table 3.31 on page 205).

OVER TO YOU!

Compare the ways in which Restoration Antiques (case study 3.2) and Phoenix Enterprises (case study 3.5) might motivate their staff.

Table 3.28 Motivational theorists

Theorist	Characteristics of leader	Summary
Warren Bennis	Leaders have four abilities in common, they are: able to turn a vision into action; able to communicate in a way that captures the imagination; consistent in behaviour so that people put their trust in them; ready to learn and make a commitment to self-knowledge.	Leadership is not rare. Leaders can be made. Leadership is required not just at the top of the organisation, but throughout the organisation. Leadership is not about the tasks of management, but about inspiring others towards a common goal.
David McClelland	There are three types of motivators: achievement (those who seek to achieve usually accept personal responsibility, are prepared to take calculated risks and are often individualistic); affiliation (those who seek affiliation are concerned with developing and maintaining relationships and prefer this to decision making); power (those that seek power look for leadership positions and wish to make an impact. Status and prestige are important to this group).	There is a mix of these motivators in all workers and the individual mix characterises a person's or manager's style and behaviour, both in terms of being motivated and in the management and motivation of others.
J Stacey Adams	People seek a fair balance between what they put into their job and what they get out of it. These are called inputs and outputs. Inputs can include effort, loyalty, commitment, skill, ability, adaptability, flexibility, tolerance, determination, enthusiasm, trust in boss and superiors, support of colleagues and subordinates. Outputs include rewards such as pay, expenses, perks, benefits, pension arrangements, bonus and commission, and also intangibles like recognition, reputation, praise and thanks, interest, responsibility, stimulus, training, development, sense of achievement and advancement, promotion. Perceptions are formed as to what constitutes a fair balance of inputs and outputs by comparing the individual situation with other reference points in the market place.	If inputs are fairly and adequately rewarded by outputs, people will be happy in their work and will be motivated to continue inputting at the same level. If inputs outweigh the outputs, demotivation occurs in relation to the job and the employer. This may lead some people to reduce effort and become disgruntled, difficult and even disruptive Others will try to improve the outputs by making claims or demands for more reward, or even seeking alternative employment.

Table 3.29 Motivational factors in the workplace

Job satisfaction	The job content will be more important than a high salary in terms of motivation.
Job rotation	Staff are trained in a number of jobs so that they can be rotated. This gives staff more variety and the employer a more flexible workforce.
Job enlargement	The employees are given a variety of duties which makes their work more interesting.
Job enrichment	This allows staff to have more responsibility and acknowledges the contribution they make towards the success of the company.
Management style	This is very important. A very autocratic style of management will act as a demotivator. Staff should be able to take part in the decision-making process and be encouraged to participate in planning work and setting objectives.
Recognition	Often overlooked by employers, but people like to feel they have worked well and made a contribution. A few well-timed words of praise and recognition can be a good motivator.
Clear and achievable targets	If the targets set are clear and achievable, this acts as a good motivator. It is then clear what needs to be done and how it is going to be achieved. People will feel secure in an environment that works in this way.
Seeing a task through	People like to see the end result of their labour.
Team working	This can act as a motivator, particularly when the work is complex. It is better to give joint responsibility to a team than to break down a task into small parts with each individual working alone.
The working environment	The physical environment will have an effect on the motivation of the staff.
Working conditions	The number of hours worked, the length and number of breaks, etc. can affect the motivation and morale of staff.
Job security	This is very important. If the company is not doing well or there are many changes, staff will feel insecure.
Skill use	Generally people enjoy doing things they are good at and if they are able to use their particular talents at work, this will have a positive effect on their morale.
Promotional prospects	If the company has good progression opportunities, staff will feel they have something to aim for.
Trust and respect	As with recognition and praise, staff like to feel that they are trusted and respected.

Table 3.30 Financial motivators

Overtime	It is usual to pay a higher rate for overtime, that is hours worked over the normal working hours per week. This is usually time and a half, which means one and a half times the normal rate, or double time, twice the normal rate.
Shift payments	If the normal hours of work are unsocial, for example evening or weekend working, an extra payment can be given or a higher rate used.
Bonus payments	An extra payment that can be used in a variety of ways, for example if staff have achieved a particular target or if the company has won a new contract.
Profit sharing	Some companies offer a profit-sharing scheme, whereby a percentage of the profits is shared among the staff.
Loyalty bonus	This may be used to persuade staff to stay with the employer for a period of time. It might be given for long service, but it can also be used for short-term contracts such as seasonal work. Some companies offer a share-owning bonus, whereby shares in the company are offered after a certain period of service.
Perks	These are usually a form of payment in kind and can include benefits such as a company car, health insurance, discounted goods and extra holiday.

Table 3.31 Demotivational factors

Boredom	If staff do not have enough to do or have to complete repetitive menial tasks, they are likely to become bored and demotivated.
Isolation	If staff have to work alone for long periods, this can have a negative effect.
Poor working conditions	Cramped workspace, lack of equipment and dull décor affect the individual at work.
Insufficient challenges	If staff are unable to use their skills or talents, this has a demotivating effect.
Management style	A poor management style can have a very negative effect on staff.
Factors outside individual control	These could be personal problems or a poorly organised distribution of work, which creates too much work

Effects of change and insecurity

No matter where you work, there will always be change at some point or other. It may be a simple change such as a colleague with whom you enjoyed working leaving the company, or more major, such as finding yourself under the threat of redundancy.

How people manage change will have a large effect on their motivation. Some people relish the idea of change and rise to the challenge. Others find it very difficult to cope with and need help to see them through the transitional period.

It is important to remember that change can be positive as well as negative. Changes at work can come through new opportunities, for example a promotion or new job.

The way in which companies manage change will also affect motivation. Those that plan carefully for change and have support systems in place may find that the disruption caused by new plans is minimal. However, if you turn up for work on a Monday morning and find that your job is under threat with no prior warning, the effects are likely to be great.

OVER TO YOU!

1 State three motivation factors for the individual at work.

2 State three ways in which companies might motivate their staff without using financial benefits.

3 List three factors that may demotivate staff.

Health and safety issues

Health and safety must be one of the main considerations of any employer. It is a legal requirement to address these issues and workplaces are subject to inspection by the Health and Safety Executive. If found to be unsuitable, the Health and Safety Executive officer has the power to shut down the premises immediately and they will remain closed until the necessary work has been completed.

The employer has to ensure that the workplace is safe for employees, visitors, the public who use the product or service and neighbours. Many accidents that happen in the workplace could be avoided with a little care and attention.

Employers' responsibilities

All employers have a legal responsibility for the health and safety of employees and visitors to the organisation. However, if an employer appoints five or more staff, extra rules apply.

Under the Health and Safety Act 1974, all employers must:

▶ appoint health and safety representatives, usually competent members of staff. (This is essential if there are five or more employees)

▶ draw up a written health and safety policy

▶ undertake a risk assessment before work begins

▶ record any significant findings from the risk assessment. (This is essential if there are five or more employees)

▶ make arrangements for implementing the health and safety measures identified as necessary by the risk assessment

▶ set up emergency procedures

▶ provide clear information and training to employees

▶ work together with other employers if sharing the same workplace

▶ provide the necessary equipment and facilities that are required for first aid

- provide equipment to deal with fires, chemical spills, broken glass, etc. safely

- provide safety equipment that reduces the risk of illness or injury as necessary

- display a Health and Safety Law poster

- report any major accidents, injuries or notifiable diseases as set out in the RIDDOR regulations (see page 208).

Risk assessment

One of the easiest ways to prevent accidents is to be aware of hazards. Your employer has a legal obligation to carry out risk assessments on a regular basis. A risk assessment means that the workplace has to be inspected for potential hazards against the guidance in the relevant regulations and an action plan drawn up and implemented. The regulations that must be used are listed in Table 3.32.

Table 3.32 Risk assessment regulations

Regulation	Key points
Management of Health and Safety at Work Regulations 1999	To identify the measures which need to be taken to comply with the requirements of the Fire Precautions (Workplace) Regulations 1997.
Manual Handling Operations Regulations 1992	To assess the need for and the risks involved in manual handling. To investigate ways of reducing injury.
Personal Protective Equipment at Work Regulations 1992	To determine whether the personal protective equipment is suitable.
Health and Safety (Display Screen Equipment) Regulations 1992	To assess workstations for health and safety risks to which users/operators are exposed.
Noise at Work Regulations 1989	To identify which employees are exposed to noise. To ensure that noise levels comply with regulations.
Control of Substances Hazardous to Health Regulations 1999	To identify risk to enable a decision to be made on the measures to be taken to prevent or adequately control exposures.
Control of Asbestos at Work Regulations 1987	To identify types of asbestos. To determine the nature and degree of exposure. To set out steps to reduce exposure to the lowest level reasonably practicable.
Control of Lead at Work Regulations 1998	To assess whether the exposure of any employees to lead is liable to be significant.

A risk assessment should identify the potential hazards of the workplace. However, hazards can occur at any time and employees also have a responsibility to be aware of these and to report them to the appropriate person.

Take a look around your workplace. Given below is a list of potential hazards of which you should be aware.

Machinery and equipment

▶ Machinery incorrectly positioned, e.g. heavy items on a top shelf.

▶ Unsafe use of machinery or equipment, e.g. not using necessary protective clothing.

Substances

▶ Unsafe storage, e.g. photocopier toner should not be stored where people are working.

▶ Unsafe usage, e.g. spillages should be cleaned immediately.

Personal conduct

▶ Unsafe behaviour, e.g. standing on chairs to reach items.

▶ Untidiness and careless working, e.g. piles of paper on the floor.

▶ Smoking, drinking and drugs, e.g. being aware of prescription drugs that may affect your capability when using equipment.

Identifying potential hazards

A risk assessment should identify the potential hazards of a workplace. However, hazards can occur at any time and employees have a responsibility to be aware of the risks and to report any hazards to the appropriate person. See Table 3.33 (p209) for a list of potential work hazards.

RIDDOR Regulations 1995

RIDDOR stands for Reporting of Injuries, Diseases and Dangerous Occurrences. These regulations require employers and those in control of premises to report specified work-related accidents, diseases and dangerous incidents to the relevant enforcing authority, which could be either the Health and Safety Executive or the local council authority.

The following work-related incidents must be reported:

▶ death

▶ major injury

▶ an accident which makes the injured person unable to work for more than three days

▶ an injury to a member of the public, which means they are taken to hospital

▶ work-related disease

▶ a dangerous occurrence, in which something happens that could otherwise have resulted in a reportable injury.

Health and Safety (Display Screen Equipment) Regulations 1992

Almost everyone uses a computer in the workplace at some point or another. There has been much concern about the injuries that can be sustained by using the computer for long periods of time. The Display Screen Equipment Regulations set out the actions that employers should take to minimise the risk of injury such as repetitive strain injury. These are shown below. Employers must:

▶ analyse workstations and reduce health and safety risks

Table 3.33 Potential hazards

Machinery incorrectly positioned	For example: ▶ a computer that is pushed too close to the back edge of a desk ▶ photocopiers, etc. placed too close to employees or being used in a poorly ventilated room ▶ leads and cables causing trip hazard ▶ equipment stored incorrectly, e.g. heavy items on top shelves.
Unsafe use of machinery and equipment	For example: ▶ incorrect use of machinery, i.e. not in accordance with instructions ▶ someone trying to repair machinery without training ▶ use of broken machinery, frayed cables, etc. ▶ failure to use necessary protective clothing ▶ failure to use the correct equipment for the task.
Unsafe storage of substances	For example: ▶ failure to store toner for photocopiers and laser printers, adhesives, correction fluids, thinners, cleaning materials, etc. in accordance with manufacturer's instructions ▶ storage of toner, cleaning materials and similar substances where people are working.
Unsafe usage of substances	For example: ▶ failure to remove and dispose of toner in accordance with manufacturer's instructions ▶ use of toner, adhesives, correction fluids, etc. in poorly ventilated rooms ▶ spillage of any of the above substances (they should be cleared immediately and in accordance with manufacturer's instructions).
Unsafe behaviour	For example: ▶ incorrect use of equipment ▶ failure to use the correct equipment for the task ▶ standing on chairs to reach items ▶ leaving filing drawers open ▶ placing items in walkways ▶ messing about in the office ▶ propping open or blocking fire doors ▶ failure to use protective clothing or equipment appropriately.
Untidiness and careless working	For example: ▶ careless disposal of waste materials ▶ leaving paper or files, etc. on the floor and in walkways ▶ failure to give due care and attention when using machinery and equipment ▶ inappropriate and dangerous storage of substances and equipment.
Smoking, drinking and drugs	For example: ▶ smoking anywhere in the building apart from designated smoking areas ▶ careless disposal of items such as matches and lit cigarettes ▶ being under the influence of alcohol or drugs (including prescription drugs) in the workplace and especially when using machinery.

- ensure workstations meet minimum ergonomic requirements
- provide information about risks and measures
- plan daily work routines for users
- offer eye tests and special glasses if necessary
- provide health and safety training.

Some of the measures that employers can take to ensure that they comply with the regulations include:

- ensuring that the desks and chairs are of a suitable size and height for the person using them. Adjustable chairs without arms are the most useful
- ensuring that the lighting is appropriate and reduces glare from the computer screens
- ensuring that an appropriate number of power points are conveniently situated so that trailing cables can be avoided
- ensuring that screens are anti-glare, adjustable and positioned to avoid glare and reflection
- staff should be given short breaks from the computer to avoid eyestrain
- where possible, staff should have their work rotated so that they spend periods of time working away from the computer
- staff should receive training on how to sit correctly at the workstation in order to avoid poor posture and resulting back and muscle problems
- if deemed necessary, special equipment should be provided such as wrist rests, foot rests and anti-glare filters
- staff should be entitled to free eye tests and where necessary help with the purchase of glasses.

Employee's responsibilities

As an employee you do have certain responsibilities to your employer with regard to health and safety. These include the following:

- to work safely at all times
- to take care of your own health and safety and that of others who may be affected by what you do or not do
- to co-operate with your employer with regard to health and safety
- to act responsibly in the workplace
- to use any protective equipment supplied to you by your employer
- to use equipment safely and in accordance with training or instructions
- to use the correct equipment for the task
- to follow any procedures with regard to emergency evacuation, dealing with accidents, fire drills, etc.
- to report hazards and potential hazards promptly

- to report accidents and injuries
- to be familiar with the first aid arrangements provided by the organisation
- to attend any training your employer provides with regard to health and safety
- not to interfere with or misuse anything provided for your health, safety or welfare.

Health and safety procedures

Your employer must ensure that you receive and are familiar with various sets of procedures relating to health and safety. These will include:

- fire drills
- emergency evacuations
- dealing with accidents
- reporting accidents
- reporting hazards.

These are important as in the case of an accident or emergency staff must know what to do. The procedures will ensure that there is a consistent approach to dealing with emergencies and that staff are calm and collected because they are fully aware of what to do.

In many companies full training on these procedures will be given as part of the induction training programme. You may also be given a written set of procedures to keep as part of your procedures manual.

Completing documentation is an important part of health and safety procedures as your employer has a legal obligation to keep records of risk assessments, accidents and injuries. Part of your responsibility as an employee is to make sure that you understand this process and give full details of any incident in which you are involved.

OVER TO YOU!

The head office of Phoenix Enterprises plc (case study 3.5) has large open-plan offices for each of the different divisions. Many of the staff at Phoenix Enterprises use computers on a regular basis.

1. State three responsibilities that the directors of Phoenix Enterprises have towards their employees with regard to health and safety.

2. Give three ways in which the directors can help reduce injuries sustained at the computer.

3. Health and safety law requires employers to take certain measures to prevent accident and injury and to ensure a safe working environment. List four of these measures.

4. Briefly explain the various procedures that Phoenix Enterprises should have in place with regard to health and safety. State why they are important.

5. State four of the responsibilities that employees have with regard to health and safety in the workplace.

Rights and responsibilities of employers and employees

Contract of employment

When you start a new job you enter into a contract with your employer. This contract is legally binding and it provides rights and responsibilities for both you and your employer.

The contract is made up of various terms and these include the following.

▶ **Express terms:** These are terms that have been explicitly agreed and might include details such as your job title, the hours your work and the salary scale.

▶ **Implied terms:** These can be:

- details that are too obvious to set out in writing, for example that you will not steal from your employer

- details that are necessary to make the contract workable, for example if you had accepted a job as a driver, it would be assumed that you have a current driving licence

- details that relate to the customs and practices of the industry.

▶ **Incorporated terms:** These are terms that are incorporated into individual contracts by reference to other documents. An example of this would be the company handbook.

▶ **Terms imposed by law:** These include employment protection and anti-discrimination legislation.

Employers are not required to set out in writing all the terms of the contract, but the main terms and conditions must be put in writing and given to the employee within two months of their employment commencing.

The main terms that must be present in the contract of employment are:

▶ the names of the employer and the employee

▶ the date when the employment (and the period of continuous employment) began

▶ details of salary or wages and the intervals at which it is to be paid

▶ the hours of work

▶ the amount of holiday entitlement

▶ the entitlement to sick leave, including any entitlement to sick pay

▶ details of any pension provision and pension schemes

▶ the period of notice needed to terminate the contract, for both employee and employer

▶ the job title or a brief job description

▶ if the contract is not permanent, the period for which the employment is expected to continue or if it is for a fixed term, the date when it is to end

▶ the place of work or, if the employee is required or allowed to work in more than one location, an indication of this and of the employer's address

▶ the details of the existence of any relevant collective agreements

▶ information on the disciplinary and grievance procedures set out by the employer.

It is acceptable for items such as sick leave and pay, pension arrangements and disciplinary rules to be mentioned in the contract and referenced to a separate document, such as the company handbook.

Once the contract has been issued, changes can only be made with the agreement of both the employee and employer. However, the majority of employers insert a term into the contract that allows them to vary the duties of the employee.

The contract confers certain rights and responsibilities on the employer and the employee.

Responsibilities

Table 3.34 shows some of the responsibilities of both the employer and the employee.

Table 3.34 Responsibilities of employers and employees

Employer	Employee
Must provide a written statement of terms and conditions within two months of employment commencing. Must provide a safe working environment. Must provide salary and benefits as dictated by legislation. Must ensure that employee is not discriminated against or treated unfairly. Must not dismiss staff without good reason and must use correct procedures.	To attend work as agreed. To work to best ability. To keep company information confidential. To show loyalty to employer. Not to discriminate against others. To work safely. To take proper care of employer's property. To give the agreed period of notice when they wish to leave their employment.

Rights

The employer has the right to expect the employee:

- to attend work as agreed
- to work the hours stated in the employment contract
- to do the work as stated in their job description
- to keep company information confidential
- to show loyalty to employer
- to comply with the terms and conditions of employment
- not to discriminate against others
- to work safely and follow health and safety regulations
- to comply with other laws relating to their work
- to take proper care of employer's property
- to give the agreed period of notice when they wish to leave their employment.

The employee has the following rights.

Rights relating to time off

- To receive four weeks' paid annual holiday entitlement.
- To have a meal break during working hours and/or rest breaks (if sufficient hours are worked).

- Not to work more than 48 hours per week (calculated over a 17-week period).
- To have paid time off for ante-natal care, carrying out trade union duties, health and safety training, looking for work or arranging training (if the staff member has been given notice of redundancy), dealing with domestic emergencies.
- To have unpaid time off for engaging in trade union duties, public duties, parental leave (up to three months).

Rights relating to pay

- To receive not less than the national minimum wage for work completed.
- To receive equal pay for doing like or similar work.
- To receive an itemised pay statement.
- To receive statutory sick pay.

Rights relating to redundancy

- To be consulted about proposed redundancies.
- To act as an employee representative in the case of redundancy or if the business is being transferred.
- To receive a statutory redundancy payment if made redundant.

Rights relating to discrimination and dismissal

- Not to be victimised, harassed or discriminated against on the grounds of gender, race or sexual orientation.
- To be accompanied at a disciplinary or grievance hearing by a trade union official of their choice.
- To receive notice of termination of employment as agreed in the contract.
- Not to be unfairly dismissed.
- Not to be dismissed for asserting a statutory right.
- Not to be dismissed for making a public interest disclosure.
- To receive a written statement of reasons for dismissal.

General rights

- To receive a written statement of the main terms and conditions of employment within two months of commencing employment.
- To belong (or not) to a trade union.
- To a safe system of working and a safe working environment.
- To be given access to their personnel record.

Disciplinary and grievance procedures

An employer will usually have two sets of procedures in place.

▶ **Disciplinary procedures:** These set out the procedures to be used if an employer wishes to take action against a member of staff because of their behaviour at work.

▶ **Grievance procedures:** These set out the procedures to be used if an employee wishes to make a complaint about the way they have been treated in the workplace.

There are a number of benefits from having the two sets of procedures in place:

▶ they help protect an employee from unfair dismissal

▶ if correctly drawn up, they help protect the employer from dismissing a member of staff unlawfully

▶ they ensure that all staff are treated in the same way should a problem arise

▶ staff who make a complaint are assured that their grievance will be investigated and, if upheld, action will be taken

▶ staff can request help from a staff representative and/or a trade union official, who will accompany them to any formal meetings if necessary

▶ the managers will know how to proceed with an investigation.

Disciplinary procedures

If an employer has a complaint about an employee, they can take action under their disciplinary procedure. However, they must ensure that the disciplinary procedure complies with employment legislation.

Usually the procedure gives the member of staff an opportunity to correct their behaviour before being told to leave the employment. A typical procedure might follow the steps given below.

1 A verbal warning will be given for a first or minor offence. The employer must ensure that the employee is aware that this is an official warning. A note of the verbal warning should be made on the employee's file and the employee will be told that this is happening.

2 A written warning will be issued for a second or more serious offence. Again, the employee must be informed that this is an official warning and that the letter will be placed on file.

3 A final warning will be issued if the employee has not corrected their behaviour after a written warning and either repeats the offence or commits a further offence within a given period. For serious offences, the employer may go straight to this step.

4 If the behaviour does not improve, the employee may be suspended, demoted, transferred or dismissed. If the offence is extremely serious, this is called gross misconduct and dismissal may be instant. Employers must be sure that the reasons for instant dismissal are strong or they could face a charge of unfair dismissal and either be prosecuted through the civil courts or face an industrial tribunal.

Reasons for dismissing employees may include:

▶ stealing from the employer

▶ passing on confidential information to people outside the organisation

- being drunk or under the influence of drugs at the workplace
- possessing illegal substances at work
- fighting on the company premises
- disregarding health and safety instructions
- smoking in unauthorised areas
- disregarding company policy on matters of discrimination, harassment and bullying
- falsifying company accounts or records
- persistent unauthorised absence
- accepting bribes from suppliers or competitors
- disregarding management instructions.

This list is not exhaustive and there are many other valid reasons for dismissing staff. Companies sometimes lose unfair dismissal cases because they have not followed the correct procedures, rather than because the member of staff did not deserve to be sacked.

Grievance procedures

If an employee feels that they, or others, are being treated unfairly then they may complain using the organisation's grievance procedures. These will clearly set out what the employee has to do and how the company will respond. Generally the procedure will follow the steps shown below. At all stages the employee may be accompanied by a colleague or trade union representative.

- The complaint is investigated within the department. The manager must investigate the complaint and respond accordingly. If the employee is satisfied at the outcome of the investigation, the matter will end there.
- The complaint may be investigated outside the department. If the employee has not received a satisfactory response to step 1 or if they feel that the complaint will not be fairly investigated within the department, they may request an investigation by a more senior manager.
- The complaint may be investigated outside the organisation. This may be because the complaint will not be taken seriously within the organisation or because of the nature of the complaint. An employee may also take this route if the first two steps have failed.

Valid reasons for making a complaint against your employer might include:

- being forced to work long hours without a break
- any infringement of employment law
- discrimination of any type
- victimisation, harassment or bullying
- dangerous working practices or environment.

Employment legislation

To ensure that the rights of employees are met, there are various pieces of legislation in force. Listed below are just a few that relate to employment.

- Sex Discrimination Act 1975
- Race Relations Act 1976
- Employment Equality (Religion or Belief) Regulations 2003
- Employment Equality (Sexual Orientation) Regulations 2003
- Protection from Harassment Act 1997
- Equal Pay Act 1970
- Disability Discrimination Act 1995
- Human Rights Act 1988
- Employment Act 1989
- Employment Rights Act 1996
- National Minimum Wage Act 1998
- Employment Relations Act 1999
- Maternity and Parental Leave, etc. Regulations 1999
- Employment Act (Flexible Working Regulations) 2002

OVER TO YOU!

1. Briefly explain the difference between express conditions and implied conditions in relation to the contract of employment.
2. State three of the responsibilities employees have towards their employer.
3. State four rights employees have with regard to pay.
4. State three responsibilities the employer has towards the employee.

Reviewing and developing office procedures

Introduction

This unit will give you all the information you need to be able to review, maintain and develop office procedures. By the end of the unit you will be able to do the following.

▶ Identify and describe activities that require office procedures

▶ Identify ways in which office-based procedures are effectively maintained and reviewed

▶ Identify the factors influencing the structure of different procedures and explain their impact

▶ Carry out a review of office-based procedures

▶ Evaluate the effectiveness of procedures

▶ Suggest improvements to procedures and design new procedures

▶ Identify ways of implementing new or revised procedures

▶ Identify issues of cost and resource management

▶ Identify training and development requirements

▶ Identify possible difficulties with new or revised procedures

The assessment of this unit is undertaken in college. You will be expected to do the following.

1 Identify and describe two different office-based procedures. This assessment will cover assessment objectives 1–3. For this you will need to write a short report describing the ways in which procedures are used and maintained.

2 Carry out an in-depth review of two separate procedures and make recommendations regarding amendments to the procedures. These can be the same procedures as you used for requirement 1 or completely different ones. This assessment will cover assessment objectives 4–10.

▼ IDENTIFY AND DESCRIBE ACTIVITIES THAT REQUIRE OFFICE PROCEDURES

What are procedures?

Procedures are instructions that you follow in order to achieve a stated outcome or objective. They are usually broken down into steps so that they can easily be followed. Steps are single tasks that are performed in a stated order so that the objective can be reached. Cookery recipes are usually broken down into procedural steps so that the recipe is easy to understand and follow. It is easy to see why you must follow a recipe in the correct order; if you don't, the food will not be cooked properly. This is the same for all procedures; the steps should lead you through the process to reach the desired objective.

Here are some other reasons for breaking down procedures into steps.

▶ **To standardise the procedure:** Everyone completes the procedure in the same way.

- **To standardise the quality of the work:** If everyone follows the same steps of a procedure, the finished task should always be of the same quality.

- **For staff training:** If you can give a new employee a set of steps to follow, the task is immediately clear and easy to follow.

- **For decision making:** To see where decisions may need to be made or alternative actions taken.

- **To find problem areas:** If the procedure is not working, it is easier to see which part of the procedure is faulty.

- **To ensure efficient and effective working practices.**

- **For monitoring purposes:** Procedures need to be monitored on a regular basis.

Procedure for making a mug of tea

Objective: a mug of tea

Steps:

1 Switch the kettle on.

2 Fetch the mug.

3 Put a tea bag in the mug.

4 When the kettle has boiled, pour boiling water over the tea bag in the mug.

5 Allow it to rest for one or two minutes.

6 Remove the tea bag.

7 Add milk to taste.

Look at the flowchart in Figure 4.1, which shows the procedure for making a mug of tea.

Figure 4.1 shows a very straightforward set of steps. You may find that for some procedures, the steps are quite complex and involve multiple choices. There may also be some alternative actions. For example, using the mug of tea procedure, after the 'remove tea bag' step there could be a decision to be made (see Figure 4.2).

Although this example is extremely basic, it should give you an idea of how procedural steps work.

When you are devising procedures you need to be able to think logically. Think about the task for which you are devising the procedure and break down the actions step by step. If you are using the flowchart method to display your procedure, you should use the following devices:

Oval	An oval or circle denotes the start and finish of your procedure.	
Rectangle	A rectangle shows where an activity must take place.	
Diamond	A diamond shape denotes where a decision must be made.	
Arrow	Arrow lines show the order in which the procedure must be worked.	

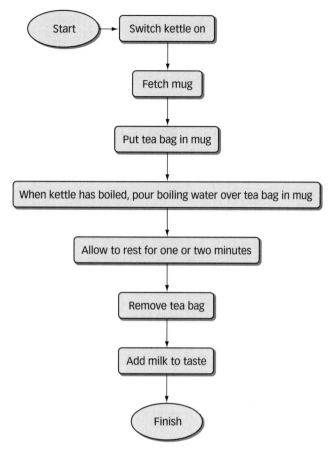

▲ Figure 4.1 Procedure for making a mug of tea

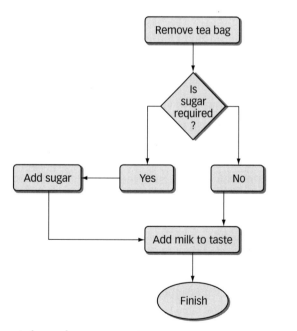

▲ Figure 4.2 Decisions to be made

Office procedures

There are many activities in the office environment that require procedures. There are activities that relate to using office equipment such as the fax machine, photocopier, shredder or laminator, and activities that relate to the usual types of office work such as filing, answering the phone or stock control of the stationery cupboard.

Depending on the type of work you are doing, there will be many other types of procedure that will be followed on a daily basis. For example, if you worked in a mail order company you would find procedures for the following:

▷ order processing

▷ credit card charging

▷ packing parcels

▷ preparing postal documentation

▷ dealing with returned goods

▷ customer refunds.

Another example would be if you worked for a company that arranged accommodation letting; there you would find procedures for:

▷ registering prospective tenants

▷ registering prospective landlords

▷ taking up references on tenants

▷ checking and making an inventory on premises

▷ setting up a direct debit from tenants

▷ setting up a method of payment for landlords.

▼ IDENTIFY WAYS IN WHICH OFFICE-BASED PROCEDURES ARE EFFECTIVELY MAINTAINED AND REVIEWED

Procedures need to be maintained, reviewed and amended on a regular basis in order to ensure that they are still the most efficient and effective way to achieve the objective. Over time people change procedures to suit the way in which they like to work. Sometimes this makes the procedure much better; however, it does mean that unless these minor changes are documented, the procedure is no longer standard to everyone who uses it and the quality of the outcome may not be as expected.

Supporting procedures

Procedures can be supported in the following ways:

▶ by training staff

▶ by documenting the procedures

▶ by tracking documents

▶ by schedules

▶ by progress chasing.

Training staff

Depending on the type and complexity of the procedure, staff may need to be trained to use it effectively. This may take the form of a demonstration on how to use a piece of office equipment through to much more formal training for complex procedures. The benefits of training staff include allowing staff the opportunity to ask questions and obtain feedback.

Documenting the procedure

Written procedures are often kept together in a **procedures manual**. These can be displayed in any or a mixture of the following:

▶ step-by-step instructions

▶ flowcharts

▶ pictures

▶ narrative.

The procedures manual is a very useful document as it can be given to new staff as part of their training. For existing staff it means that they can easily refer to the document if they require any help with their work. However, in order to maintain the procedures manual, it must be checked and updated on a regular basis.

The procedures manual for a large company may run into hundreds of separate procedures. It would not be necessary to issue all procedures to all staff. Each member of staff can receive a custom-made procedures manual that is tailored to the procedures that they are likely to use.

Tracking documents

These can be particularly useful if the procedure involves two or more people in a chain of activities. For example, if you were following a procedure to take an order from a customer by telephone, the first step would involve a member of the call centre staff taking the order from the customer.

The resulting order may then be passed on to the order processing team, which will arrange for the goods to be picked from the warehouse shelves and packed into parcels. The order will also be passed to the finance department, which will raise an invoice for the items. After a period of time, the finance department will check that the invoice has been paid and if it hasn't, chase the customer for payment.

You can see from this chain of events that there is plenty to go wrong. A tracking document that is signed and dated as each part of the procedure is completed will help to ensure that nothing is forgotten and that hold-ups are traceable.

In order to help this process the work may be given a job number or ticket so that all the elements of the job can be linked together easily. This also provides a reference number for the work as it goes through the system.

Tracking documents can be paper-based, but are most useful when they form part of the computer record. This means that everyone has access to the tracking of an order for example just by looking up the customer on screen. An example of a tracking document is shown in Figure 4.3.

Customer order tracking document	Date	Signed
Date order received		
Customer order number		
Details logged on computer		
Order sent to warehouse		
Goods picked (note any omissions)		
Goods packed		
Despatch documentation prepared		
Date despatched		
Order passed to finance		
Customer invoiced		
Payment received		

▲ Figure 4.3 A tracking document

Schedules

Schedules can be useful to see where you are in a procedure, the timescale you are likely to be to working to and can also be used as a checklist to ensure that nothing is omitted or forgotten. They are most useful for following procedures that are lengthy. For example, if you were to organise a training event, you may have to follow a set procedure. The schedule would ensure that you follow the procedure correctly and is easily referred to if you need to see what to do next.

The schedule shown in Figure 4.4 could act as a standard schedule for any training course that has to be arranged. The words in brackets can be replaced with the correct information for a specific event.

Schedule for human resources training (Date) (Venue) (Times)		
Task	**Comments**	**Actioned (Please sign and date this column when task completed)**
Week commencing (6 weeks before event) Book hotel conference room		
Book catering		
Inform delegates		
Confirm date with trainer		
Confirm hotel booking and request special equipment		
Week commencing (4 weeks before event) Log delegate confirmation		
Prepare presentation materials		
Week commencing (2 weeks before event) Prepare delegate handouts		
Week commencing (1 week before event) Confirm numbers with hotel		
Confirm catering		
Confirm special requirements		
Week commencing (1 week after event) Chase late feedback forms		
Week commencing (3 weeks after event) Prepare analysis of feedback		
Pass report to HR Director		

▲ Figure 4.4 A sample schedule

Progress chasing

It may be that when following a procedure over a period of time, it will be necessary to check on the progress of yourself and others. A progress chasing step can be written into the procedure so that at a given point others can be asked to report where they are with their work. This will show whether set deadlines have been met and when the overall objective is likely to be achieved.

Another method of progress chasing is to have a member of staff responsible for this as part of their duties. This person may be asked to report to their supervisor or manager on a regular basis the progress of work as it is going through a procedure.

OVER TO YOU!

Using the two procedures you chose in the exercise at the bottom of page 222, describe how they are supported in your organisation or college.

Maintaining procedures

Procedures can be maintained by the above methods. However, it is important that they are also maintained by ensuring that staff are aware of the following.

▶ **Knowing that the procedure exists in the first place:** A company may have developed lots of very efficient procedures, but if staff are not aware of them, they will be useless.

▶ **Knowing where to get information:** If the company has a procedures manual, it is important that staff know where it is kept. If there is no procedures manual, staff must be aware of how they can access the necessary information elsewhere.

▶ **Where staff can access the training they require:** Is there a training manual? If so, where is it kept? If this is not available, who will show them what to do?

▶ **Knowing who to ask for help:** This should really form part of the procedure, but in any case, it should be clear who to turn to if help is required.

▶ **Amending or updating procedures:** If a step in the procedure needs amending or updating, it is useful to know whom to contact. If amendments are made on a regular basis, the procedure is more likely to remain effective and efficient. However, if all the staff who use the procedure each amend it slightly to suit themselves, before long the procedure will be completely worthless as it is no longer a standard for carrying out the task.

▶ **Monitoring the procedures:** Some procedures will have monitoring built in as a procedural step, however all procedures should be monitored.

OVER TO YOU!

Find out how the procedures you chose in the exercise on page 222 are maintained.

Reviewing procedures

Procedures should be reviewed on a regular basis to see if:

▶ the procedure is still needed

▶ the procedure is still working effectively

▶ staff are still following the stated procedure

- it is cost effective; there is no point in having a procedure that costs more in time and resources that the benefits that it gives

- the procedure maintains the required standard of quality

- the procedure meets current legislation, including health and safety

- changes in technology or equipment mean that the existing procedure is now out of date, for example if your company bought a new photocopier, the existing procedures will no longer be relevant

- any small amendments can be made that will benefit the procedure

- changes in working practice have affected some of the procedures.

In order to review procedures, it is essential to undertake some research. It may be necessary to consider the following.

The users of the procedure

It will be necessary to look at the people who are following the procedure. What is their job role? Where does the procedure fit into their work? What is their authority level? This information will help the reviewer to see whether the procedure is appropriate both in terms of the level of the work and the way in which the procedure is written. For example, if the procedure is to be followed by an inexperienced administrator, it will be difficult for him or her to work the procedure accurately if it is written in technical language with no further explanation.

The views of the user on the procedure

This can be done by observation, questionnaire or interview and will enable the reviewer to find out the user's views of the following:

- whether the procedure is easy to follow

- whether all the necessary steps are included and the procedure follows a logical progression

- whether the procedure always leads to the successful completion of the objective

- whether the procedure takes the stated time.

The views of the user on the end product

The end user here could be an external customer or a colleague. The views of the end user will show the following:

- whether the service can be improved

- whether the end product is of a consistent and high quality

- whether the task is completed within a reasonable or stated timescale.

Manufacturer's instructions

Procedures for using equipment must comply with the manufacturer's instructions and guidelines. These can be found in the handbooks that accompany the equipment, but are often supplemented with advice on helplines or the Internet.

Alternative methods of completing the task

Are there other ways in which the task could be completed? It can sometimes be better to take a completely fresh approach, particularly if the procedure is not working well. It may be that it was written many years ago and hasn't been changed. People may be reluctant to look at the task in any other way because 'it's always been done that way'. However, a fresh look and perhaps some lateral thinking may produce a completely new and more efficient way of handling the task.

Sometimes the task itself will involve alternative methods for completing it. For example, if you were recording a customer's order on a database and they have ordered before, you would use their existing record; however, if it was a new customer, you would have to follow the procedure for opening a new record.

Legal requirements and restrictions

Before embarking on a thorough review of a procedure, it is essential that you have access to current legislation. There is no point in reviewing and amending sets of procedures only to find that they do not comply with current legislation. This is particularly important if you are involved with health and safety procedures.

Table 4.1 shows the types of legislation that need to be considered before a procedure can be written or amended. This list is not exhaustive; you will need to ensure that you keep up to date with relevant legislation and be prepared to undertake some research on this topic. The Internet will provide you with plenty of information on current legislation.

Table 4.1 Types of legislation

Health and Safety	Employment	Other
Manual Handling Operations Regulations 1992	Equal Pay Act 1970	Data Protection Act 1998
Provision and Use of Work Equipment 1992/Regulations 1998	Race Relations Act 1976	Copyright, Designs and Patents Act 1988
European Directives 1992	Sex Discrimination Act 1975	Employers' Liability 1969
Control of Substances Hazardous to Health Regulations 1999	Disability Discrimination Act 1995	
The Offices, Shops and Railway Premises Act 1963	Fixed-Term Employees Regulations 2003	
Management of Health and Safety at Work Regulations 1999	Employment Act 2002	
Electrical at Work Regulations 1989		

▲ Figure 4.5 Filing systems need to have a procedure that is easy for everyone to follow

Observation

This is a useful review method as the supervisor or manager can watch staff perform tasks following the procedure. This method will quickly show if staff are following the procedure to the letter or if they have introduced their own amendments, which are not documented. For example, if staff always omit one or two steps, but still achieve the required objective at the correct standard, this might be a case for amending a procedure.

Questionnaires

These are a good way of obtaining feedback from the users of the procedure. The advantage to using a questionnaire is that the person completing it can take his or her time and give a considered reply. However, designing a useful questionnaire can be difficult. You need to consider the following when writing questions.

▶ What is the aim of the questionnaire?

▶ What do you want to know?

▶ Who are you going to ask?

▶ How will you measure the results?

▶ What will you do with the results?

Before you hand out your questionnaire to a number of people, trial it on one or two people to see if you get the response you expected. One of the most common mistakes when designing questions is to make the question too narrow or too broad. For example, if you asked 'Does the procedure work?' the response might well be 'Yes'. There are two problems with this:

▶ You haven't found out if there are any problems with the procedure.

▷ The lack of explanation from the answer 'yes' will not give you any information as to the quality of the outcome or the time it took to complete the procedure.

It would have been more helpful to ask the following questions

▷ When following the procedure, are the instructions clear and unambiguous? If no, please explain.

▷ Do you have to make decisions that are not stated in the procedure? If yes, please give details.

▷ Is the task completed to the stated standard and within a reasonable time scale?' If no, please explain.

These more specific questions will give you plenty of feedback for your analysis.

Once you have received the completed questionnaires, you will need to analyse the responses. One of the most efficient ways of reading the results is to put them into chart format. This could be a pie, bar chart or even a table giving the tally marks. The point of this is that the results are clear and easy to read.

OVER TO YOU!

Design a questionnaire to find out the shopping habits of your colleagues. You will need to find out the following:

▶ where they shop

▶ how often they go shopping

▶ how much they spend

▶ what they buy

▶ their favourite shop.

Present your findings in chart format.

Interviews

As with questionnaires, the key to a successful interview is in the preparation and planning. You will need to think carefully about the questions you want to ask and you must bear in mind that you are taking up the time of someone who is probably very busy. Make sure that your questions are specific and that you keep the interview on track. Make notes of the responses you receive to your questions or record the interview (after checking that the interviewee is agreeable to this).

After you have completed the interview, don't forget to thank the person for their input. Ask if you can contact the interviewee again either by telephone or email if you require any further information.

Timescales

Often a procedure will have a built-in timescale. For example, a procedure for dealing with customer complaints might state that the customer must receive at least an acknowledgement of their complaint within five working days. By checking the dates of receipt of the complaint and the date of reply, a reviewer can see if the procedure is working correctly. This is an important area to review as there is no point in setting unrealistic timescales for work if it will prove impossible for the user to keep to them. This is particularly important if these expectations are to be published, for example in a customer charter.

Quality control

By checking the end result or objective of the procedure it is easy to review whether the procedure is working correctly. Quality control can also be undertaken by random or sample checking, which will show whether the procedure works consistently and whether all work is completed to the same standard. If the work is of an inconsistent standard, the reviewer will know that further investigation is necessary.

Some companies have instigated **total quality management (TQM) systems.** These implement standards and procedures in order to reach certain levels of quality. Others use **quality circles** to good effect. These are usually made up of teams of employees from across the workplace, who meet to discuss improvements that can be made to working practices. This is normally a voluntary involvement. Quality circles can be very useful to a company as it is the users of the procedures who can give the most valuable feedback. They also help to promote a feeling of pride and responsibility among staff.

Internal audits

An internal audit should take place at regular intervals to check that the procedures are still relevant and working correctly. The audit can involve observation, consultation with the users and quality control. It may be necessary to involve external specialists for complex procedures. Upon completion of the audit, recommendations will be made as to whether the procedure needs to be amended or updated.

Testing

One of the easiest ways to review a procedure is to test it yourself. Follow the instructions carefully and see if it works. It doesn't matter if you do not have any experience of the task, the procedure should be written so that you can achieve the objective just by following the instructions.

OVER TO YOU!

Use the same two procedures as you chose for the exercise on page 222. For one, design a short questionnaire to find out if there are any problems with the procedure. For the second, interview someone who regularly uses the procedure. Present your findings in the form of a short report.

External quality assurance procedures

Many companies and organisation are keen to show others that they are working to best practice in the workplace. Quality Assurance Awards such as Investors in People (IiP) or ISO 9000 give recognition to organisations that implement and maintain procedures that ensure quality throughout the organisation in terms of its work, standards, management systems, training and development.

INVESTORS IN PEOPLE

© Investors in People, UK

▲ Figure 4.6 IiP logo

Investors in People (IiP) is a national standard that sets out a level of good practice for training and developing people to achieve business goals. It provides a framework for improving business performance and competitiveness through a planned approach to setting and communicating business objectives and developing people to meet these objectives. The end result should mean that people are trained and motivated to do what their organisation needs them to do. The Investors in People standard is based on four key principles:

▶ **commitment;** to invest in people

▶ **planning;** how skills, individuals and teams are to be developed to achieve these goals

▶ **action;** taking action to develop and use the necessary skills in a well-defined and continuing programme directly tied to business objectives

▶ **evaluating;** evaluating outcomes of training and development for individuals' progress towards goals, the value achieved and future needs.

In order to be recognised as an Investor in People, it is important that an organisation does the following:

▶ understands the standard and its strategic implications for the organisation

▶ undertakes a review against the standard to identify gaps in current practice

▶ makes a commitment to meet the standard and communicates that commitment to all members of staff

▶ plans and takes action to bring about change

▶ puts together the evidence for assessment against the standard.

Each of the broad principles is broken down into a number of actions, which are used as evidence indicators. An organisation must be able to produce evidence that these actions have been completed.

Once the evidence has been gathered an assessor will visit the organisation, examine the paperwork and speak to various members of staff. Once the assessor is satisfied that all the evidence indicators have been met, the standard will be awarded.

In order for an organisation to show its commitment to the standard, it is likely that procedures will be needed to ensure that the development of staff is continuous and effective. These procedures may well have an impact on the culture of the organisation and the way in which in works.

If you were to review or develop procedures in an organisation that has been awarded the IiP standard, or is working towards achieving the standard, you would need to ensure that your work complies with any procedural plan that has been implemented by your organisation.

ISO 9000 is the name given to a set of standards that has been developed by the International Organization for Standardization to provide a framework in which a quality management system (QMS) can be implemented. The QMS will help to ensure that the company has consistent working practices that are continually improved and updated. This will help the company to provide products and services that meet customers' requirements. A company awarded the ISO standard shows that it has made a commitment to quality.

There are a number of different standards contained in the ISO awards. This unit will look at the ISO 9000:2001 standard. If a company decides to register for this particular award it will have to implement a QMS in accordance with the published standard.

The ISO 9000:2001 includes the following sections:

▶ quality management system

▶ management responsibility

▶ resource management

▶ product realisation

▶ measurement, analysis and improvement.

The organisation would need to be able to do the following:

▶ define why the organisation is in business

▶ determine the key processes that state 'what' the organisation does

▶ establish how these processes work within the organisation

▶ determine who owns these processes

▶ agree these processes throughout the organisation.

Basically, this means to look at what and why the organisation is in business, set procedures to help maintain the process of what it is the company does and then set a standard that is used throughout the organisation, i.e. implement procedures.

If an organisation is considering applying for the standard they will have to put together a QMS, which will involve input from the senior management. A quality manual must be developed, which outlines the organisation's intentions to operate in a quality manner. It must outline the following:

▶ why the organisation is in business

▶ what the organisation's intentions are

▶ how the standard is applied

▶ how the business operates.

Support documentation must then be developed and this will take the form of a procedures manual. The procedures will link with the QMS. The QMS can then be implemented and staff trained. Documentation must be produced to show that the organisation is following the correct procedures to the stated standard. As with the IiP award, an external assessor will look at the systems and speak to staff before deciding whether the organisation deserves the award.

▼ IDENTIFY THE FACTORS INFLUENCING THE STRUCTURE OF DIFFERENT PROCEDURES AND EXPLAIN THEIR IMPACT

There are many factors that influence the structure of procedures and these include the following:

- resources such as time, equipment and cost
- legal regulations and restrictions
- the staff who will be using the procedure
- safety regulations
- technology
- external changes
- quality awards such as IiP or ISO 9000:2001.

Resources

When devising procedures it is important to take into account the resources that will be required.

- **Purpose:** This is the most obvious consideration, but one that is often overlooked. It is easy to forget that procedures should have a stated and useful objective. Some organisations put in place many procedures that are not necessary and not used. This is a waste of resources and can restrict the workflow. Questions that should be asked include 'Is the procedure necessary?' 'What is the procedure going to do?'

- **Time** is one of the biggest resources used when developing, implementing and reviewing procedures. Time costs money as staff time is expensive. Therefore when devising procedures it is important to keep in mind the amount of time it will take to develop, implement and follow the procedure.

- **Equipment** costs should also be considered. If a large amount of new equipment will need to be purchased in order to implement a procedure, this will require careful consideration. It may be that existing equipment can be used, but the creator of the procedure will have to look at the existing use of the equipment and whether it will be available and appropriate for the new procedure.

- **Cost:** The cost of a procedure in terms of staffing, equipment and time should not outweigh the benefits of the procedure. For example, if the cost of developing, implementing and maintaining a procedure is estimated to be around £10,000 and the procedure is developed to save the organisation around £2000 per annum, the cost benefit may not be considered sufficient to go ahead with the development.

Legal regulations and restrictions

These must also be researched and reviewed on a regular basis. It is no use having procedures that are in breach of legal regulations. Legal restrictions may also mean that additional procedures have to be developed in order to comply with the law. For example, an organisation may have produced procedures that deal with stock control in the stock room. However, the COSHH regulations (Control of Substances Hazardous to Health), which deal with the safe storage of substances, would mean that certain procedures are required.

Staffing

This is a very important issue as staffing resources must be looked at very carefully, not only in terms of how many staff will be needed to use the new procedure, but also the capabilities of the existing staff. The results of this part of the research will help determine the form the procedures will need to take.

Training is another staffing issue that needs to be taken into account. The time it takes to train staff will have an impact on the cost of the procedure. Even training that takes an hour or so in the office will need to be costed as it will remove staff from their normal work. Training may also need to be formal with staff attending external training such as a health and safety course.

Safety regulations

Specific procedures relating to health and safety, including the fire or emergency evacuation and accident reporting procedure, must be adhered to when devising procedures.

External changes

A change in external circumstances may mean that existing procedures need to be amended or new procedures developed. An example of this would be if an organisation had a procedure that customer orders were to be despatched within 21 working days, but customers felt that this was not acceptable. Customers would put pressure on the organisation to send their goods more quickly. This may result in a change to the procedure to ensure customer satisfaction.

The above factors will strongly influence why and how procedures are devised, developed and maintained. It is important when reviewing procedures to know the impact these factors have. For example, if a procedure was devised because of safety regulations that have now changed, this can be taken into account during the reviewing process.

OVER TO YOU!

Describe the factors you think would have influenced the structure of each of the procedures you chose for the exercise on page 222 at development stage. Present your findings in the form of a short report.

Assessment requirement 1

The first part of the assessment for this unit states that candidates must identify and describe two different office-based procedures, including how each is maintained and reviewed, and the factors that influence the form and content of each. Candidates must address each of the items listed on the candidate information sheet in order to meet assessment objectives 1–3.

The candidate information sheet contains the following instructions.

Choose two procedures with which you are familiar. For each procedure:

▷ identify at least six steps, i.e. single tasks that have to be performed and that together make up a procedural chain

▷ choose a suitable method of presentation, e.g. a narrative or a flow chart, to provide a task-by-task breakdown of each step:
  – indicate the roles of the individuals undertaking tasks at each stage
  – indicate where alternative courses of action are possible and where these may lead
  – suggest any occasions where the procedure may not apply.

▷ describe at least three different ways in which the procedure is maintained (e.g. manuals, schedules and forms, etc.) and reviewed (e.g. system audits, quality circles, etc.)

▷ identify at least two factors that have affected the form and content and explain how.

In short, you must prepare a report or reports that discuss in detail the two procedures you have chosen. All of the information requested above must be included. It is much better to produce two separate reports so that the examiner or moderator can see clearly that you have met all the assessment objectives on both occasions.

The following example covers all the assessment objectives and shows you how a report might look. There is no need to produce masses of supporting evidence. The procedural steps, together with a clear, concise and informative report, should provide sufficient evidence to cover the three assessment objectives.

PROCEDURE FOR DEALING WITH A TELEPHONE CATALOGUE REQUEST

This report will look at the catalogue request procedure for Eagle Group plc, a company that sells stationery direct to the public through its mail order catalogue and website. It also wholesales stationery to small and medium-sized businesses. Customers may call and request a copy of the latest catalogue which is sent free of charge. The company uses the Royal Mail software that is designed to link to the company's database to provide access to the Royal Mail address database. This will enable the user to quickly find the correct address.

There is no requirement for the operator to print the label as this forms part of a separate procedure for batch printing. This takes place twice a day.

Procedural steps
The steps for this procedure are shown on a separate sheet.

Users
The users of this procedure are the call centre operators.

Alternative courses of action

If the customer's postcode does not appear on screen, after checking that it is correct with the customer, the alternative course of action is to take down the details on paper. This is because the Royal Mail software will not allow the operator to enter a postcode that is not correct. The details are then passed to a supervisor who will check with the Royal Mail Address Finder service as it may be a new postcode that has not been entered on to our version of the software.

If the customer is an existing customer, details are checked and so a number of procedural steps are not required.

Customers may also request an up-to-date or additional catalogue when they place an order. A different set of procedures then apply because they are existing customers.

Supporting and maintaining the procedure

The procedure is supported in the following ways:

- induction training for new employees
- inclusion in the procedures manual
- screen prompts by the software
- laminated copies are kept by each monitor.

The procedure is maintained in the following ways:

- the supervisor observes call centre operators on a regular basis to check that the procedure is being followed correctly
- the procedure must be followed correctly in order for the software to accept the new customer record
- updates and additional training during staff training sessions.

The procedure is reviewed in the following ways:

- as part of the systems audit, which takes place on a regular basis
- when new software updates are issued from Royal Mail, the procedure must be reviewed in case of changes or problems. This is carried out by testing.

Factors that influenced the structure of the procedure

- The main factor was that the company decided to purchase the Royal Mail software. This was to ensure that catalogues were sent to the correct address, saving money and making the company more efficient. Royal Mail gives discounts on large mailings that have been sorted by postcode. This is easy to do with the software.
- The second factor was that the company offers a freephone service to customers requesting a catalogue. Using this software keeps the phone calls short and therefore saves money.
- The third factor was the software itself. The instructions for using the software make up the procedure. If the instructions for using the software are not followed correctly, the outcome will not be achieved as the software will not allow changes to the procedure.
- The Data Protection Act was the fourth factor. Organisations must ensure that the data held relating to customers complies with the Data Protection Act. As Eagle Group plc sells mailing lists to other companies, it is important that customers are asked if they would not like to have their name passed to other companies for mailing purposes. Any amendments to the Data Protection Act might affect this procedure.

This review covers all the assessment objectives of assessment requirement 1. The report has been structured so that it is easy to see where the assessment objectives have been met. It is a good idea to use headings for your report as your work will look much more professional.

OVER TO YOU!

Choose a procedure you are familiar with. Write a review, making sure that you fully cover assessment objectives 1–3.

▼ CARRY OUT A REVIEW OF OFFICE-BASED PROCEDURES

For assessment requirement 2 you will need to carry out a review of two different sets of procedures. You have looked at how to carry out the necessary research and consultations, but how would you conduct a thorough review of an existing procedure? Read the following case studies to see how procedures have been reviewed in different situations.

CASE STUDY 4.1

Samir has just started employment as a senior administrative officer at a public relations company. He has a very demanding job and is directly responsible for a team of 15 staff. Samir's duties include ensuring the smooth running of the office on a day-to-day basis. Emma, one of the administrative assistants, has complained to him that there have been lots of problems when trying to do the photocopying.

Given below are the notes that Samir made during his discussion with Emma.

▶ The glass screen of the photocopier is often marked with correction fluid or glue, which causes shadows on copies.

▶ The photocopier is often set to produce large numbers of copies and if staff have not checked this before they use the copier, they make far more copies than necessary.

▶ Staff do not check to see if the photocopier requires more paper or toner. This can be very inconvenient for the next person to use the photocopier, especially if he or she is in a hurry.

▶ If there is a paper jam, some staff just walk away leaving the paper stuck in the machine.

▶ There appears to be a large amount of personal photocopying taking place.

▶ Documents are often left in the photocopier and Emma has recently found some highly confidential information left there for all to see.

Some of these problems are quite serious, particularly those concerning confidential information. Samir knows that one of his tasks is to update the procedures manual for the staff to use. He feels that now is a good time to make a start. First of all he decides that he should make some notes reminding himself of the things that need to be considered before tackling the procedures manual. The notes that he made are shown below.

1 Updating a procedure

▶ The need for the procedure must be clearly identified.

▶ The procedure should have a clear, identifiable outcome.

▶ The procedure should be easy to implement.

▶ The procedure should be easy to follow.

▶ The procedure should comply with the law and health and safety regulations.

▶ Staff should be clear about the purpose of the procedure.

▶ The procedures should not cost too much to develop, implement and follow, otherwise the costs will outweigh the benefits.

▶ Consultation with the users of the procedure must take place.

▶ The procedure should be carefully documented so that this can be referred to when necessary.

▶ The procedure must be easy to monitor and review.

First of all Samir needs to decide whether a procedure for photocopying is really necessary.

2 Identifying the need for a procedure

There is obviously a need for a procedure as problems have been reported. However, Samir draws up a list of pros and cons of implementing a photocopying procedure. Given below is his list.

Pros

▶ There will be a clear, stated outcome.

▶ Staff will be clear about how and for what purpose to use the photocopier.

▶ Work would be more efficient.

▶ There would be less wastage, both in terms of time and resources – such as paper and toner.

▶ The company would save money through time and resources savings.

▶ The procedure would act as a training guide.

▶ The procedure would mean everyone would use the photocopier in the same way – a standardised approach.

▶ Quality standards can be set, reviewed and maintained more easily.

Cons

▶ Staff may not follow the procedure.

▶ Staff may not like the idea of having a stated way of doing things.

▶ Staff may be resistant to change.

▶ The procedure will need to be written, developed, reviewed and maintained, which may be time consuming and therefore costly.

As can be seen, the pros of having a procedure clearly outweigh the cons. Samir moves on to the next stage of the development.

3 Reviewing the existing procedure

Evaluation of relevant documentation

Samir looks at the existing procedure manual. He finds that a photocopying procedure exists, but it is very out of date. It was written for a much older machine that the company no longer has. It does give basic information that is still relevant, but many of the problems encountered by the staff are not covered in the manual. Samir decides that there is little in the existing procedure that can be used and so he will have to start from scratch.

Observation

As there are no recorded procedures to see what the staff should be doing, Samir has to observe the staff at work to see what they are doing. He spends an afternoon in the photocopying room and then draws a diagram of what he discovers (see Figure 4.7).

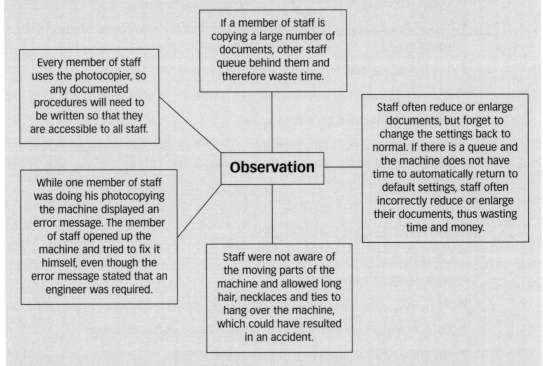

▲ Figure 4.7 Samir's observation of staff photocopying

Samir is now convinced that a procedure needs to be put in place. He knows that everyone uses the photocopier and so calls a staff meeting to discuss the proposed procedure. In the meantime he researches regulations surrounding the use of photocopying equipment.

Health and safety and other legislation

Samir checks for any rules and regulations that affect the use of the photocopier. He finds that although there are recommendations from the manufacturer that the machine should be situated in a well-ventilated room away from direct heat, etc. there are no legal requirements. The safety regulations state that staff must be properly trained to use the equipment and that the storage of toner and paper must be in line with recommendations.

With regard to other legislation, Samir is aware that the Copyright Act restricts the amount of photocopying that can be taken from books, periodicals, journals, etc. As the photocopier is used only for copying information that has been produced in-house, he feels confident that he doesn't have to consider the Copyright Act in preparing his procedure.

Consultation process

Here are Samir's notes from the staff meeting.

▶ Staff are fairly receptive to having set procedures because they feel it will make them more efficient.

▶ The most common problems include:

  – staff not resetting the machine after using it

  – staff not refilling the machine with paper and toner when necessary

  – staff often doing large amounts of non-urgent copying towards the end of the afternoon when others need to copy documents that need to be posted.

▶ Staff are clearly unaware of the implications of health and safety.

▶ Staff are using the photocopier for their own personal use.

▶ The glass needs to be cleaned on a regular basis.

Samir has now completed his review of the procedure, the next thing he must do is evaluate the effectiveness of the existing procedure.

CASE STUDY 4.2

Melinda and Joshua work as editors at a company that publishes fiction books. They receive a large number of unsolicited manuscripts each week. Although they are unsolicited, the company has a policy stating that these will be read by an editor and a decision made as to whether they could be published, within three months of receipt.

There is a procedure in place to ensure that the manuscripts are not forgotten; however, it does not seem to be working properly and there are a large number of manuscripts piled up in the office. The new administrator, Anita, is responsible for ensuring that the correct procedure is followed so that the manuscripts are dealt with efficiently.

Melinda feels that something must be done about these outstanding manuscripts. She decides to conduct a review of the procedure.

Reviewing the documentation

The procedure for receiving unsolicited manuscripts is written and contained in the procedures manual. Anita has her own manual, which contains the procedures that are relevant to her work. Melinda reads through this documentation, which takes the form of a flowchart (see Figure 4.8 on page 242).

Consultation

Melinda discusses with Anita the problems that have been occurring with unsolicited manuscripts. Anita says that she didn't know what to do with the manuscripts after the second reading as the instructions were not clear. She realises she should have asked for help, but hasn't found the time. The previous administrator knew what to do and so didn't refer to the procedures. From this, Melinda is clear that the problem lies in the design of the procedure and that it needs to be updated.

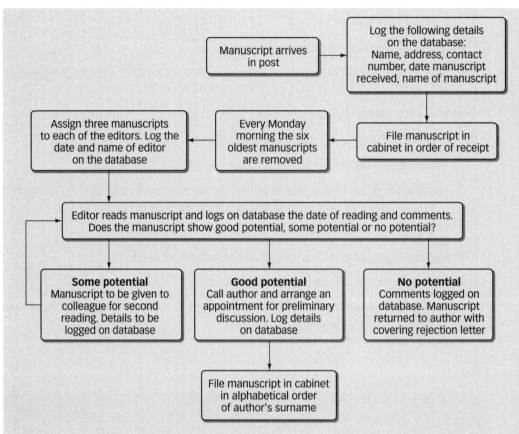

▲ Figure 4.8 Procedure flowchart

Melinda also discusses the procedure with Joshua. He feels that the second reading of a manuscript should take priority over reading new manuscripts; currently they are passed on as extra manuscripts in addition to the three new ones each week. Joshua suggests that if this idea was adopted, it would speed up the process of getting these back to the authors.

Health and safety and other legislation

Melinda feels that the way the paper manuscripts are piled around the office and post room is a health and safety hazard. They should be kept securely in fireproof cabinets. The procedure states that the manuscripts should be filed.

The Data Protection Act must be considered as the authors' personal details are being kept on the organisation's database. Melinda makes a note to read up on the Act to see if there is anything they should be doing to ensure that they comply with the stipulated rules.

OVER TO YOU!

In a small group of three or four, choose a procedure that you are familiar with. Carry out a review of the procedure using the methods given above. Present your findings to the rest of your class.

It is important to evaluate existing procedures. This means that you should consider your findings from the research you have undertaken. This should show you where things are going wrong or working well. From this you will be able to do the following:

▷ identify the strengths of the procedures

▷ understand the difference between weaknesses and omissions

▷ identify any weaknesses or omissions

▷ find the source of weaknesses and omissions

▷ identify the consequences of the weaknesses or omissions.

Strengths of a procedure

There could be a number of strengths within a procedure, even one that doesn't work properly. Some strengths are shown in Table 4.2.

Table 4.2 Examples of strengths within a procedure

Cost	Time	Quality	Training
The procedure saves the organisation money.	The procedure saves the organisation time.	The procedure always produces work of a stated quality.	The procedure acts as a training guide.

Weaknesses of a procedure

The weaknesses of a procedure could include those shown in Table 4.3.

Table 4.3 Examples of weaknesses within a procedure

Cost	Time	Quality	Training
The procedure costs the organisation more money than it saves.	The procedure costs the organisation more time than it saves.	The procedure does not produce work of a stated quality.	The procedure fails to act as a training guide; it assumes that the user is already experienced in some aspects of the work.

Omissions in a procedure

Omissions in procedures can cause real problems. These could be missing steps or explanations. A missing step means the procedure may not work properly. It may be that the users of the procedure are so familiar with the way in which it works that they do not notice the missing step. However, when new staff are using the procedure they will encounter problems.

If the procedure requires the user to make decisions, it is important that all possible decisions are also covered. This can make the procedure very complicated. However, if this information is not present, the procedure will not work effectively.

Another area where omissions can occur is if the unexpected happens. For example, if you were following a procedure for using the photocopier and the paper jams in the machine, this may not be covered by the procedure. This would result in the user having to go and find out how to clear the paper jam, wasting time and effort. Including paper jams in the general photocopying procedure is unnecessary and would make the procedure more complicated than it needs to be. A better way to cover this problem would be to write into the main procedure the name and whereabouts of a separate secondary procedure that has been devised to deal with the problem.

Sources of weaknesses and omissions

The source of the weakness could be one or more of the following:

▶ the design of the procedure; it could be overcomplicated for the task

▶ ambiguous or confusing instructions

▶ incorrect assumption of user's skills and knowledge.

Consequences of omissions and weaknesses in procedures

These could include any of the following:

▶ wasted time and money

▶ poor or variable quality outcome

▶ health and safety issues that could result in injury to staff, damage to equipment, etc.

▶ breaking the law

▶ damaging the organisation's reputation.

Some of these sound rather dramatic, but they are all possible consequences of omissions and weaknesses in procedures. They must be taken into account when reviewing procedures as, for example, it would easily be possible to have a procedure that works well, but in fact breaks employment law. This would obviously need to be put right.

OVER TO YOU!

From the review you undertook in the exercise on page 242, use your findings to evaluate the effectiveness of the procedure. Present your findings to the rest of your class.

You have already seen how Samir carried out a review of the photocopying procedure. He must now evaluate the effectiveness of the existing procedure.

It is easy for him to evaluate the existing procedure because the written procedure contains instructions that are not applicable to the new photocopier. However, even if the procedure gave the correct instructions for the photocopier, there are significant omissions and these include:

▶ there are no instructions for refilling the machine with paper and/or toner

▶ there are no instructions for resetting the machine after it has been used with non-standard settings

▶ there are no instructions for dealing with paper jams

▶ there is no method for recording faults with the machine

▶ staff are not sufficiently trained to use the equipment

▶ health and safety is being compromised as staff are endangering themselves and others in both the way they use the equipment and by trying to fix faults.

The consequences of these omissions from the procedure are obvious; they are the problems that staff have been experiencing. There may also be health and safety consequences; a member of staff could easily suffer an injury if current working practices are allowed to continue.

Melinda now moves on to evaluating the existing procedure for dealing with unsolicited manuscripts. She has read through the documentation and has spoken to Anita. After looking at the procedure, Melinda feels that the flowchart gives a reasonable set of instructions for it, but she also sees that there are a few weaknesses. These are as follows.

1 The second step states the details need to be logged into the database. However, there is no instruction to set up a new record. A minor point, but one that could be confusing to new staff.

2 The third step does not tell the member of staff which cabinet must be used to house the manuscripts.

3 The fourth step does not tell you where to log the date and name of editor; this should be in the manuscript's record.

4 The fifth step should also state where the information is to be logged; again this should be the manuscript's record.

5 The instruction for manuscripts that show some potential states that the manuscript should then be given a second reading. After it has had the second reading there is no clear instruction for what to do next. This would result in the manuscript getting stuck in a loop.

6 If the manuscript shows good potential, the author is contacted and the manuscript filed. The instructions do not state where the manuscript is filed; is it the same cabinet as when they are received?

7 The procedure states that both Melinda and Joshua are to be given three new manuscripts each week to review. This is unrealistic as they have not got time to consider three unsolicited books during the working week.

8 The customer charter states that manuscripts will be returned within three months of receipt. The current backlog of manuscripts means it will be nearer six months before return. This will cause the organisation problems as the customer charter is part of the total quality management system.

With the exception of problems 5, 7 and 8, these are minor problems that can easily be sorted out by asking a member of staff with some experience. However, the design of the procedure is in fact quite poor. The procedure assumes that the user is already familiar with the system in that they will automatically know which cabinet to use, that they are familiar with the database and that they will know how to proceed after a manuscript has had a second reading.

It is easy when developing procedures to leave out steps that seem to the writer to be obvious. It should be remembered that the one of the reasons for developing procedures is to provide instructions for completing a task; these steps will not be obvious to people without any experience.

Melinda's conclusion is that the procedure needs to be amended in order to eliminate the weaknesses. Joshua's idea of the second reading of manuscripts taking priority is a good one and should be incorporated into the procedure. There should also be some form of monitoring included. This will allow the staff to see not only how the procedure is working, but also the current status of unsolicited manuscripts.

▼ SUGGEST IMPROVEMENTS TO PROCEDURES AND DESIGN NEW PROCEDURES

Once the review and evaluation have been completed it should be quite clear where improvements are necessary. In some instances completely new procedures will be required. Whatever is the case, you will need to do the following:

▶ identify reasons why the improvements or new procedures need to be devised

▶ ensure that the improvements or new procedures are fit for the purpose

▶ consider the various factors involved in the design or amendment of the procedure.

If there are serious weaknesses or omissions in the procedure you are reviewing then it will be easy to identify reasons why new or amendment procedures should be devised. Remember though that there may be other reasons and these could include legal or organisational factors, changes to technology or equipment or external factors. These should be clear from your research.

Whether you make amendments to an existing procedure or devise a new procedure altogether, it is important that you ensure they are fit for their purpose. The research you undertook when reviewing the procedure will be useful here as you will need to consider issues such as legislation, regulations, company policy, the user and the place for the procedure within the workplace. Your research will give you a good idea of what is required and what must be considered.

You have looked at factors that influence the design of procedures on pages 234–235. Some of these may influence the amendment of existing procedures. You will need to take these into account and see what impact they or any other external factors will have on the design or amendment of the procedure.

Samir has decided that a new procedure needs to be devised for staff using the photocopier. He has identified a number of reasons for his conclusion. These are:

▶ staff are experiencing problems when using the photocopier

▶ health and safety of the staff is being compromised

▶ time and money are being wasted by inefficient working practices.

Samir needs to separate out from his notes and observations the elements that should be incorporated into the new procedures and those that need addressing in other ways.

Here is his conclusion.

Procedures need to be written for the following:

▶ general use of the machine, including leaving the machine as you find it

▶ refilling the machine with paper and toner

▶ how to deal with a paper jam

▶ what to do when the machine states there is a fault.

Issues that need to be addressed include the following:

▶ health and safety training on how to use the equipment safely

▶ use of the photocopier for personal documents

▶ prioritising the use of the photocopier so that staff can work more efficiently and effectively

▶ regular servicing of the machine.

▲ Figure 4.9 Efficiency can be affected when procedures are not in place

The factors that will influence the design of the new procedure are as follows:

▶ health and safety legislation

▶ the time involved in designing, implementing and training. As Samir has to review all the current procedures, he does not have much time to spend on this work.

Melinda has decided that the existing procedure needs to be amended so that the system for dealing with unsolicited manuscripts runs smoothly. She has identified the following reasons for doing so:

▶ the procedure is not working correctly

▶ Anita has not been given all the necessary information to use the procedure effectively

▶ the number of unsolicited manuscripts in the office is causing problems

▶ the organisation is not meeting its customer charter because the unsolicited manuscripts are being kept longer than stated.

▲ Figure 4.10 Efficiency can be affected when procedures are out of date

The factors that will influence the amendments are:

▶ the knowledge and ability level of the user

▶ the findings of Melinda's research on the Data Protection Act

▶ the estimated number of manuscripts received by the organisation each week

▶ the number of manuscripts that it is possible to read during each week

▶ the organisation's customer charter.

The proposed amendments are:

▶ to redraft the procedures assuming the user has no previous knowledge of the system

▶ to make the instructions for dealing with a manuscript after its second reading much clearer

▶ to take into account the Data Protection Act when storing personal details of authors

▶ to change the customer charter so that the timescale for dealing with manuscripts is more realistic

▶ to add a monitoring process to the procedure so that each week the number of manuscripts waiting for first reading is reported to the commissioning team and manuscripts that have been held on file because they show some potential are dealt with promptly.

▼ IDENTIFY WAYS OF IMPLEMENTING NEW OR REVISED PROCEDURES

Once the new or amended procedures have been designed, they have to be implemented. With a new piece of equipment, the implementation of the procedure is quite straightforward; you have to follow the new procedure in order to use the equipment. However, with more complex procedures there must be a plan of implementation in order for the change to be made effectively and efficiently.

You will need to identify the ways in which the amendments or new procedures can be implemented. These might include:

▶ writing the documentation

▶ delivering training

▶ updating training and procedural manuals

▶ consulting staff.

It is a good idea to write a plan of implementation as this will ensure you do not forget anything and you can ensure that progress is made at a reasonable rate. When you are drawing up your plan of implementation you will need to take into account the factors described below.

Timescale

Allow yourself plenty of time to implement your new or revised procedure. This is because it almost always takes longer than you imagine. There are many reasons why your plan will be delayed and these could include:

▶ your colleagues are busy and it is difficult to obtain feedback, arrange training sessions, etc.

▶ you will probably have to seek approval from your line manager or other senior staff

▶ writing new documentation is time consuming

▶ you will have other work that needs to be completed.

Communication

In order to implement the new or revised procedure successfully, you will have to communicate the changes to others. This not only takes time, but needs to be planned to ensure that it is effective. In order to communicate the changes effectively you should ensure that you have completed or planned for the following:

▶ preparing all necessary documentation

▶ seeking and obtaining approval from your line manager

▶ preparing any required training materials

▶ planning any in-house training or booking external trainers.

Drawing up a plan

It is much easier if you draw up a schedule of implementation. This will ensure that you remain on track and that all elements have been covered. You will also be able to see if your timescale is realistic and make amendments if necessary.

CASE STUDY 4.1

Samir is realistic about the amount of time he has to spend on writing the new photocopying procedure. He decides to draft a plan that allows plenty of time for implementation. He feels that if he finds he has any spare time, he can always bring forward some of the dates. Table 4.4 shows a copy of his draft plan for implementation.

Table 4.4 Implementation plan

Photocopying procedure

Action	Timescale	Comments	Completed (date and sign)
Draft new instructions for using the machine	1 week		
Test instructions are correct	2 days	Work through the instructions I have written.	
Give instructions to colleagues for trialling	2 days	Ask four or five people to trial my instructions.	
Obtain feedback and collate results	1 week		
Make amendments	3 days		
Organise training session	1 week	Arrange separate health and safety training. Include other issues such as wasting time and personal photocopying in session.	
Make any amendments after training	2 days		
Prepare final documentation	1 week	Prepare laminated sheet for wall, paper copies for each member of staff.	
Issue documentation	2 days	Prepare a checklist for staff to sign to confirm receipt.	
Log procedure in manual	1 day		

At first glance it would appear that Samir has allocated far too much time for writing the new procedure, but he has been very realistic. The various activities will not actually take 1 whole day or 1 week to complete, but he has written the schedule bearing in mind his other work commitments. He has also been realistic about the amount of time it will take to organise and prepare a training session.

Melinda decides that because the procedure is not working satisfactorily and the customer charter is not being adhered to, she will make the revision a priority. She draws up the following plan of implementation.

Table 4.5 Implementation plan

Procedure for dealing with unsolicited manuscripts

Action	Timescale	Comments	Completed (date and sign)
Consult senior mangement regarding change to customer charter	1 week	If the customer charter cannot be changed, we will have to look at our general work commitments to see where other changes can be made to ensure manuscripts are read on time.	
Research our responsibilities regarding the Data Protection Act	1 week	The results may have an impact on the procedure.	
Amend new procedures	1 day	Ensure that all steps are now clear.	
Check new procedure	1 day	Ask Joshua to read the new procedure to ensure that it is clear and nothing has been forgotten.	
Check current state of manuscripts	1 day	Go through all the manuscripts in the office and log on database if necessary. Place in relevant filing cabinets so that the work is correctly logged and filed.	
Training	Half a day	Work through the procedure on Monday morning with Anita to ensure she understands it and that it works. Joshua must also be present.	
Amend documentation	Half a day	If there are any problems with the training, I may need to amend the documentation.	
Issue documentation	Half a day	Anita.	
Log procedure in procedure manual	Half a day		

Melinda has been more ambitious in her plan of implementation. During the first week, while she waits for a reply from the senior management team, she will also be undertaking her research on the Data Protection Act. Once she knows whether the timescales can be amended she will be able to complete her implementation in just one week.

OVER TO YOU!

Plan the implementation of the procedure you revised in the exercise on page 249.

▼ IDENTIFY ISSUES OF COST AND RESOURCE MANAGEMENT

There are always costs involved in reviewing and amending procedures, even if it is just staff time. However, for some procedures the cost of amending and reviewing them can run into many thousands of pounds. For example, if an organisation decided to seek approval for the Investors in People award, the amount of staff time in setting, reviewing and presenting the procedures would cost a great deal.

Remember, every hour spent by a member of staff working on reviewing a procedure costs the organisation the sum of their hourly wage plus the employer's payment towards National Insurance contributions, their pension plan and any other benefits. It must be pointed out that at this level you would not be expected to research the salary details of every member of staff who will be using the procedure or assisting with its development. However, you need to remember that staff time is not in fact free.

If the cost of developing, supporting, maintaining and reviewing a procedure is higher than the benefits it produces, it may not be worth the expense. Sometimes the procedure, particularly if it relates to health and safety, must be implemented no matter what the final cost.

Given below is a list of costs that must be considered:

▶ staff time

▶ training staff (includes staff time, room hire, refreshments, any external trainers, hire of equipment, etc.)

▶ equipment; a new procedure may require additional or more up-to-date equipment

▶ stationery

▶ time and resources required for maintaining and monitoring the procedure.

Once the cost of the work has been estimated, it will be necessary to obtain approval from a senior member of staff before the work can go ahead.

CASE STUDY 4.1

Samir needs to look at the cost of developing new photocopying procedures. Here is his list of estimated costs:

Staff time (approximately 40 hours, to include in-house training)	£420
Health and safety training event	£547
Resources from general stationery budget	£10
Total	£977

This may seem like a large sum of money just to write some photocopying instructions. However, the main cost in this estimate is the health and safety training. This is an essential requirement for companies and will cover other topics, not just using equipment. This cost will save the company money in the long term as the amount of staff time taken to instruct new members of staff will be reduced because there will be paper based instructions for them to work through.

CASE STUDY 4.2

The cost element of amending the procedure for unsolicited manuscripts cannot really be determined until Melinda has received an answer regarding the change to the customer charter. If the senior management decides to change the customer charter, the cost could be considerable, especially if the company's literature needs to be reprinted. However, if this is not the case, the cost of revising and implementing the procedure will be very small.

Staff time (20 hours)	£240
Stationery and resources (including new filing cabinet)	£200
On-going training and support (20 hours per annum)	£240
Total	£680

OVER TO YOU!

Work out the cost of revising and monitoring the procedure you used for the exercise on page 252.

▼ IDENTIFY TRAINING AND DEVELOPMENT REQUIREMENTS

It is essential that training and development are carefully considered when amending or devising procedures. There is no point in putting together a procedure if no one knows how to use it. You will need to consider the following:

▶ the current skills of the users

▶ the skills required to use the procedure

- training facilities available in house
- any requirement for external training
- ongoing training for the procedure
- the cost of the training.

You may simply need to document the procedure and then show staff how to work through the instructions. In the case of using equipment a demonstration would be useful. More complex procedures will require a higher level of training and may involve staff attending external training courses. For example, a member of staff who has responsibility for first aid would need to attend a specialist training course run by professionals.

Ongoing training and support

As well as the initial training, it is important to consider on-going training for the procedure. The requirement for this will depend on one or more of the following circumstances:

- if more staff are asked to use the procedure
- if any amendments are made to the procedure
- as part of staff development
- if there are any changes to regulations.

Delivering the training

Once you have determined the training requirements you will need to assess who can deliver the training to the staff. The human resources department should be able to help with finding a suitable trainer, whether in-house or externally. However, if you have to research this yourself, you could explore the following possibilities:

- local college or training provider
- the Internet to find names of specialist training providers
- business consultants
- trade organisations
- local Business Enterprise Agency.

Training costs

The cost of the training is an important consideration. If you require any external training, you will have to agree a budget with your superior. He or she will expect you to put together a detailed proposal including a breakdown of all cost elements. These may include:

- room hire
- refreshments
- delegate materials
- trainer fees
- staff expenses
- hire of any necessary equipment.

Devising a training plan

It is important to plan the training carefully so as to ensure the staff receive maximum benefit from the training. If staff are to attend an external course, it is simple – they must attend on the date of the course at the designated time. However, if you are planning an in-house session you will need to consider the following.

▶ **Who will attend?** How many staff will need to attend the training event? Obviously this must be considered first of all so that you can work out the size of the venue required, etc.

▶ **When it will take place?** Some organisations have time set aside each week for staff training. If your organisation does not, you will need to choose a time when staff are most receptive to training.

▶ **How many sessions will be required?** Hopefully you will be able to train staff during one session, but time constrictions or the number of staff that require training may mean that the training has to take place over a period of time.

▶ **Where it will take place?** Is there a suitable room at the workplace to undertake training? If there is, do not forget to book it. If there isn't, you will need to find a suitable venue. This might be at a local hotel or conference centre.

▶ **What equipment and materials will be required?** If you are planning to produce a training manual or similar, you will need to ensure that you have sufficient supplies of resources in stock. You will also need to ensure that you give yourself plenty of time to prepare the training materials.

▶ **How will you keep staff informed?** Obviously you must let staff know when and where the training event is being held. It is always a good idea to ask staff to confirm their attendance so that you are sure that they are aware of the course.

▶ **Be prepared for absences.** If staff cannot make your training event, how will you ensure that they receive the training? You will need to factor this into your plan.

CASE STUDY 4.1

Samir has decided that a demonstration of how to use the photocopier will be the most appropriate method of training. However, he also decides that as a separate issue, he should organise some health and safety training for his staff.

After some consideration he decides that a short 15-minute training session on the use of the photocopier will be all that is needed. He will demonstrate how to use the equipment and will go through the written procedures to ensure that staff have understood what is required. In addition, he will also take the opportunity to discuss wasting time waiting for the photocopier to be free and personal photocopying.

In order to minimise the disruption to the working day, he thinks it would be a good idea to hold these sessions at 2 pm and have a maximum of three staff attending. The sessions will take place every day for one week. Samir does not have to worry too much if a member of staff is absent. As the session is very short, he can easily train on a one-to-one basis if necessary.

The health and safety training is more complex. Samir feels that a half-day session on general health and safety in the workplace would be a good idea for all staff. In order to keep the office running, there will need to be two half-day sessions. He decides to employ an external trainer for this event. It is agreed with the trainer that the sessions will be held a month apart to ensure that all staff can attend.

Samir puts together a training proposal, including a cost analysis, and submits it to his line manager for approval. The training proposal is shown in Figure 4.11.

Training proposal

Aim

To ensure that staff are fully trained in health and safety in the workplace, to include:

▶ safe use of equipment

▶ awareness of hazards and reporting procedures

▶ accident reporting

▶ emergency procedures

▶ awareness of display screen regulations.

Staff involved

15 administration staff and Samir Rachid, Administration Manager.

Event details

Two half-day sessions for eight staff to be held in the conference room on 10 November and 10 December. The sessions will start at 9.30 am and finish at approximately 12.30 pm. Refreshments will be provided at 11 am. The trainer will be Joanna Bruce from Edmonds Ltd, a specialist health and safety training agency.

Cost

Trainer's fees	£180 × 2	£360
Delegate packs (provided by trainer)	£10 × 16	£160
Refreshments (coffee and biscuits)	£1.50 × 18	£ 27
	Total	£547

Equipment

The trainer has requested the following to be made available:

▶ flip chart

▶ general stationery such as pens and paper

▶ computerised presentation equipment

▶ video player and television screen.

All equipment is available in house at no extra expense.

Comments

It is felt that the administration staff would benefit from attending a health and safety course as part of their on-going staff development. I have also witnessed some poor working practices by staff in this department and the proposed content of these sessions would address this issue.

Dated   *12th November*   Signed   *Samir Rachid*

▲ Figure 4.11 Samir's training proposal

Samir receives approval from his line manager and he confirms the training events with Joanna Bruce from Edmonds Ltd. An email is sent to each member of staff requesting their availability for the two planned sessions. Once these have been received, Samir will allocate places for the staff. He will provide written confirmation to staff so that they are clear as to the date, time, venue and duration of the training.

He then draws up a training plan for the photocopying sessions (see Table 4.6).

Table 4.6 Samir's training plan

Date	Time	Staff attending	Comments
27 October	2 pm	Greg, Jake and Lorinda	
28 October	2 pm	Cathy, Emma and Marc	
29 October	2 pm	Ewan, Jasminder and Winston	
30 October	2 pm	Alison, Tom and Sarah	
31 October	2 pm	Vicky, Declan and Angus	

This will be emailed to each member of staff and a notice placed on the board. As all the staff work in the same office, if someone forgets they are easily contactable.

OVER TO YOU!

Draw up a training schedule for the procedure you used in the exercise on page 249.

The training requirements for the new procedure are quite basic. Melinda will need to spend an hour or so going through the procedure with Joshua and Anita. They will be able to discuss any issues that arise. Although there is no need for a formal training proposal to be written, they will need to agree a time and be able to keep to it.

The problem when arranging informal training, particularly when several people are involved is that the commitment to attending is often poor. It is important in this case to book a specific time and give an indication of how long you think the session will last. It is a good idea to give this information in a written format; it makes it appear more formal and others are less likely to forget.

Melinda decides to write a memo to Joshua and Anita (see Figure 4.12).

Memorandum

To:	Joshua and Anita
From:	Melinda
Date:	25 June

Unsolicited manuscript procedure

I have now written the amendments to the procedure and would like to hold a training session to discuss these with you.

We will need to spend approximately 1 hour on this and I suggest we meet at 10 am on Tuesday, 1 July in my office.

Please let me know if this is inconvenient. A copy of the proposed procedure is attached for your reference.

▲ Figure 4.12 Melinda's memo

▼ IDENTIFY POSSIBLE DIFFICULTIES WITH NEW OR REVISED PROCEDURES

When you are revising a procedure or developing new ones, it can be difficult to identify possible problems. However, you should try to think about what might go wrong as you work through your revisions.

The research you undertake should give you some ideas as to where there may be problems. These may include:

▷ staff being resistant to change

▷ cost factors

▷ timescales

▷ omissions.

Staff

The way in which you undertake your review, present your findings and plan the implementation of changes or new procedures will have an impact on how smoothly the process will run. Remember that you are dealing with the way in which your colleagues work and few people enjoy being criticised.

Some members of staff may not take kindly to having their working practices changed. They may have felt comfortable with the way in which they have been doing something and feel that the revision is 'change for change's sake'. People often feel threatened by change and will need careful handling if they are to accept your recommendations and work with you to improve their working practices.

If you are looking at procedures that are used by more senior members of staff, you will have to tread very carefully indeed. If, during your research you find that they are not using the procedure properly or do not understand what is expected of them, report this very tactfully. Unit 2 explains in detail how to work with colleagues effectively.

Cost factors

Your cost estimates should have shown you whether the new procedure or amendments are feasible. However, it may be that you underestimate the time the process takes or you may encounter other problems along the way, which involve more time and money. This is why it is important to research and plan as thoroughly as possible before drawing up your recommendations.

If you find as you work though the revision process that the costs are spiralling, you should report this to a senior member of staff as soon as possible. You will need to explain why the costs have risen and be able to justify the extra cost. It is not acceptable to tell your line manager that the costs have risen because you forgot something or that you didn't know how expensive certain elements would be.

Even the most thorough plans can go wrong and over-running the timescale is one of the most common errors people make. Think how often you get this wrong in other areas of your life. Sometimes, the problem you have with keeping to your timescale is unavoidable. You may be given extra, urgent work to complete or people do not respond to your questionnaires as quickly as you thought.

In order to overcome this problem, it is far better to be over-generous in your time planning when you are drawing up your implementation plan. It looks far more professional to complete the revision of the procedure two weeks early than it does to do so two weeks late.

Omissions

We all forget things from time to time and if you are working on a procedure that you are not completely familiar with, it is easy to leave out steps or get them wrong. This is why it is very important that you should trial your revisions or new procedure with people who have some experience of it. Therefore, you should also allow for adjustments in your implementation plan. Again, it is more professional to plan for adjustments than to have to admit that you haven't got things right and go back over something.

CASE STUDY 4.1

Samir is confident that his implementation plan is realistic and achievable. He thinks he has covered everything that needs to be done and as he is responding to staff complaints regarding the procedure, he is sure that staff will act positively towards the changes.

However, he is keeping in mind that there may be difficulties with the new procedure. Given below are his two main concerns.

▶ Staff may not follow procedures for changing toner and refilling the machine with paper if they are short of time.

▶ Staff may not remember to report faults in the book that will be provided.

These are very minor concerns and with on-going support should be eliminated. These areas can also be highlighted during the initial training sessions.

CASE STUDY 4.2

Melinda is worried that if the senior management will not agree to changing the customer charter, the procedure will not work correctly after a very short period of time. This is because the number of unsolicited manuscripts received each week seems to be increasing all the time. However, dealing with this problem is not within the scope of Melinda's authority. All she can do is report problems to senior management as and when they happen. The design of a reporting step in the procedure will enable her to report problems as soon as they occur.

OVER TO YOU!

Identify any possible problem areas you may have with the procedure you revised in the exercise on page 257. If you cannot find any, you should justify this.

Assessment requirement 2

The second part of the assessment for this unit states that candidates must, for either of the two procedures discussed in assessment requirement 1 or for two other procedures with which he or she is familiar, write a report reviewing those procedures.

The candidate information sheet contains the following instructions.

You must include in your report the following items of information.

▶ A description of the research carried out: the research methods, the reasons for using them, any groups or individuals consulted, key documents consulted.

▶ The findings of your review: weaknesses/omissions in procedures, consequences/implications of omissions/weaknesses, reasons for each weakness/omission (you must reference your findings back to your methods of research, i.e. show that your findings have been guided by the research).

- Suggestions for improvements to existing procedures and/or suggestions for new procedures. For each weakness/omission, you must suggest at least one improvement to a procedure/new procedure. You must also include the rationale behind the suggestion (this must be suggested from your consultation) and any general issues arising from your suggestions (obstacles to change).

- Ways of implementing each improved/new procedure. This must include a plan of implementation for each improvement/new procedure (which must take into account issues of cost, physical resource management, professional development/support of staff, timescales and the communication of plans to relevant people at appropriate times).

- Issues arising relating to additional training/support requirements. This must include a description of the way in which training/support requirements will be met and dealt with.

- The anticipated difficulties of introduction of the improved/new procedures (if candidates do not anticipate difficulties, they should state this and give reasons).

You will need to carry out a piece of research on a procedure used in your college or workplace. Any weaknesses or omissions must be identified and relate to your research. You should then be able to suggest improvements to the procedure or design a new procedure based on the findings of your research. A plan of implementation will need to be devised and the issues of costs, training and resourcing must be taken into account. A report detailing all of the items given above must be produced for each procedure. It is much better if you produce two separate reports.

The following example covers all the assessment objectives and shows you how your report should look.

RECRUITMENT PROCEDURE: CARLTON CARE HOMES LTD

1 Background

Carlton Care Homes Ltd is a company that owns six residential care homes for the elderly in the south west of the UK. The company has an administration office in Exeter, which deals with all the general administration, finance and recruitment for the organisation. The organisation provides a high level of care for the residents and has been approved for the IiP award.

The human resources department deals with the recruitment of staff throughout the care homes and at head office. When a new member of staff is required, a request is made by the manager of the home and the recruitment procedure is then followed.

2 Research
The need for a recruitment procedure

As Carlton Care Homes employs a large number of staff throughout the organisation, it was considered essential that a procedure was put in place to standardise the recruitment process. The very nature of the company means that there is a high turnover of staff and the procedure ensures that the progress of recruitment for each vacancy is easily tracked.

The recruitment procedure is included in the training manual issued to new members of staff in the human resources department.

Written procedure

In order to find out exactly how the procedure works, the written procedure was read (it is logged in the procedure manual). It consists of a flowchart setting out all the steps and two sets of written instructions. One set gives the steps to be completed by the manager, the other gives the steps to be completed by the HR function. A copy of this procedure and the written instructions can be found in Appendix A.

Interview: Mrs Sutton, human resources manager

An interview was held with Mrs Sutton, the human resources manager of the company. A transcript of the interview can be found in Appendix B.

Questionnaire

A questionnaire was sent to all managers of the organisation. This included both the managers at head office and the care homes. A copy of the questionnaire can be found in Appendix C.

Legislation

Current legislation that relates to staff recruitment was also researched and this included the following:

▶ Equal Pay Act

▶ Sex Discrimination Act

▶ Race Relations Act

▶ Disability Discrimination Act

▶ Employment Act.

3 The effectiveness of the procedure

The findings of the research proved interesting. The human resources manager felt that procedure worked well and that there were no problems with it. Her answers indicated that the time from the request for a new member of staff being made to the new recruit starting work was acceptable.

Mrs Sutton felt that the outcome of the procedure was always successful. It was easy to track the progress at any time and the procedure was extremely useful as a training guide. Mrs Sutton said she felt that it would be unnecessary to amend the procedure as there was nothing wrong with it.

The views of the managers, both at head office and in the care homes, were very different. From the results of the questionnaire, it can be seen that 95 per cent of all managers felt that the amount of time needed to recruit a member of staff was far too long (see Appendix D). The process can take as long as 4–6 weeks and this is unacceptable when a replacement member of staff is urgently required. This is particularly the case for domestic staff, i.e. cleaners and kitchen assistants.

More than 50 per cent of the managers felt that one of the problems with the procedure was that references were not taken up until the applicant had been selected and had sent back a letter of acceptance. The new member of staff cannot start work until satisfactory references have been received. It can sometimes take several weeks for this activity to be completed.

Over 75 per cent of managers felt that they should be allowed to recruit domestic staff without any involvement from head office. They stated that word of mouth was one of the most effective ways of finding suitable domestic staff. This was not accepted by head office. Quite often existing domestic staff were asked to work double shifts in order to ensure a high level of cleanliness in the residential homes.

The written procedure is divided into two parts. Part one is used by the manager requesting the new member of staff. The second part is followed by the human resources staff. The written procedure appears to be clear and easy to follow. There are only a few decisions to be made and these relate to the type of staff being employed. For example, if the vacancy is for a care worker, the advertisement is checked against a particular set of guidelines. This is because it is acceptable for organisations to advertise specifically for male or female staff in these circumstances.

Training for using the procedure is effective. New members of staff in the human resources department are given the written instructions as part of their training manual. On the first occasion that they use the procedure, they are shadowed by an experienced member of staff who goes through the procedure with them and checks their work at each stage. On the second occasion, they are allowed to work by themselves, but their work is checked at each stage. If they have followed the procedure successfully, they are then able to work unsupervised.

Managers receive training on the recruitment procedure as part of their induction programme. They also have a copy of the written procedure. As their input is relatively small, they all felt confident that they were able to use and understand the procedure correctly.

The research conducted on employment legislation showed that the procedure ensures the recruitment process is in line with current regulations. The procedure also meets the standard stated by the company.

The monitoring of the procedure appears to have been satisfactory.

4 Strengths and weaknesses of the procedure

The procedure appears to have the following strengths:

- it is easy to follow
- it provides a standardised approach
- it is a useful training guide
- it produces a successful outcome.

The weaknesses found with the procedure are:

- the length of time it takes to recruit staff
- the fact that references are not requested until the selection process has been completed
- it does not take into account the high turnover of domestic staff and the need to replace them quickly
- if the successful applicant turns down the job offer, there are no instructions on how to proceed.

The problem areas are generally caused by the procedure's failure to respond quickly when there are staff shortages.

5 Consequences of the weaknesses found in the recruitment procedure

The consequences of the weaknesses are that there are often staff shortages in the various care homes. This costs the organisation money in terms of having to pay existing staff overtime rates in order to have the necessary work completed. It also causes problems in that existing staff are not always willing to work extra hours, particularly during weekends and holiday periods. This could have a far-reaching consequences if the homes are not providing the correct standard of hygiene and cleanliness.

At head office, the consequences are less dramatic, but include staff being overworked, which results in a higher turnover of staff than might otherwise be expected.

From the research undertaken, it would appear that the following amendments could be made to the procedure, which would allow a quicker response to filling staff vacancies.

- The job specification should be held by managers. When they need to recruit a new member of staff they could send an updated copy of the job specification with their request. This would allow human resources to deal with the request as soon as it is received.
- References should be taken up when the shortlist for interview is made. This would have three benefits:
  - the references should be received by the interview date, providing extra information for the interviewing panel
  - time would be saved, thus allowing the successful applicant to start work earlier
  - if a reference is not received or is not particularly good, time would be saved as the following up could be done within a shorter timescale.
- The managers of the care homes should be allowed to request that human resources deal with an application as a priority if the vacancy is likely to cause a staffing problem.
- For domestic staff, local advertising such as in newsagents and job centres should be considered.

These improvements would reduce the time it takes to complete this procedure, but would also allow human resources to remain in control of the recruitment process. This is important as company policy does not allow managers to recruit their own staff. This means that the procedure cannot be amended to allow staff to be recruited by managers.

There should also be an amendment to the procedure so that if a successful applicant refuses the position, the procedure continues.

The factors to consider when making these improvements are:

- employment legislation; the procedure must comply with employment legislation
- company policy; the amendments to the procedure must comply with company policy.

It should be relatively easy to implement the amendments to the procedure. This will take place by:

- rewriting the procedure to incorporate the amendments
- communicating the changes to the relevant staff
- logging the amended procedure in the procedures manual
- issuing new documentation for training guides.

A plan of implementation has been drawn up and can be found in Appendix E.

6 Cost and resource management

The main cost of amending the procedure will be staff time. It is estimated that the redrafting and implementation of the procedure will take approximately 25 hours. There will be a small cost in reproducing the new written materials.

The on-going cost of this procedure will not involve any extra expense as there are no significant changes to the resourcing, training and staffing currently required to operate the existing procedure.

7 Training and development requirements

The training and development requirements of this procedure are minimal. Staff working in the human resources department will require a short training session on the amendments to the procedure. This can easily be undertaken during the company's regularly scheduled training sessions and will not therefore require any financial funding. The documentation for the amendments will be updated in the training manual for new staff.

The various managers will be sent an explanatory note with a copy of the updated procedure. This should be sufficient for their needs.

8 Possible difficulties with revised procedures

As the amendments to the procedure do not require any extra staff, training or cost, there should be few difficulties. However, one possible difficulty may be staff resistance to change. The human resources department did not perceive any difficulties with the existing procedure and may not welcome the amendments

This can be overcome by explaining the benefits of the amendments both to the company as a whole and to the staff in the human resources department in particular as they will provide a better service to their customers and be able to work more efficiently.

Appendix A

Recruitment procedure: Logged in procedures manual, reference RECRUIT1.1

INSTRUCTIONS FOR MANAGERS

1 Inform HR of job vacancy.
2 Receive job specification from HR. Amend and return.
3 Receive completed application forms from HR.
4 Shortlist applicants for interview within three days. Return forms to HR.
5 Agree interview date with HR.
6 Interview applicants.
7 Select applicant.
8 Receive start date from HR.

INSTRUCTIONS FOR HUMAN RESOURCES

1 Request received from manager to start recruitment process.
2 Retrieve correct job specification from file and send to manager for approval.
3 Receive job specification from manager.
4 Make any amendments and send copy to manager.
5 Draft advertisement for vacancy. Set a closing date for applications, two weeks after the date of publication.
6 If the advertisement is for care staff, ask the HR manager for approval.

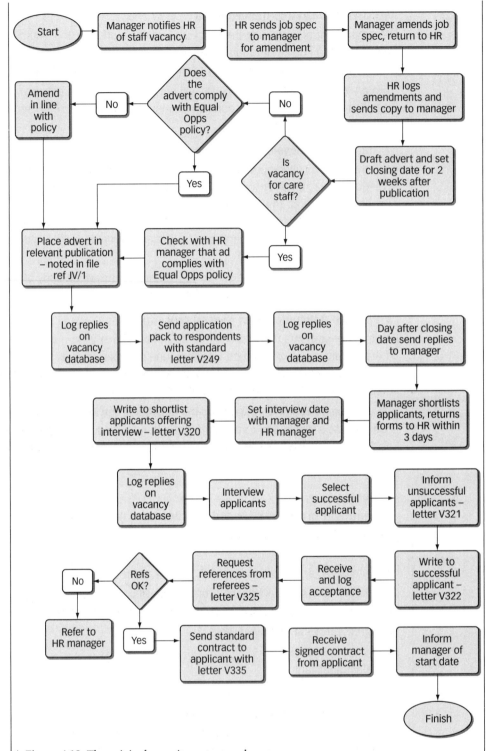

▲ Figure 4.13 The original recruitment procedure

7 If the advertisement is not for care staff, check it complies with the company's Equal Opportunity Policy, reference EQP 1.3.

8 Place advertisement in relevant publication. Current list will be found on computer, reference JV/1.

9 Log replies on database, VACANCY.

10 Send application pack to respondent with standard letter V249.

11 Log completed application forms on VACANCY database.

12 Day after closing date send application forms to manager.

13 Receive shortlist applications three days after sending to manager.

14 Set interview date with manager and HR manager.

15 Send interview letter V320 to shortlisted applicants.

16 Log replies on VACANCY database.

17 Interview candidates.

18 Inform unsuccessful applicants by letter V321.

19 Write to successful applicant by letter V322.

20 Receive and log acceptable on VACANCY database.

21 Request references from referees using letter V325.

22 Receive references. Satisfactory references log on VACANCY database and proceed to step 24.

23 Unsatisfactory references received log on VACANCY database and refer to HR manager.

24 Send standard contract to applicant with letter V335. Log on VACANCY database.

25 Receive signed contract. Log on VACANCY database.

26 Inform manager of start date of new staff member.

Appendix B
Transcript of interview with Mrs Sutton, human resources manager

Interviewer: Thanks for agreeing to speak to me about the recruitment procedure. I believe that the recruitment procedure relates to all staff employed by Carlton Care Homes. Is this correct?

Mrs Sutton: No, if the vacancy is for a manager or temporary staff, different procedures apply.

Interviewer: How would a member of staff know this?

Mrs Sutton: Well, if a manager is leaving, I will have received their resignation and will deal with the recruitment process myself. Therefore staff will not receive the request that triggers this procedure. In the case of temporary staff, managers have to make their request to Mr Greenslade, the director. If Mr Greenslade agrees, he will pass the request directly to me.

Interviewer: Do you think the procedure is easy to use?

Mrs Sutton: Yes.

Interviewer: Have you identified any problems with the procedure?

Mrs Sutton: No.

Interviewer: How do you train staff to use this procedure?

Mrs Sutton: Well, new managers are given training during their induction programme. However, as you know, their input is limited and so a short explanation is sufficient. For new members of HR staff, they work with a senior or more experienced colleague the first time they follow the procedure. On the second occasion they use the procedure, their work is checked at each stage by a more experienced member of staff. Only if they are confident that they can follow the procedure are they authorised to follow it without supervision. The written instructions provide quite an efficient method of training and so they are able to refer to this document if they require help.

Interviewer: How is the procedure monitored?

Mrs Sutton: All procedures are subject to a systems audit on a yearly basis. Apart from that the procedure is, I suppose, self-monitoring in that if it doesn't work, there is a fault with the procedure which is looked at. If this happens, it tends to be the fault of the user. In this case we retrain the user and they are shadowed again until they feel confident.

Interviewer: Do you think that the length of time it takes to complete the recruitment process is acceptable?

Mrs Sutton: Yes. I am aware that managers are not always happy, but things have to be done properly and they cannot just employ staff without going through the proper channels. I don't think that the process can be made any faster.

Interviewer: Do you think it would be helpful to have different procedures for different types of staff? For example, if employing domestic staff would it be possible for managers to deal with this by themselves?

Mrs Sutton: No. Because company policy insists that the recruitment procedure is in line with current regulations with regard to employment protection, equal opportunities, human rights, discrimination, etc., it was felt that in order to ensure we meet these standards the procedure should remain in the control of HR.

Interviewer: Are there any amendments you would like to make to this procedure?

Mrs Sutton: No, absolutely not. It works well and I always think that if you start messing around with procedures when they are working you will end up with more problems than before you started.

Interviewer: Those are all my questions. Thank you very much for talking to me – it's been very helpful. Would it be possible to contact you if I need any further information?

Mrs Sutton: Yes, of course. I am pleased to have been of some assistance.

Appendix C

Questionnaire given to managers of Carlton Care Homes Ltd

Please complete this questionnaire and return in the envelope provided. Please note that all replies will be treated in confidence.

1 Did you receive training to use the procedure RECRUIT1.1? If so, were you then able to use the procedure without any further help?

2 When using the procedure, do you experience any problems in following the instructions? If yes, please explain:

3 Are you satisfied with the way in which the procedure works? If no, please explain.

4 Please answer yes, no, or not sure to the following.

▷ Is the length of time taken to recruit staff acceptable?

▷ Are references taken up too late?

▷ Is the procedure difficult to understand or follow?

5 Do you have other suggestions for improvement?

Thank you for completing this questionnaire.

Appendix D

Questionnaire findings

Were you able to follow the procedure unaided after training?

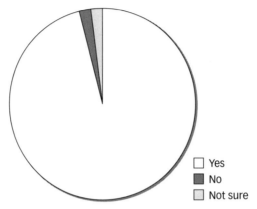

▲ Figure 4.14 Pie chart showing the percentage of managers able to follow the procedure

Do you experience any problems when following the procedure?

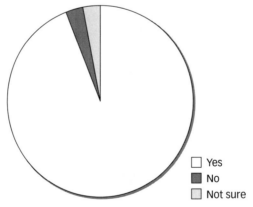

▲ Figure 4.15 Pie chart showing the percentage of managers who experience problems with the procedure

Are you satisfied with the way in which the procedure works?

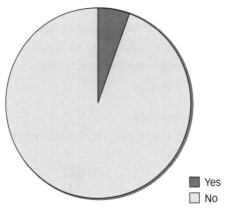

▲ Figure 4.16 Pie chart showing the percentage of managers satisfied with the procedure

Is the length of time taken to recruit staff acceptable?

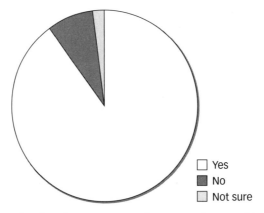

▲ Figure 4.17 Pie chart showing the percentage of managers happy with the length of time taken to recruit staff

Are references taken up too late?

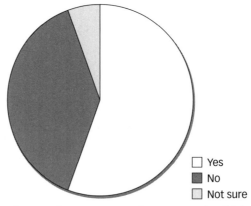

▲ Figure 4.18 Pie chart showing the percentage of managers who think that references are taken up too late

Is the procedure difficult to understand or follow?

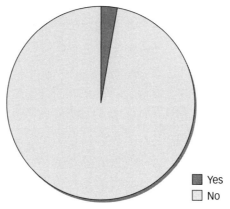

■ Yes
□ No

▲ Figure 4.19 Pie chart showing the percentage of managers who think the procedure is difficult to follow

5 Other suggestions for improvement. This section was only answered by one manager.

▷ Allow managers to recruit domestic staff.

▷ Advertise in different media.

Appendix E

Implementation plan

Recruitment Procedure RECRUIT1.1

Action	Timescale	Comments	Completed (date and sign)
Draft new written procedures	1 week		
Check instructions are correct	1 week	Ask Mrs Sutton and one HR staff to check through amendments	
Obtain feedback and collate results	1 week		
Make amendments	3 days		
Organise training session	Next available session	Book topic into next staff training session (HR staff)	
Prepare final documentation	1 week		
Issue documentation	2 days	Manager training guide, HR staff training guide, Prepare a checklist for staff to sign to confirm receipt	
Log procedure in manual	1 day	Full procedure plus both sets of instructions	
Update publications list	1 day	Include new places to advertise	
Organise for all job specifications to be sent to managers	2 weeks	Ensure that managers receive the relevant and most up-to-date job specifications	

Index